OXFORD PHILOSOPHICAL M

THE ONTOLOGY OF MIND

ALSO PUBLISHED IN THE SERIES

The Justification of Science and the Rationality of Religious Belief
Michael Banner

Individualism in Social Science
Forms and Limits of a Methodology
Rajeev Bhargava

Causality, Interpretation, and the Mind
William Child

The Kantian Sublime
From Morality to Art
Paul Crowther

Kant's Theory of Imagination
Sarah Gibbons

Determinism, Blameworthiness, and Deprivation
Martha Klein

Projective Probability
James Logue

Understanding Pictures
Dominic Lopes

False Consciousness
Denise Meyerson

Truth and the End of Inquiry
A Peircean Account of Truth
C. J. Misak

The Good and the True
Michael Morris

Nietzsche and Metaphysics
Peter Poellner

Things that Happen because They Should
A Teleological Approach to Action
Rowland Stout

The Ontology of Mind
Events, Processes, and States

HELEN STEWARD

CLARENDON PRESS · OXFORD

OXFORD
UNIVERSITY PRESS

Great Clarendon Street, Oxford OX2 6DP

Oxford University Press is a department of the University of Oxford.
It furthers the University's objective of excellence in research, scholarship,
and education by publishing worldwide in

Oxford New York

Athens Auckland Bangkok Bogotá Buenos Aires Calcutta
Cape Town Chennai Dar es Salaam Delhi Florence Hong Kong Istanbul
Karachi Kuala Lumpur Madrid Melbourne Mexico City Mumbai
Nairobi Paris São Paulo Singapore Taipei Tokyo Toronto Warsaw

with associated companies in Berlin Ibadan

Oxford is a registered trade mark of Oxford University Press
in the UK and in certain other countries

Published in the United States
by Oxford University Press Inc., New York

British Library Cataloguing in Publication Data

Data available

Library of Congress Cataloging in Publication Data
Steward, Helen.
The ontology of mind : events, processes, and states / Helen
Steward.
(Oxford philosophical monographs)
Based on the author's doctoral thesis.
Includes bibliographical references and index.
1. Philosophy of mind. I. Title. II. Series.
BD418.3.S74 1997 128.2—dc21 96-52313

ISBN 0-19-824098-8
ISBN 0-19-825064-9 (Pbk.)

Printed in Great Britain
on acid-free paper by
Biddles Ltd
Guildford and King's Lynn

ACKNOWLEDGEMENTS

MANY people have provided me with ideas, criticism, discussion, and encouragement which have enabled me to clarify and defend the claims made in this book and I am very glad to have the opportunity to thank them here. Much of the material has been presented at different times to various discussion groups and philosophy societies, and I have benefited enormously from the comments of those audiences. David Charles's discussion group in Oriel College, Oxford, in particular, has been the source of feedback on almost every portion of the book at some time or another—I thank all its members warmly for the intellectual stimulation they have provided over the years. Among those who have influenced my thinking at various points in ways that I can still recall, both in this discussion group and elsewhere, are Helen Beebee, David Bell, John Biro, Bill Brewer, John Campbell, Bill Child, Martin Davies, Lizzie Fricker, Greville Healey, Jennifer Hornsby, Frank Jackson, Alan Millar, David Owens, Rowland Stout, Peter Sullivan, and Tim Williamson.

The earlier portions of the book grew out of my D. Phil. thesis, which was supervised by Paul Snowdon and David Charles, both of whom were enormously generous with their time, incisive in their criticisms, and thoroughly supportive throughout. Jennifer Hornsby and Simon Blackburn examined the thesis, and their comments on it have helped me to make the book a substantial improvement on the original work. Jennifer Hornsby, in addition, read the entire manuscript of the book prior to publication, in the capacity of Oxford University Press reader, and I have benefited immensely from her thoughtful suggestions.

I also acknowledge the support of a number of institutions. The bulk of the D. Phil. thesis from which this book has finally emerged was written whilst a Junior Fellow at University College, Oxford, and a Darby Fellow at Lincoln College, Oxford. Balliol College, Oxford granted me a sabbatical term in which to complete the book, without which it would undoubtedly never have seen the light of day. In addition, it deserves a mention for its nursery, which has considerably eased the task of combining motherhood with authorship. I would also like to thank the other PPE tutors at Balliol, who cheerfully took up the extra workload created by my sabbatical, and those lecturers who took over much of my teaching in the meantime: Paul Matthewson, Alan Bailey, and Sean Hall.

Many friends cheered me up through what was sometimes a very difficult writing process. I would like to thank, in particular, everyone who came on the New Year holiday to Amsterdam, Nilly Sarkar and Patrick Costello, Miranda Fricker, Lucy Allwood, and Susanne Bobzien. My partner, David Hesmondhalgh, provided constant practical and moral support throughout, and helped by laughing at my examples to put philosophy of the kind of which this book is an instance into a helpful, if not always gratifying, perspective. Jones and Smith, unfortunately, remain here and there, taking arsenic and believing that p. Our daughter Rosa was born as I was nearing completion of the manuscript—over a year ago now—and Dave's support through the pregnancy and thereafter have been invaluable.

It remains to thank my parents, Cathy and Ernie Steward, and Dave's parents, John and Maureen Hesmondhalgh, for their willingness always to be on hand, despite living many miles away, to help out with Rosa in times of need. Their love and support is gratefully acknowledged.

H. C. S.

Oxford, March 1996

CONTENTS

Introduction   1

PART I: EVENTS AND PROCESSES   17

1. Events, Particularity, and Properties   19

   1. Kim: Exemplifications of Properties at Times   21
   2. Property Exemplifications and Theories of Mind   28
   3. Particularity and the Secret Life Requirement   35
   4. Bennett: Events as Tropes   41
   5. Bennett's Argument against Anomalous Monism   44

2. Events as Changes   56

   1. Happenings   57
   2. Events as Changes in Objects   58
   3. Is there a Motivation for the RCO?   61
   4. Composite Events and the Composition Relation   65
   5. Are there Changeless Events?   69
   6. States and Change   72

3. The Temporal Strategy: Time and Aspect   75

   1. Vendler and Kenny   78
   2. Types of Verb versus Types of Predication   82
   3. Aspect   84
   4. Nominalization Transcriptions: Events and Processes   88
   5. Non-paradigmatic Events   92
   6. *Event* and *Process* as Ontological Categories   94
   7. Temporal Shape   97

PART II: STATES, CAUSATION, AND CAUSAL EXPLANATION   103

4. States and the Type–Token Distinction   105

   1. States and Properties   107
   2. Nominalization Transcriptions: States   110
   3. The 'State of . . .' Locution   115

4. The Type–Token Distinction   120
5. Token States in Philosophy of Mind   127

5. Particulars, Facts, and Causal Explanations   135

   1. Forms of Causal Explanation   139
   2. Singular Causal Claims   141
   3. Sentential Causal Explanations   146
   4. The Existential Generalization Account   153
   5. Causation and Causal Explanation   163

6. Efficacy, Causing, and Relevance   168

   1. Child on Causation and Causal Explanation   169
   2. Program and Process Explanations   186
   3. Sentential Explanations as Program Explanations   192
   4. Why there are no Causally Efficacious Properties   197

PART III: STATES AND CAUSALITY IN
PHILOSOPHY OF MIND   203

7. The Network Model of Causation in Philosophy
of Mind   205

   1. The Network Model of Causation   206
   2. What's Wrong with the Network Model of
     Causation?   213
   3. The Network Model in Philosophy of Mind   221
   4. Causal Relevance and Isomorphism   225

8. Token Identity Theories   232

   1. Understanding Identity Statements   235
   2. Token State Identities and the Network Model of Causation   242

9. Eliminativism and the Problem of Epiphenomenalism   247

   1. Two Characterizations of Eliminativism   248
   2. An Argument for Eliminativism   250
   3. The Problem of Epiphenomenalism   254
   4. The Solution to the Problem of Epiphenomenalism   257
   5. Concluding Remarks   263

References   265

Index   271

Introduction

FEW philosophers now believe in the existence of a substantial soul. The mind has lost its status as a special kind of persisting object in the ontological frameworks presupposed by contemporary philosophical debates. But it has not lost its place as a central concept in those debates; on the contrary, it is a concept which organizes the very discipline. A whole field is known as 'Philosophy of Mind'. The 'Mind–Body Problem' appears regularly on lists of major philosophical issues in introductory books. And in general, many philosophers continue to take it for granted that 'mind' is a term which succeeds in singling out a distinctive and philosophically awkward domain which demands investigation—and which, depending on one's inclination, requires either incorporation into some physicalistic picture of the world, or rescue from the pretensions of such views.

Without the support provided by the metaphysics of what Ryle termed 'the dogma of the Ghost in the Machine',[1] however, philosophers have had to restate many of their traditional questions about mentality. Ryle himself, deprived by his own arguments of the freedom to suppose that the distinctive domain of philosophy of mind was the nature and properties of a special kind of substance, forged his subject-matter by means of semantic ascent. For Ryle, the proper subject of investigation became the *concepts* which go to constitute our idea of mentality: the concepts, for example, of believing and desiring, intending and understanding, thinking and wishing, being proud, generous, or vain. But some philosophers fretted about what they perceived to be the replacement of proper metaphysics by Ryle, and the tradition he inaugurated, with trivial investigations into language.[2] They complained that Ryle's

---

[1] G. Ryle, *The Concept of Mind* (London, 1949; repr. Harmondsworth, 1983), 17.

[2] This shift away from Ryleanism and back towards metaphysics is well exemplified by D. M. Armstrong in *A Materialist Theory of the Mind* (London, 1968);

treatment amounted to the denial of the existence of the mind, and
demanded a descent back down again from the semantic to the
genuinely ontological. And in time the descent was duly effected, so
that today, philosophers are happy to talk not only about the
concepts of belief, desire, etc., but of beliefs, desires, and the rest,
themselves, and worry about what they are and how to fit them into
the world as impersonally conceived, the world of neurons and
synapses where human actions seem somehow to originate.

In the light of the prevalent conviction, though, that there is no
such 'thing', strictly speaking, as the mind, philosophers have had
to draw on new ontological resources to state their concerns about
the mental. The boundaries of mentality are mostly drawn up by
means of what is by now a fairly standard lexicon which includes
terms associated with the propositional attitudes, sensations, perception, emotions, actions, memory, and imagination—though it is
often conceded that the realm thus delineated may perhaps have no
real unity over and above the more or less loose association of its
constituents with the puzzling phenomena of meaning and consciousness, in which philosophers have an abiding interest. But the
acceptance of this lexicon as a means of defining the scope of the
mental, together with the demise both of the metaphysics which
suggested that beliefs, desires, feelings, thoughts, etc. were modifications of a distinctive kind of substance, and of the Rylean alternative which suggested that the conceptual investigation of
'mind-talk' was the only properly philosophical task that might be
salvaged from the wreck of substance dualism, has left new ontological categories propping up the traditional questions and suggesting new ways of formulating and responding to them. Different
ways of conceiving of the mode of existence of such entities as
beliefs, thoughts, and sensations have given rise to a new ontology
of mind, in which mental events, states, and processes have replaced modifications of the soul.

These categories have been crucially important in permitting the
reformulation of the mind–body problem, because they have pro-

D. K. Lewis in 'An Argument for the Identity Theory', *Journal of Philosophy*, 63
(1966); repr. rev. in Lewis, *Philosophical Papers*, 2 vols., i (Oxford, 1983), and
'Psychophysical and Theoretical Identifications', *Australasian Journal of Philosophy*, 50 (1972); repr. in N. Block (ed.), *Readings in Philosophy of Psychology*, 2
vols., i (London, 1980); and H. Putnam in 'Brains and Behaviour', in R. J. Butler
(ed.), *Analytical Philosophy: Second Series* (Oxford, 1963); repr. in Putnam, *Mind,
Language and Reality* (Cambridge, 1975).

vided philosophers with the ontological means of retaining a brain-independent purchase on the mental realm. For the collapse of substance dualism might otherwise have threatened entirely to subvert the dualistic underpinnings of traditional questions about the nature of mind—to make these questions redundant, dualism being straightforwardly replaced by a monism in which no questions about the 'relation' between mind and brain remained to be asked. Of course, many philosophers profess to be monists of one kind or another; but monism as we have it in contemporary analytic philosophy usually requires to be understood in such a way that the conceptual and epistemological independence of the mind from the brain is conceded, even while their ultimate metaphysical distinctness is denied.[3] Some contemporary monists, for example, are identity theorists who believe that the identity theory makes a substantive and informative claim about the nature of mind. But to make sense of this supposition, they must start by insisting that there is something—the mind, or mentality—whose ultimate nature, previously obscure to us, has now been determined to be physical, something on which we can get pre-theoretical semantic and epistemological purchase, prior to belief in the identity theory. The mind, as one might put it, must have a different mode of presentation from the brain, if the contention that the two are identical is to have any significant content.

Mental events, states, and processes have been essential in permitting this reconstruction of the mind–body problem, because the exploitation of these categories has enabled philosophers to substitute for the view of the mind as a thing the alternative picture of the mind as a kind of collection of things—a collection of events, states, and processes about whose connections with the physical world questions can then arise. These categories have enabled us to perpetuate the thought that these questions are essentially open

---

[3] It seems to me that despite the hold which mind–*body* dualism is often alleged to have on Western thought, it is certainly a philosophers' myth that the mind–*brain* distinction, as we have it in contemporary analytic philosophy, simply sharpens up on a pre-theoretical contrast already given to us by our immersion in that cultural tradition. On the contrary, the philosophical distinction between mind and brain is something one has to learn to understand. The relation between mental activity and the brain is so firmly entrenched in contemporary consciousness that it requires some effort to come to understand the philosophical concept of mentality, which is constructed precisely so as to deliver the mental–physical contrast which purports to allow for a coherent, post-Cartesian formulation of the mind–body problem, and for possible solutions to it.

questions, questions about a set of entities whose identification and individuation we are supposed to be able to understand quite independently of having obtained any answers to questions about their metaphysical nature. In some cases, this independence is secured by the distinctive epistemological access to these entities which introspection is alleged to provide (e.g. pain-events, current trains of thought, etc.); in other cases, where our commitment to the entities in question is supposed to be based more on quasi-theoretical considerations than on any direct introspective acquaintance (e.g. beliefs), the independence is rather a matter of the existence of an allegedly distinctive mode of interpretation—the propositional attitude mode of interpretation—which appears to demand reference to the existence of intentional, and so distinctively psychological, states. But in both kinds of case, what is important is that we appear to be able to get a grip on the idea of mental entities concerning which the question whether or not they are also physical entities remains an open one. Events, states, and processes have therefore assumed enormous importance in the philosophy of mind; for they are the key to our contemporary understanding of its subject-matter.

Given the overwhelming significance of these entities for modern philosophy of mind, then, it seems important that we should have some idea of what kinds of things they are and what the differences between them might be. Events have attracted a lot of attention over the last thirty years or so, largely because of the legitimacy that has been accorded the category in the light of the writings of Donald Davidson, and the widespread interest in his argument for anomalous monism, which is couched in the language of events.[4] Following Davidson, many arguments relating to the mind–body problem are now expressed entirely in terms of events. But states

---

[4] See D. Davidson, 'Mental Events', in L. Foster and J. W. Swanson (eds.), *Experience and Theory* (Amherst and London, 1970); repr. in Davidson, *Essays on Actions and Events* (Oxford, 1980). It should perhaps be remembered that the widespread use of the concept of 'event' in philosophy of mind is a relatively recent development. The earliest identity theorists usually spoke not of events, but rather of states and processes, perhaps at least partly because these terms are in more frequent use in our ordinary talk about mental and psychological phenomena. The phrases 'mental state' and 'mental process' blend fairly comfortably into everyday language; we speak unhesitatingly, for example, of states of depression and states of consciousness and of going through the processes of decision-making or of working out mathematical problems. But the phrase 'mental event' stands out as something of a philosopher's intrusion.

and processes are rarely given separate treatment. More often than not, it is simply stipulated by philosophers of mind that they will be using the term 'event' in a broad sense, so as to encompass states and processes.[5] This seems rarely to be considered philosophically dangerous, and it appears to be widely held that states and processes are somewhat event-like in their nature. States, it is sometimes said, are simply rather longer-lived than events and (usually) involve no change, while the nature of processes and their relation to events is seldom discussed, though it often seems to be assumed that nothing crucial hangs on the distinction.[6] And on the basis of this assumption, it is very commonly accepted that arguments and positions in the philosophy of mind which are formulated explicitly in terms of events may be applied without adjustment of any kind also to states and processes. Anomalous monism is a good example of a theory of mind which has been extended in this way; though Davidson's argument for the position is an argument about mental *events*, it is frequently taken to be a general theory of the nature of mind, rather than a claim about the nature of a limited class of mental items.

In this book, I shall be examining these assumptions. Philosophers have been surprisingly slow to ask about the distinctions between the categories in terms of which they characterize the mind. It is not, of course, that nobody has ever investigated the differences between events, states, and processes; indeed, I shall draw in later chapters on some philosophical and linguistic work in this area which seems to me to be extremely illuminating as regards the sources of the trichotomy.[7] It is rather that work specifically in philosophy of mind has largely proceeded as though it could simply

[5] Some examples: Lewis, 'An Argument for the Identity Theory', 99: 'I shall not distinguish between processes, events, phenomena, and states in a strict sense'; J. Kim, 'Events as Property Exemplifications', in M. Brand and D. Walton (eds.), *Action Theory* (Dordrecht, 1976), 159: 'there are ... good reasons for not taking this dichotomy ... of events and states, too seriously'; T. Horgan and J. Woodward, 'Folk Psychology is here to Stay', *Philosophical Review*, 94 (1985), 198: 'we shall use the rubric "event" in a broad sense, to include not only token changes, but also token states and token processes. Thus, non-momentary folk-psychological token states will count as mental events, in our terminology.'

[6] F. Dretske is a significant exception; see his *Explaining Behavior: Reasons in a World of Causes* (Cambridge, Mass., 1988).

[7] Notably Z. Vendler, *Linguistics in Philosophy* (Ithaca, NY, 1967); A. Kenny, *Action, Emotion and Will* (London, 1963); and A. P. D. Mourelatos, 'Events, Processes and States', *Linguistics and Philosophy*, 2 (1978).

afford to ignore these discriminations, thinking them perhaps to be too subtle to be of any great moment, or too tightly rooted in linguistic considerations to matter much to metaphysics. But I think this neglect has been a mistake. Indeed, I shall try to argue in what follows that the category of state has been so grossly misunderstood that some theories of mind which are supposed to encompass entities traditionally regarded as falling under the category, e.g. beliefs and desires, cannot so much as be sensibly formulated, once we are clearer about the nature of states.

Lest the subtitle of the book should mislead, it is perhaps necessary to say here that I shall not be devoting an equal amount of attention to each of the three categories of entity. Indeed, most of what I have to say is really about the misuse of the concept of a *state* in philosophy of mind. I have rather little to say about processes, though I shall try to say something about how they might differ from events in Chapter 3; and though I have considered events in some detail in the first three chapters, I have done so mainly in order to be clearer about how they differ from states. My aim in these early chapters has been to defend a particularist conception of events against what I regard as a range of mistaken views centred on the assumption that events have something rather special to do with properties—that they are, for example, instances or exemplifications or exemplifyings of properties.[8] These theories, I think, have made it seem tempting to suppose that events and states must be entities of much the same sort. I shall claim, however, that a proper understanding of events and states reveals them to be entities almost as different from one another as substances are from properties. For events, I shall argue, belong with substances in the more general category of *particular*, a category about which I shall attempt to say something in Chapter 1; but states, I shall suggest—even so-called 'token' states—cannot properly transcend

---

[8] Jaegwon Kim, whose view of events I shall consider in some detail in Chapter 1, has perhaps defended this view with more vigour and in more detail than anyone else. But he is by no means the only proponent of the idea that events are best considered, in some sense or other, to be instances of properties. Jonathan Bennett's view in *Events and their Names* (Oxford, 1988), though different from Kim's in many respects, shares the crucial assumption that events bear some relation to properties which is other than simply *having* them; and several philosophers of mind and action (e.g. Alvin Goldman, in *A Theory of Human Action* (Englewood Cliffs, NJ, 1970) and Cynthia Macdonald in *Mind–Body Identity Theories* (London, 1989)) invoke the view when detailed argument requires them to be specific about the nature of events.

their association with the predicative parts of language, and ought not to be granted particular status.

This is perhaps the best place also to enter a second caution. I will say very little in what follows about the distinction between the mental and the physical; and I have used the terms for the most part uncritically throughout. I have traded, by and large, on an already existing philosophical consensus about which terms belong to physical, which to mental discourse, and have not attempted to supply any criteria or precise definitions for marking the bounds of either category. I have not insisted, for instance, that a physical predicate must be a predicate of *physics* (a neurophysiological description will thus often count as physical for my purposes), or that a mental description must be essentially intentional, as some philosophers have done in attempting to make their conceptions of physicalism precise. I hope, and believe, that no harm has come of this imprecision; indeed, that it may even have been necessary to leave some questionable dogmas standing in order to be able better to challenge others.

The book falls into three parts. The first part is concerned with the nature of events, and includes a critical review of some of the most influential and important positions in what is now a colossal literature. I think it is fair to say that the philosophical literature on events is not characterized by even a basic framework of shared assumptions. Some philosophers regard events as literally repeatable, so that if I make myself a cup of tea every morning, one and the same event occurs each time.[9] Others treat events as concrete, datable particulars which do not literally recur.[10] Some think events necessarily involve change;[11] others are inclined to regard this as a metaphysical prejudice without substantive justification.[12] It has

[9] This view is put forward by R. Chisholm, 'Events and Propositions', *Nous*, 4 (1970), and 'States of Affairs Again', *Nous*, 5 (1971).

[10] Davidson explicitly defends this view against Chisholm in 'Events as Particulars', *Nous*, 4 (1970), and 'Eternal vs. Ephemeral Events', *Nous*, 5 (1971), both collected in his *Essays on Actions and Events*.

[11] L. B. Lombard puts forward this view in *Events: A Metaphysical Study* (London, 1986), and it is endorsed (with qualifications) by C. Macdonald in *Mind–Body Identity Theories*.

[12] For this view, see e.g. C. D. Broad, *Scientific Thought* (London, 1923), 54: 'We usually call a flash of lightning or a motor accident an event, and refuse to apply this name to the history of the cliffs of Dover . . . the only relevant difference between the accident and the cliffs is that, if successive slices, each of one second long, be cut in the histories of both, the contents of a pair of adjacent slices may be very different in the first case and will be very similar in the second case. Such . . . differences as

even been suggested that events are sets.[13] With this bewildering variety of accounts to choose from, how should one go about deciding which is correct? That is to say, what are the constraints on a theory of events?

I think it ought to be admitted from the outset that many philosophical views about the nature of such items as events can only pass muster if they are regarded as stipulative—as defining a class of items useful for the purposes of some general theory or other. Certainly, it is hard to understand some of the suggestions in the recent literature as elucidations of the ordinary-language concept of event. For it seems plain that many currently popular views would include as events entities which do not conform at all to the ordinary-language conception of an event, in so far as such a conception exists.[14] The accurate reflection of common-sense views

these give no good ground for calling one bit of history an event and refusing to call another bit of history by the same name.' N. L. Wilson also appears to endorse this view in 'Facts, Events and their Identity Conditions', *Philosophical Studies*, 25 (1974), 313: 'Davidson is of the opinion that every event is a change. This . . . seems a bit restrictive . . . In general, I don't see why a remaining-the-same shouldn't be classed as an event.' And Bennett follows suit in *Events and their Names*, 7: 'any philosophical theory of events should be extended to cover states as well, because the differences between them are of the superficial kind that would seem significant only to someone doing the kind of "conceptual analysis" that shades off into mere lexicography.'

[13] I have seen this view attributed, not without reason, to Jaegwon Kim. This does sometimes appear to be Kim's view in at least some of his writings. In 'Events as Property Exemplifications', for example, he says explicitly that some ordered triples are events. But I think it is reasonably clear from what Kim says elsewhere that he does not really want to *identify* events with sets; just that they may be conveniently represented by means of set notation. For a start, Kim's events only exist where the constituents of the triple stand in particular kinds of relations to one another, whereas the triples themselves are presumably guaranteed existence, provided only that the members of the triple exist. Kim also says several times that he regards events as spatiotemporal particulars; see e.g. 'Events and their Descriptions: Some Considerations', in N. Rescher (ed.), *Essays in Honor of Carl G. Hempel* (Dordrecht, 1969), 198. Barry Taylor, on the other hand, does explicitly commit himself to the identification of events with sets in his *Modes of Occurrence: Verbs, Adverbs and Events* (Oxford, 1985).

[14] For example, Kim's account of events as property exemplifications by substances at times would appear to countenance as an event my bedroom carpet's being blue at *t*, not something we would ordinarily think of as an event at all. I am not entirely confident about attributing this view to Kim, since he does accept that some restrictions will have to be placed on the kinds of properties whose exemplifications count as events (see 'Events as Property Exemplifications', 162). Kim's view seems to be that it is not possible to pick out these properties, or 'generic events', as he calls them, completely a priori; that they may be best picked out relative to a scientific theory. But it seems certain that whatever the basic properties turn out to

does not seem to be a prime consideration in the philosophical literature in this area.

But if this is right, it will not be possible, or useful, to consider theories of events in a vacuum. Presumably, argument will have to revolve rather around considerations to do with the usefulness of singling out this category of things rather than that for philosophical attention. If someone wishes to insist, for instance, that events need not be happenings—that, for example, the history of the cliffs of Dover ought to be accounted an event—she will just be stipulating that the term 'event' applies to a different category of items from that to which certain other philosophers would prefer to see its application restricted. And she might defend her stipulation, as her opponents would defend theirs, by giving details of the use to which she wishes to put the theory—of what, precisely, it is intended to elucidate and explain. Indeed, I think it is clear that the present disparate array of views about events is at least partly due to the fact that different philosophers have introduced events, for quite different purposes, into quite different contexts of inquiry.[15]

Since my context of inquiry is that range of post-war discussions of different forms of physicalism and functionalism which has generally been accounted English-speaking philosophy's recent contribution to the mind–body problem, my concern is to develop a view of events on which they are able to perform the role which I have suggested above makes them so significant for that area of philosophy—that of providing an ontological framework which permits the coherent formulation of its theories, which makes sense of the intuitions which those theories embody, and on which the arguments usually given in support of the theories do at least appear to justify them. It will be argued, in what follows, that the needs of

be, a view of events which gives no special place to the idea of change or of happening will have to recognize as events at least some entities which would not normally be thought of as belonging to that category.

[15] Kim, for example, is primarily concerned with events in connection with explanations. Davidson wants them to serve as the relata of the causal relation. Yet other philosophers, assimilating events to facts, have hoped that they can be made to serve some purpose in a general theory of semantics. Wilson's view in 'Facts, Events and their Identity Conditions' seems to be of this kind. R. M. Martin, in the preface to *Events, Reference and Logical Form* (Washington, 1978), construes the term 'event' so broadly as to embrace 'all kinds of entities whatsoever, physical objects, acts, states, processes, mental events, linguistic events, natural numbers, and so on'.

these theories make it crucial to develop a theory of events according to which they are proper particulars, rather than so-called 'fine-grained' entities like property exemplifications or facts. This in turn supplies us with a good reason for sticking with a view that remains close to the ordinary-language conception of an event in making the idea of a happening central to the concept. On this view, wars, football games, nuclear fissions, Jane's suddenly remembering that she has left the kettle on, the death of John F. Kennedy, would all count as events. The history of the cliffs of Dover, some traffic-light's being green, my bedroom carpet's being blue at *t,* would not. I think people have been inclined to feel that various kinds of unphilosophical arbitrariness are involved in the attempt to restrict the concept of event in this way. I shall try to show that this kind of fear is misplaced and that, on the contrary, distortions and difficulties are more likely to be introduced in the attempt to make the class of events more inclusive than the ordinary-language concept permits. One particular distortion is precisely the view that states are not importantly distinguishable from events and that therefore we can formulate theories and arguments in the philosophy of mind using an ontology which, whatever it is called, is designed to include entities from both categories.

I shall begin, in Chapter 1, by examining Kim's property-exemplification view of events and the account offered by Jonathan Bennett in his book *Events and their Names,* which can be regarded, in some ways, as a development of Kim's. Neither view, I shall argue, permits events the particular status which I regard as utterly crucial to their role in the formulation of physicalist claims. Then, in Chapter 2, I shall look at the account of events offered by Lawrence Lombard in *Events: A Metaphysical Study.* Lombard thinks that events are changes, which is a view which fits well with the particularity constraint. It is therefore quite promising as a candidate for a view of events which might permit them to perform the sort of role which they ought to play in philosophy of mind. It is also undeniable, I think, that it is a very natural view. But I shall argue that, its appeal notwithstanding, it cannot be quite right. There seem to be events which cannot be fitted into Lombard's account; and reflection on these examples reveals that it is not change, but something else, which is really fundamental to the category.

Philosophers other than those on whom I have chosen to concentrate have, of course, expressed views about the nature of events and I am conscious of having neglected some major contributors to the literature; limitations on space, for example, prevented the inclusion of chapters on Chisholm and Quine. But the absence of a chapter on Davidson's views is perhaps so glaring an omission as to require comment. There is no such chapter mainly because those aspects of Davidson's position which seem to me to be particularly relevant to the issues I wish to discuss are treated extensively in Chapters 5 and 7, where I consider Davidson's views on event causation. His particularist ideas are also discussed in the criticism of Kim and Bennett in Chapter 1. In the light of the extent to which Davidson's views figure in all these discussions, it simply seemed unnecessary to devote a separate chapter to them. It is not neglect of his work on events, therefore, but rather the extent to which discussion of it has been unavoidable throughout, which explains the absence of such a chapter.

None of the three theories I shall be considering in Chapters 1 and 2 seems to me at all satisfactory—though Lombard's is certainly closest to the view of events which I shall eventually espouse. That view will be developed in Chapter 3, in connection with a discussion of the linguistic phenomenon of aspect, which in my opinion is the source of the distinction between events and processes, and which is also important to the understanding of the difference between events and states. It might be said, with justice, that the view developed in that chapter is too thin to amount to anything that might be called a 'metaphysical theory of events'; but then I am, I think, rather sceptical about the possibility of saying anything very informative about the 'metaphysical nature' of events—there seems to be too much variety amongst the entities which fall into the category to allow for any very rich characterization of this 'nature'. If I have a 'metaphysical view of events', it is based on the not terribly grand-sounding idea that what is distinctive of events, what is common and peculiar to them all, is a certain relation to time; as I shall put it, the category of *event* is defined by a certain 'temporal shape'.

In Part II, I move from events and processes to consider states. States have frequently underpinned the various formulations of functionalism and physicalism which have been offered us over the last forty years.[16] They are now firmly entrenched as part of the furniture in most contemporary versions of the ontology of mind, and given that this is so, it is perhaps surprising that they have not been the focus of more philosophical attention. The neglect is all the more astonishing, considering the vast literature that the topic of events has generated. Why have states failed to arouse comparable interest?

I have two hypotheses, one more cynical than the other. First, stative vocabulary is just sufficiently homely and familiar to give us the impression that we do not need to take much trouble to understand it. As I have already noted,[17] we are comfortable talking of states of mind, states of consciousness, emotional states, being in a state, etc. And perhaps this has lulled us into a false sense of security as far as states are concerned. Perhaps the very familiarity of these idioms has prevented philosophers from giving the concept of a state the attention it deserves.

The second hypothesis is less charitable. It is probably not unreasonable to speculate that the scale, generality, and impressiveness of a philosophical theory sometimes bears a direct relation to the freedom with which certain key concepts used in its construction are deployed. The use of the term *idea* in the seventeenth and eighteenth centuries might be an example. It is often pointed out that the British Empiricists traded on ambiguities and vaguenesses in the word 'idea' to support some of their more extravagant claims. I suspect states may be shoring up many of the grander-sounding theories in current philosophy of mind in much the same way, and if this is right, perhaps their neglect is best explained by a certain over-enthusiasm in philosophy for sweeping claims about 'the nature of mind'.

This is a neglect which Chapter 4 attempts, in some measure, to rectify. I try to explain how we come by the nouns and nominal phrases which suggest reference to states, before going on to argue

---

[16] David Armstrong, for example, formulated his materialism as the thesis that 'mental states are nothing but physical states of the brain' (*A Materialist Theory of the Mind*, p. xi); and David Lewis defined the Psychophysical Identity theory as 'the hypothesis that—not necessarily but as a matter of fact—every experience is identical with some physical state' ('An Argument for the Identity Theory', 99). Putnam stated his functionalism originally as the theory that mental states were functional states of whole organisms ('The Nature of Mental States', in *Mind, Language and Reality*). Such examples could be multiplied.

[17] See n. 4 above.

that the idea that events and states are close relations in the same ontological family, an idea present either explicitly or implicitly in the writings of many philosophers, has been a huge and serious mistake. I try to suggest, in particular, that the concept of a token state has been widely misunderstood and that the sorts of stative nominals which are sometimes alleged to refer to these entities are usually best understood as nominalizations of whole sentences, and as expressions, therefore, which refer to facts rather than to particulars. In Chapter 5, I argue that the distinction between particulars and facts is crucial to the understanding of the workings of our causal explanations; and that we need to recognize two rather different varieties of causal statement, which I call 'singular' and 'sentential'. The chapter attempts to explain the difference between the two kinds of explanation, and argues that the idea that token states must be recognized as a variety of causally efficacious particular stems from the existence of a certain class of sentential causal explanations in which the *explanans* is a stative predication. I argue that it is a mistake to think that these explanations have their basis in interactive or productive relationships in which token states figure. Rather, they involve us in commitment to causal relationships between *facts* and effects of various kinds. There is therefore no need at all to recognize token states as a class of particulars. In so far as the category is legitimate, I argue, the entities it subsumes are not particular but rather fact-like—hence my claim that events and states are not close relations but rather species very different from one another.

Chapter 6 attempts to deal with the very natural thought that facts (especially in the 'thin' sense in which I use the term) are unsuited in various ways to serve as relata of the causal relation, and considers the suggestion that facts can be, at most, relata only of the relation of causal explanation. I argue that facts certainly cannot stand in anything like the *same* sort of causal relation to their effects as that in which events stand to theirs. But that is not to say that we need to retreat to a position in which facts can stand only in explanatory relations. I argue that we ought to recognize a relation which I call 'causal relevance', a relation which facts can bear either to particular events or to other facts, and which is to be understood in terms of the truth of counterfactuals: very roughly, a fact F is causally relevant to an event E only if E would not have occurred, or would have been less likely to occur, had F not been a fact (i.e. had the sentence which expresses F been false instead of true). The distinction between program and process explanations which has been developed in some detail by Frank Jackson and Philip Pettit[18] is used to loosen the grip of the thought that the causal relevance of a fact must always involve the fact's being efficacious, and to show that there is no need for the theory to be committed to facts producing or interacting or 'doing causal work' for which they are eminently unsuited. But I argue that Jackson and Pettit wrongly think of the program–process distinction as characterizing a difference in the various ways in which *properties* can matter to an effect. The truth, I claim, is rather that properties always matter causally in what Jackson and Pettit call the 'program' way, even when they are the basic properties of physics. For a claim about the causal relevance of a property is really just another way of making a claim about the causal relevance of a fact—and so properties belong with facts in discussion of causation. Properties, on the view suggested, are therefore never efficacious; their role in causation is always a matter of a fact's standing in the relation that I call 'causal relevance' to some effect or other.

Part III is concerned with the role which has been played by states in the philosophy of mind. In Chapter 7, I try to use the conclusions of Chapters 5 and 6 to argue against a model of the causation of events which I regard as wholly misconceived; I call this the network model of causation. Then in Chapters 8 and 9, I try to argue for the strong claim that once we have rejected the mistaken picture, a number of questions, problems, and theses in philosophy of mind need to be discarded as mere products of the mistaken model. Amongst the casualties are the token identity theory of propositional attitudes, a popular form of argument for eliminative materialism, and the worries about the epiphenomenalism of content that have dogged recent attempts to formulate a physicalism that respects the intuition that at least sometimes we do the things we do because of what we believe and want.

Broadly speaking, the overall aim of the book is to suggest that

---

[18] The most important papers are the following: 'Functionalism and Broad Content', *Mind*, 97 (1988); 'Program Explanation: A General Perspective', *Analysis*, 50 1990; 'Causation in the Philosophy of Mind', *Philosophy and Phenomenological Research*, 50, supp. vol. (1990); 'Structural Explanation in Social Theory', in D. Charles and K. Lennon (eds.), *Reduction, Explanation and Realism* (Oxford, 1992).

approaches to the mind–body problem which persist in treating philosophical questions about the relation of mentality to the physical world as though they were primarily questions about the status of *entities* are misguided, and inapplicable to vast areas of the domain which has traditionally been thought of as the realm of the mind. I call such approaches *particularist* approaches; they are generally characterized by a concentration on relations like identity and milder alternatives like composition relations between *things*. My view is that the important, wide-ranging, and interesting questions associated with the mind–body problem ought rather to be construed as questions about relations between *facts*—and that we ought to shift our attention, accordingly, to relations like supervenience and dependence which can hold between facts. To a certain extent, this is already happening; the arguments of eliminative materialists against identity theories of mind have done a great deal to shake the faith of physicalists in one–one token identifications between mental and physical entities, even if they have not always persuaded people of the truth of their own views.[19] Content-externalism may also have played a part in convincing some people that a move away from particularist theories of mind is needed. But the view that beliefs and other mental states just *must* be states of the brain if we are to do justice to the common-sense thought that mental states are among the causes of our actions is still sufficiently widespread to warrant a demolition attempt from a different kind of angle—an angle from which it can be shown not only that many general theories of mind cannot be true of states, but from which it can also be seen why they do not need to be true in order to account for the part played by what are called mental states in the causal explanation of our actions. I hope, in this book, to have gone at least some way towards providing such an account.

---

[19] Stephen Stich, Paul Churchland, and Patricia Churchland, for example, have argued on a posteriori grounds that it will probably never be possible to identify individual belief states with states of the brain, no matter how complex the latter. See S. P. Stich, *From Folk Psychology to Cognitive Science: The Case against Belief* (Cambridge, Mass., 1983); P. S. Churchland, *Neurophilosophy* (Cambridge, Mass., 1986), ch. 9; and P. M. Churchland, 'Eliminative Materialism and the Propositional Attitudes', *Journal of Philosophy*, 78 (1981).

I

Events and Processes

Events, Particularity, and Properties

IN this chapter, I shall be considering two theories of events which connect the category of *event* quite closely to the category of *property* by utilizing the notion of a property exemplification. Both Jaegwon Kim and Jonathan Bennett have defended views according to which events are exemplifications of properties; and though there are significant differences between the two accounts, both share the thought that events relate to properties not merely by having them, in the ordinary way in which anything which is characterizable in any manner at all can be said to have properties, but in a special way, whereby the event is deemed to be something whose identity is actually tied to some particular property (Kim) or to a collection of properties (Bennett). The aim of the chapter is to argue that views of this sort result in a conception of events on which they have really ceased to have any status as genuine particulars, in a sense which I shall attempt to explain. Kim's events, I shall suggest, despite his frequent claim that they are particulars, are better classified as fact-like entities. And Bennett, I shall argue, relies illicitly on a particularist conception of events in order to develop his anti-particularist theory of what they are, so that his view ultimately founders in incoherence.

There cannot, of course, be any very deep philosophical objection to someone's defining a category of entity for some purpose or other and deciding that the term 'event' serves as well as any other to name the category thus defined, though one might be able to argue that the term is confusing or inappropriate if the entities in question are very different from those which the term ordinarily designates. As I have already stressed, theories of events can only really be assessed properly relative to some broader design. My aim, therefore, will be to try to show that whatever else they may be useful for, property exemplifications are not the right kinds of thing in terms of which to understand and assess the various theories and ideas about the relation between mental and physical realms which have been formulated using an ontology of events: theories like anomalous monism, other sorts of so-called 'token' identity theory, and what might be called token constitution or composition theories (which hold that the relation between mental and physical events is not identity but rather constitution or composition, the relation that an object bears to its parts).[1] These theories attempt to give expression to what is really a very natural and straightforward thought about the relation between mental and physical phenomena—namely, that they are, in some sense or other, the very same things, viewed from two different perspectives, or described in two different ways. The events which figure in these theories therefore ought to be the sorts of entities which could conceivably present themselves to a conscious observer in two (or more) radically different ways, which could be the object of two or more very different descriptions. A mental event, in particular, ought to be something about which one could envisage there being some mystery, about which the question 'Is this event identical with, or composed from, some event or set of events which are purely bodily?' is a sensible and substantive one, neither trivially true nor trivially false. Such an event should be something which it makes sense to suppose has hidden aspects, properties one does not know about, descriptions which one does not realize apply to it; it should be the sort of thing that it makes sense to suppose might have what I shall call a 'secret life'. But property exemplifications, I shall argue, whether of Kim's or of Bennett's sort, do not allow for the diversity of perspective which could make such mystery intelligible.

I shall begin in Section 1 by outlining Kim's view; then, in Section 2, I shall explain why Kim's events cannot provide a useful ontology for the formulation of a number of theories of mind which have generally been stated in terms of events, tracing their unsuitability to their failure to satisfy what I call the 'secret life requirement'. In Section 3, I argue that the distinction between entities which do and entities which do not satisfy the requirement is a philosophically significant one, and that its satisfaction ought to be made a necessary condition of particularity. For it is often important in philosophy to distinguish particulars not just from traditional 'universals', but from things which, for want of a better designation, I call

---

[1] See R. Boyd, 'Materialism without Reductionism: What Physicalism does not Entail', in Block (ed.), *Readings in the Philosophy of Psychology*, i, for a view of this kind.

'fact-like' entities. Traditional criteria for particularity (e.g. spatio-temporal locatedness), I shall argue, do not clearly distinguish particulars from certain sorts of fact; and so the traditional criteria need supplementation by a further condition, one which Kim's property exemplifications clearly fail to meet.

In Section 4, I shall move on to describe Bennett's version of the property exemplification account. In my view, Bennett's account does not really succeed in avoiding versions of the problems which confront Kim's position; indeed, it faces its own additional difficulties. I shall try to show in Section 5 why Bennett's events cannot meet the secret life requirement any more easily than Kim's, unless we smuggle into our understanding of the view an assumption which ultimately undermines it.

1. KIM: EXEMPLIFICATIONS OF PROPERTIES AT TIMES

In a series of papers, Jaegwon Kim has developed a view of events which he calls the property exemplification account.[2] Events, according to Kim, are 'exemplifications of properties at times', and are to be represented by means of a canonical notation which is specifically designed to reflect their metaphysical character. Every event, according to Kim, can be represented by an expression of the form $[S, p, t]$, where S stands for a substance, p for a property, and t for a time—either an instant or an interval. Of course, not every such expression stands for an event. Kim supplies an 'existence condition' for his events; event $[S, p, t]$ exists just in case the substance S has the property p at time t. And events $[S_1, p_1, t_1]$ and $[S_2, p_2, t_2]$ are identical just in case $S_1 = S_2$, $p_1 = p_2$, and $t_1 = t_2$.

As I have already mentioned, there seems to have been some confusion in the literature, not without cause, as to whether Kim intends his events to be particulars, or rather abstract objects of some kind, perhaps sets.[3] Sometimes Kim says explicitly that events

---

[2] The most important papers are 'On the Psycho-physical Identity Theory', *American Philosophical Quarterly*, 3 (1966); 'Events and their Descriptions: Some Considerations'; 'Causation, Nomic Subsumption and the Concept of Event', *Journal of Philosophy*, 70 (1973); and 'Events as Property Exemplifications'; the latter two repr. in his *Supervenience and Mind* (Cambridge, 1993).

[3] See Intro., n. 13. Terence Horgan also notes the confusion in 'The Case against Events', *Philosophical Review*, 87 (1978), 29.

are ordered triples; in other places he is insistent that his events are particulars:

My events are 'particular' and 'dated'. That they are dated is obvious. I am not clear what 'particulars' are; but events in my sense have location in space, namely the location of their constitutive substances ... And my events are not 'eternal' objects; they do not exist in all possible worlds; they exist only if the existence condition is met, which is a contingent matter of fact. If this doesn't show that something is 'concrete' or 'particular', what does?[4]

Much of the confusion stems, I think, from the fact that Kim himself does not see that the two views are crucially different. In 'Events as Property Exemplifications', for example, after suggesting that the predicate '... is an event' might be defined over ordered triples, he suggests that taking this new approach would not materially affect his former account,[5] and goes on to reaffirm, a little later in the same paper, his commitment to the view that events are dated particulars.[6] But as Horgan notes, this seems to be a mistake.[7] If events really are sets, they cannot also be ordinary spatio-temporal particulars. The two views are not mere notational variants of one another, as Kim seems to believe.

In my opinion, the view that events are spatiotemporal particulars is clearly predominant in Kim's writings. In several different papers, he stresses that events have spatial location and are dated.[8] At any rate, I shall be proceeding on the assumption that this is his intention, and that the talk of defining the predicate '... is an event' over ordered triples is best regarded as an aberration. The alternative view is uninteresting, in any case, as far as philosophy of mind is concerned, for the question whether mental events are, or are somehow composed of or constituted by, physical ones is surely not a question about relations between sets.[9]

---

[4] 'Events as Property Exemplifications', 165.
[5] See ibid. 161–2: 'the use of the set-theoretic machinery *may* have certain metaphysical consequences, depending on one's metaphysical views of sets ... But I regard these as peripheral issues pertaining largely to the mode of presentation of the theory ...'.
[6] Ibid. 165.
[7] 'The Case against Events', 30.
[8] See e.g. 'Events and their Descriptions', 198; 'Events as Property Exemplifications', 165; 'Noncausal Connections', *Nous*, 8 (1974), 42.
[9] At least, only in the uninteresting sense in which any question about the identity of something is also a question about the identity of any set of which it is an element.

It is rather unclear, though, even if we accept that Kim intends his events to be spatiotemporal particulars of some sort, whether his theory is supposed to be a theory of (among other things) the happenings to which we ordinarily apply the term 'event', or whether he is attempting rather to define a wholly different category of entity, within which ordinary events are not included. His own statements of intent hover uneasily between the two interpretations. On the one hand, Kim mentions earthquakes, collisions of particles, and expansions of metals as examples of the kind of entity he wishes his theory to encompass, and these certainly seem to be ordinary, particular events.[10] On the other hand, Kim is wedded to two philosophical assumptions which seem to have been inherited from Hempel's discussion of events in *Aspects of Scientific Explanation*[11] that are in considerable tension with the claim that his theory of events is a theory of these ordinary particulars. First, Kim wants the individuation of events to be closely tied to considerations about intersubstitutability in explanatory contexts. This he gives as his reason for regarding as distinct Brutus' stabbing of Caesar and his assassination of Caesar: 'we are interested in events primarily in so far as they are objects of explanation and relata of the causal relation, and it is by no means false or absurd to say that to explain why Brutus stabbed Caesar is not the same as explaining why Brutus assassinated Caesar'.[12] And secondly, Kim seems to want to use the term 'event' as a general name for what is 'described' by a whole host of sentences of the form '*Fa*' or '*Rab*'. The linguistic structures with which he associates events are not definite descriptions or names, like 'Brutus' stabbing of Caesar' or 'The Falklands War'; rather, his linguistic 'event-describing' paradigm is a simple sentence of ordinary predicative or relational form. But as Davidson has argued, it is highly doubtful whether any theory of events organized around these two assumptions can be a theory of the happenings to which we ordinarily apply the term 'event'.

The two assumptions are, of course, related. Kim's insistence on the primacy of what he calls event-describing sentences stems partly from the fact that he is mainly interested in events because of the

---

[10] 'Events and their Descriptions', 198.
[11] C. G. Hempel, *Aspects of Scientific Explanation* (New York, 1965), 421–3. I think it is not insignificant that one of Kim's earliest forays into the question of events was written for a collection of essays in honour of Hempel.
[12] 'Events and their Descriptions', 213.

role they play, or appear to play, in explanation. These sentences appear frequently both in the formulation of questions, as *explananda*, and in the formulation of answers to those questions; we can ask, for example, why Socrates drank hemlock or why Xanthippe wept, or assert that Socrates died because he drank hemlock. Because Kim assumes that what gets explained by such a sentence is an individual event, he assumes also that the role of these sentences is to designate individual events—that, for example, in asking why Socrates drank hemlock, we are asking for an explanation of why some individual event of Socrates' drinking hemlock occurred, or that in saying that he died because he drank hemlock, we are referring to the particular, individual hemlock-drinking event which caused his death. If this were indeed so, Kim's insistence that we should individuate the events in question according to the intersubstitutability in explanatory contexts of the corresponding 'event-describing' sentences might be defensible. But for reasons that are now very familiar, it is a mistake to assume that sentential constructions single out particular events (though of course they may contain singular terms which do so).

Someone who asks or tries to explain why Socrates drank hemlock, for example, is not asking or explaining, of any individual event, why it occurred. None of the particular features of the particular drinking event which in fact brought about Socrates' death are up for explanation, other than its being a hemlock-drinking; it is not the particular event, but rather the fact that an event of that *type* occurred, which is the *explanandum* (if indeed it is correct to think of such an explanation as one which pertains to the occurrence of events at all).[13] There is, strictly speaking, no reference at all to any individual occurrence either in the question 'Why did Socrates drink hemlock?' or in any purported answer of the form 'Socrates drank hemlock because . . .'. Given that this is

---

[13] The parenthetical qualification is due to the fact that I have reservations about the general idea that explaining why a person did something is always equivalent to explaining why some kind of event occurred. Jennifer Hornsby has observed that a question of the form 'Why did *S* do such and such a thing?' may not be asking for the same sort of enlightenment as a question of the form 'Why was there an event of such-and-such a kind?' and that the distinction between the two can be important for philosophy of action: 'Asking why *a* φ-ed, we hope to learn something about *a*, the person; but if we ask why *a*'s φ-ing occurred, *a* might not be a subject of concern at all' ('Agency and Causal Explanation', in J. Heil and A. Mele (eds.), *Mental Causation* (Oxford, 1993), 166).

so, it is of course not at all surprising that the failures of substitutivity which Kim notes should occur—that, for example, an answer to the question why Brutus stabbed Caesar does not always serve also as a good answer to the question why Brutus killed Caesar. For a good explanation of why an event of the Brutus-stabbing-Caesar variety occurred might not succeed in explaining also why an event of the Brutus-killing-Caesar kind occurred. But this has absolutely no tendency to imply that a single individual event—Brutus' stabbing of Caesar—might not be identical with his killing of Caesar, as Kim's criterion of event-individuation implies. If explanations of the form 'S_1 because S_2', where S_1 and S_2 are sentences, are never explanations of why an individual, particular event occurred, it can be no argument against the identity of any individual, particular events to point out that certain of these sentences are not intersubstitutable in explanatory contexts.

Kim's difficulties here can be traced directly to the second assumption mentioned above, the view that ordinary sentences of subject–predicate or relational form succeed in singling out individual events. The problem with this suggestion, as Davidson has emphasized, is that such a sentence might be made true by the occurrence of any of a number of individual happenings.[14] A sentence like 'Doris capsized the canoe yesterday', Davidson points out, is no less true if Doris capsized the canoe twelve times than if she capsized it only once. The sentence is general, not particular, in its claim; in so far as we take it to involve some kind of commitment to events, that commitment needs to be expressed by means of an existential quantification over events, not by a sentence with a singular term for an event in subject position. And this is no less true even if Doris did as a matter of fact capsize the canoe only once yesterday—this is merely a contingent fact which has no bearing on the logical function of the sentence. Davidson compares the sentence 'Doris capsized the canoe yesterday' to 'There is a mosquito in the room', which, similarly, is an existential claim, true even if the room contains seven mosquitoes, and which makes no *reference* to any individual mosquito even if the room contains only one.

[14] D. Davidson, 'The Individuation of Events', in N. Rescher (ed.), *Essays in Honor of Carl G. Hempel* (Dordrecht, 1969); repr. in Davidson, *Essays on Actions and Events*, 167–8.

Kim's difficulties here are masked, to some extent, by his attempt to enlist the aid of times in order uniquely to identify individual events. The idea is that any true event-describing sentence could be supplemented so as to incorporate reference to a particular time, to yield sentences such as 'Doris capsized the canoe at 1 p.m. yesterday'—and that by this means an individual event could be singled out. But as Davidson points out, such sentences still make existential claims; the mere addition of a temporal modifier will not serve to turn a sentence containing no singular term into one which does contain such a term:

Some actions are difficult or unusual to perform more than once in a short or specified time, and this may provide a specious reason in some cases for holding that action sentences refer to unique actions. Thus with 'Jones got married last Saturday', 'Doris wrote a cheque at noon', 'Mary kissed an admirer on the stroke of midnight'. It is merely illegal to get married twice on the same day, merely unusual to write cheques simultaneously, and merely good fortune to get to kiss two admirers at once. Similarly, if I say, 'There is an elephant in the bathtub', you are no doubt justified in supposing that one elephant at most is in the bathtub, but you are confused if you think my sentence refers to a particular elephant if any.[15]

It would seem, then, that Kim's event-describing sentences, even when they specify times explicitly, cannot be understood as making reference to particular events. What, then, are we to say about the exemplifications of properties at times (henceforth, EPTs) which are supposed to stand (more or less) in one–one correspondence with those sentences, when they are true?[16] Presumably, we cannot suppose them identical with ordinary particular events, since ordinary particular events, as we have seen, do not necessarily stand in one–one correspondence with those sentences. But that is not to say that EPTs might not be entities of some philosophically important kind, which we might be at liberty to *call* events. What sort of entities might these be? What sorts of entities might stand in one–one correspondence with ordinary, true sentences of predicative or relational form? The natural answer, surely, is that EPTs must be

---

[15] D. Davidson, 'The Individuation of Events', 167.

[16] 'More or less' because Kim does seem to be prepared to countenance some restrictions on the 'generic properties' which can be constitutive properties of EPTs. But the details of these restrictions are irrelevant to my particular objection to his view; and so I shall not describe them here.

facts. When a sentence is true, what is thereby guaranteed unique existence is a fact, not any kind of particular thing.[17]

That EPTs are facts, not particular events, is supported by a number of considerations. I have already noted that the *explananda* in which Kim is interested are really facts, not particulars—for example, if I want to know why Brutus stabbed Caesar, what I am looking for is an explanation of a fact, an answer to the question why *P*, where *P* is the fact that Brutus stabbed Caesar, not an explanation of any particular stabbing (if indeed we can make sense of the idea of particulars serving as *explananda* at all). The criterion of identity that Kim gives for EPTs also suggests that they are facts, not individual events. According to Kim's identity criterion, exemplifications of distinct properties always count as distinct EPTs. An exemplification of the property of capsizing, on this criterion, for example, could not also be an exemplification of the property of having a disaster or having an accident, because capsizing, having a disaster, and having an accident are distinct properties which might all figure in different explanations of other events—and which might themselves require different explanations. But it is much more plausible to think that this kind of 'fine-grainedness', as it is sometimes called, is a feature of the individuation of facts than it is to associate it with the individuation of particular events. The fact that Doris capsized the canoe, for example, is certainly not identical with the fact that she had an accident; and neither is the fact that she capsized the canoe at 1 p.m. yesterday identical with the fact that she had an accident at 1 p.m. yesterday. But it is quite natural to suppose that an individual event can be described in many ways—as a disaster, an accident, a capsizing, and so on.

I shall take it to have been established from now on that Kim's events are best understood to be fact-like, structured entities that correspond to sentences rather than to singular terms. In the next section, I want to try to show why such fact-like entities are not useful for the formulation of the thoughts and theories in philosophy of mind which have been given expression in terms of an ontology of events.

---

[17] I intend here—and in all the discussion of facts which follows—a very modest understanding of what it is for a fact to exist; this formulation should not be taken to imply commitment, for example, to a correspondence theory of truth, even though I have used the word 'corresponds'. A fact, in my sense, exists simply in virtue of some proposition or other's being true.

2. PROPERTY EXEMPLIFICATIONS AND THEORIES OF MIND

In a paper entitled 'Identity, Necessity and Events', Fred Feldman has argued that what he calls 'structural' views of events, by which he means accounts like Kim's, according to which events are exemplifications of properties at times, will not allow space for a proper distinction between type and token versions of physicalism.[18] I shall start by outlining this argument, which seems to me perfectly sound, before going on to diagnose the failure of Kim's events to supply a coherent ontology for token physicalism as due to their failure to satisfy a condition which I call the 'secret life requirement'.

Feldman's argument to the conclusion that Kim's events cannot be used to support the formulation of token physicalism goes as follows. Token physicalism, as usually understood, is supposed to be compatible with the assumption that mental and physical *properties* are distinct from one another. That some particular occurrence of a feeling of pain, for example, is identical with or composed from some physiological event or set of physiological events, is usually held not to imply that the property of being in pain can be identified or associated specifically in some other way with any physiological property. But if this line of thought is coherent, we need a way of conceiving of events which makes it possible to understand how event identities (or compositional relations between individual events and sets of events) could hold in the absence of any corresponding relationships between properties. The trouble with Kim's theory of events, according to Feldman, is that it does not appear to allow for such a possibility.

On Kim's view, if events are to be identical, they must be exemplifications of the same property by the same substance at the same time. If a mental event is to be identified with a physical event, on Kim's account of events, therefore, it would seem that the mental property of which the mental event is the exemplification will have to be identifiable with the physical property of which the physical event is the exemplification—presumably a physical property. But

---

[18] F. Feldman, 'Identity, Necessity and Events', in Block (ed.), *Readings in Philosophy of Psychology*, i. Later, I shall question whether the type–token distinction is really the right distinction in terms of which to differentiate between these different versions of physicalism; but for now, I shall follow conventional usage. The term 'token physicalism', as I use it, is intended to cover both token identity theories and theories which are stated in terms of constitution or composition relations.

this is the position of the type identity theory. There does not seem to be any logical space, on Kim's view of events, for the token identity theory. There is no space for a view that combines property dualism with event monism.[19]

As far as I can see, there are only two possible responses Kim might make to Feldman's challenge, neither of which coheres with his theory of events.

1. It might perhaps be wondered whether Kim might be able to allow that so-called mental events could be exemplifications of physical properties at times—perhaps *as well as* being exemplifications of mental properties. If this were permissible, identifications between mental and physical events would not be out of the question. But Kim certainly seems unwilling to make any such concession. There is never any indication, in Kim's writings, that a single 'exemplification' might be an exemplification of more than one property at a time. In so far as it is possible to understand what sorts of things exemplifications are supposed to be, it seems to be a necessary truth, for Kim, that every exemplification is an exemplification of exactly one property—what counts as a single property to be determined by the explanatory criterion mentioned above. But if this is right, there is no room in Kim's theory for the admission that exemplifications of mental properties might be identical with exemplifications of physical ones.

2. Perhaps it might be suggested that mental events are *simply* exemplifications of physical properties (or that physical events are *simply* exemplifications of mental ones)—that an individual occurrence of a feeling of pain, for example, might be simply an exemplification of some (perhaps rather complex) physical property, and not an exemplification of a mental property at all. But this is not something which Kim can countenance, either. Recall that, for Kim, our commitment to events is demonstrated by our use of 'event-describing' sentences—which are sentences of simple subject–predicate form, such as 'Xanthippe wept' and 'Socrates died'. Our commitment to an ontology of mental events, according to Kim, is signalled by our use of sentences in which a mental predicate

---

[19] That this is indeed a consequence of Kim's view of events is admitted by Kim himself in 'On the Psycho-physical Identity Theory', 232: 'the problem of the identity of Socrates' being in pain and Socrates' being in brain state B reduces to the problem whether or not the property of being in pain and the property of being in brain state B are the same property'.

is used—'Christopher felt a sharp pain', for example. There is thus no way of understanding the classification of an event as *mental*, except by conceiving of it as the event 'described' by a sentence in which a mental predicate is used. The suggestion that an event might be mental and yet not be an exemplification of a mental property just seems to be incoherent, given this framework.

In a paper entitled 'Phenomenal Properties, Psychophysical Laws and the Identity Theory',[20] Kim seems to recognize some of the consequences which his view has for the philosophy of mind. For example, after explaining his own view of events, he writes that: 'One consequence of our interpretation of the identity theory . . . is that it entails the thesis that all psychological events have nomically correlated physical events.'[21] But Kim, far from being concerned by this, welcomes the result. He goes on to contrast his theory of events with the alternative view that events are 'structureless particulars', a view on which nothing follows from the assertion that 'all mental events are physical events' except 'the rather weak assertion that a mental event happens to an organism when and only when it is undergoing some physical event'.[22] This seems to confirm that it was right to deny that Kim has the resources to accommodate token physicalism; at any rate, this certainly seems to be his own view.

It is important to emphasize that it is not only those who believe some version of token physicalism to be *true* who will need to reject Kim's account of events, if this is right. Anyone who claims to think it even intelligible owes us an account of how the commitments of type and token physicalism may be supposed to differ, given a view of events as EPTs. On the whole, I think most philosophers think they understand what it would be for a mental event, the occurrence of a feeling of pain, say, to be identical with or perhaps to be composed out of some neurological event, or set of events, and that they can make sense of the thought that such relations might hold quite independently of any commitment to any thesis at all about the relations between mental and physical properties. But then the items which are the objects of these thoughts cannot be Kim's

---

[20] *The Monist*, 56 (1972).
[21] Ibid. 184.
[22] Ibid. 185. Though if the 'are' here is the plural equivalent of the 'is' of identity, it does not seem to be true that nothing follows from the assertion that all mental events are physical events except for this weak correlation thesis.

events. Token physicalism requires for its coherent formulation entities which might intelligibly be singled out by means of both mental and physical descriptions—and exemplifications of single properties clearly do not fit the bill.

What is it, exactly, about EPTs that unsuits them for the formulation of token physicalism? It is here, I think, that it is useful to reflect on the capacity of a thing to have what I earlier referred to as a 'secret life'. Token physicalism (whatever the precise version under consideration) seems to need for its cogent formulation entities about whose nature and properties questions can intelligibly arise which are not simply dependent on answers to prior questions about relations between other entities. We need to be able to make sense of the thought that one and the same event, unbeknownst to someone who can identify that event in one way—say, from the psychological point of view, by means of a demonstrative thought, e.g. as 'that decision I just made' or 'my thinking of this thought'— might be identifiable also by means of some physiological or neurophysiological description, or a different demonstrative, targeted via a physiological indication of which event, or events, are meant—e.g. 'that flow of electrical impulses'. And this thought seems clearly to raise a question which is in an utterly basic way a question simply about *this thing*, not a question which requires the prior settling of questions about the identity, nature, or properties of anything else. But the only model we have for the identification of a single EPT by more than one means is a model on which two different descriptions of the [S, p, t] form are judged equivalent. This means that any question which might arise about an identity between EPTs will turn necessarily on a prior question about the identity of the constitutive substances, properties, or times specified by the two alternative canonical descriptions. We cannot make sense, therefore, of the idea that an exemplification of some mental property by a person might, unbeknownst to someone who singles it out, at the same time be an exemplification of some physical property, *except* by supposing that an unknown property, substance, or time identity holds. One can make no sense of the idea that an exemplification of a property might have a secret life *qua* token. Whatever diversity of perspective is possible on such an entity is entirely derivative from different ways of characterizing its constitutive substance, property, and time. It cannot be guardian of any mysteries which are genuinely its own; it can only have a secret life vicariously, as it were, by relying on whatever multifacetedness might exist in the entities by means of which it is identified.

I shall say that an entity satisfies the 'secret life requirement' if and only if it is intelligible to suppose that:

1. the entity might be uniquely identified by means of some referring expression which is not known to apply to it by someone who is, nevertheless, in a position to single that entity out in some other way;

2. for some such referring expressions, the subject's not knowing that they provide an alternative means of uniquely identifying the entity in question is not simply a matter of her being ignorant of an alternative means of uniquely identifying some *other* entity;

3. for some such referring expressions, the subject's not knowing that they provide an alternative means of uniquely identifying the entity in question is not simply a matter of her not knowing about one of the entity's *relational* properties (where spatial and temporal properties are not accounted relational).

What I now want to suggest is that the events needed for the formulation of token physicalism need to satisfy the secret life requirement.

A word of explanation is needed about the details of the secret life requirement. Condition (1) is simply intended to capture the idea of an entity's being available from more than one point of view, the possibility of its having hidden aspects. Condition (2) is intended to exclude the kind of case where an entity's secret life is only vicarious in the sense suggested above—i.e. the kind of case in which the fact that an entity has hidden aspects is entirely a matter of some other entity's having hidden aspects, in the way in which, for example, an EPT can have hidden aspects if its constitutive substance, property, or time can be singled out in more than one way. Condition (3) is intended to exclude the kind of case in which an entity can be uniquely identified by means of a relation it bears to something else—as, for example, an EPT might be identified as 'the EPT I just thought of' or 'the EPT mentioned on such and such a page of this book'. The possibility that some such description might be true of an EPT unbeknownst to someone who can single that EPT out in another way (say, by giving its canonical description) does not render the EPT multifaceted in the sense in which I am interested—and so this sort of relational means of singling out an entity uniquely needs to be ruled out. Genuinely being able to have a secret life involves having intrinsic properties about which someone might be ignorant, not just relational ones.[23] But it is important that spatial and temporal properties count as 'intrinsic' for these purposes. Particulars which genuinely present more than one face to the world can sometimes only be singled out from other entities of the same sort by means of spatial and temporal criteria—so these need to count as non-relational if the secret life requirement is not to be too difficult to satisfy.

What sorts of events might fulfil the secret life requirement? The answer would seem to be—precisely entities of that 'structureless' variety which Kim eschews—particular events whose individuation is independent of the prior identification of specific properties, and about which questions can therefore arise the answers to which are not simply dependent upon answers to prior questions about properties.[24] I do not mean to suggest, of course, that properties play no

---

[23] It might be objected that the distinction between intrinsic and relational properties is unclear. But even if this is true, I do not think it will matter for the purposes of the secret life requirement. The point is just to exclude a certain sort of property which entities like EPTs and facts (and indeed any sort of thing at all) can have from counting as contributing to their multifacetedness—and the properties in question, properties like 'having just been thought of by Jim', are *clearly* relational, if any property is.

[24] The question whether *actions* satisfy the secret life requirement has been put to me by Jennifer Hornsby. Her worry is that it is more obvious that actions are particulars than that they satisfy the secret life requirement. On Hornsby's conception of the individuation of actions (which I share), actions can be described in many ways, but typically, these redescriptions identify actions by way either of their effects or their causal-explanatory predecessors. It might therefore be thought that actions cannot satisfy conditions (1) and (2) without violating condition (3).

For those who believe that actions are events which can be given descriptions which make no reference whatever to persons—descriptions which utilize only physiological or neurophysiological vocabulary, say—there is no danger that actions might fail to satisfy the secret life requirement. Each action, on this view, would be available, in principle, to be picked out uniquely by any of a number of possible referring expressions, none of which fall foul of conditions (2) or (3). For a start, actions presumably have definite spatiotemporal locations, on this view, which would provide one means of identifying them uniquely without contravening conditions (2) and (3); and they would presumably also have a number of suitable physiological descriptions. But Hornsby does not believe that actions can be singled out by such means as these (see her 'Which Physical Events are Mental Events?', *Proceedings of the Aristotelian Society*, 81 (1980–1); and 'Agency and Causal Explanation'); and I think her arguments for this claim are convincing. Actions, then, might seem to present a challenge to the secret life requirement, for one who accepts that 'actions are not in fact accessible from the impersonal point of view' (ibid. 162).

role in the singling out of structureless particulars as objects of thought, for of course they often (perhaps even always) do. But the properties which thus aid the singling out of these structureless particulars are *their* properties, not properties of which they are the exemplifications, but properties which they *have*. A structureless particular will always possess a number of such properties, which is what makes it intelligible to suppose that there might be more than one way of singling it out, that someone might be able to identify

There are, as far as I can see, two possible responses (not counting the straightforward denial that actions *are* particulars, which I regard as unacceptable). The first is to note that it is a condition of an entity's satisfying the secret life requirement only that it be *intelligible to suppose* that that entity might be uniquely identified by means of some referring expression which is not known to apply to it by someone who is, nevertheless, in a position to single that entity out in some other way (where the referring expression satisfies conditions (2) and (3)). One might then try to say something about the kind of intelligibility which is involved here which might make it seem plausible that, although it is not true that actions have physiological descriptions, it is not in fact unintelligible to suppose that they might have had such descriptions—that they are the sorts of things (perhaps because they are events?) which might have had such descriptions (though they do not). Certainly, it seems to me that even if there is a sense in which it could be said to be unintelligible that actions can be singled out by means of physiological or other kinds of impersonal descriptions, the reason why this is unintelligible (if it is) is quite different from the reason why it is unintelligible that facts or EPTs should be uniquely identified by a range of different referring expressions, none of which violate conditions (2) or (3); and perhaps for the purposes of the secret life requirement, this difference could be somehow built into the relevant notion of 'intelligibility'.

The second possible response, which I am inclined to favour, is to try to argue that actions can be described from the *personal* point of view in a number of different ways, such that (1)–(3) are in fact satisfied. Hornsby herself has suggested to me one possible way of arguing for this claim. If one believes, as Hornsby does, that (nearly) every action is someone's *trying* to do something, and indeed that there are typically quite a few descriptions of any given action which are of this form, then it does seem to be intelligible to suppose that an action might be uniquely identified by means of a referring expression which is not known to apply to it by someone who is, nevertheless, in a position to single that entity out in some other way. I might, for example, know that your hitting the tennis-ball into the net was your trying to get it over the net—but not that it was also your trying to get the ball into the bottom right-hand corner of the court or your trying to win match point. Provided one accepts that, in such a case, my not knowing that these descriptions provide an alternative means of uniquely identifying your action is not a matter of my not knowing about one of your action's relational properties, then the action satisfies the secret life requirement.

Is it true that my not knowing that these descriptions provide an alternative means of uniquely identifying your action is *not* a matter of my not knowing about one of your action's relational properties? Without a clearer account of the distinction between intrinsic and relational properties than I have provided here, it is obviously difficult to say; but I can see, at least, no immediately obvious reason for thinking that an action's being someone's trying to φ should be accounted a relational property of it.

and provide one or more definite descriptions (or demonstratives) which referred to it without being able necessarily to say of *any* such description whether or not it referred to the particular in question. But this is just another way of saying that structureless particulars are precisely the sorts of entities which might satisfy the secret life requirement, that such an entity might be singled out successfully by someone who does not know all the ways in which it might be uniquely identified, and whose ignorance might genuinely and fundamentally be an ignorance about *it*; not ignorance that is simply derivative from ignorance about some other entity, or from ignorance of some relation that that entity bears to something else.

It seems to me that the distinction between entities like facts and EPTs which cannot have a secret life, except to the extent that other entities on which they are dependent for their individuation have such a life, and those like genuinely particular events and substances whose mysteries may be their own, is an immensely important one. In the next section, I want to try to argue that the secret life requirement ought to be made a necessary condition of particularity, i.e. that only those entities which can have a secret life in the sense specified by that requirement should count as particulars.[25] Of course, just as with the concept of 'event', there is a sense in which there can be no genuinely philosophical interest in an entirely context-free debate about what constitutes particularity; doubtless there are a number of different, equally admissible understandings of what particularity is. My claim, therefore, will simply be that for the characterization of so-called 'token' physicalism, we must have a conception of the relevant tokens which is such as to enable them to satisfy the secret life requirement.

3. PARTICULARITY AND THE SECRET LIFE REQUIREMENT

Particulars are traditionally contrasted in philosophy with 'universals'. Unfortunately, though, there is not sufficient consensus about how this distinction should be drawn, nor even about its

---

[25] I do not, though, think that the secret life requirement is a sufficient condition of particularity; it seems to me that it might perfectly well be satisfied by substances in the mass sense, e.g. gold, water; and perhaps also by certain properties, if one thinks there can be informative property identities.

legitimacy, to make this a very useful starting-point. Roughly, though, a particular is usually supposed to be an entity like Socrates or the Taj Mahal, which has contingent existence in a reasonably well-defined place at a reasonably well-defined time or through a period of time, while universals are things like properties and relations, like redness, or the property of being a horse, which are in principle multiply instantiable, are usually (though not universally) thought not to have spatiotemporal location, and which have been argued by some to be necessarily existent rather than contingent entities. This contrast, or something like it, is the contrast on which Kim relies when he defends himself against the claim that EPTs are not particulars; for he points out that EPTs have location both in space and in time, and that their existence is not necessary but rather contingent on the truth of the corresponding 'event-describing' sentences.[26] But is this enough for particularity? I shall argue (1) that for anyone who thinks that no fact ought to count as a particular, Kim's criteria are not sufficient for particularity, (2) that anyone who thinks it is all right for facts to count as particulars is not utilizing a conception of particularity which could be useful for the formulation of token physicalism, and (3) that the condition which ought to be added to Kim's criteria to ensure a conception of particularity which would be useful for the formulation of token physicalism is the secret life requirement.

Kim is surely right to suggest that his EPTs are contingent existents. He is also right that there is a sense in which it is usually possible to assign a place and a time non-randomly to any given EPT.[27] But I think it might be doubted whether the possibility of doing so is enough to make them truly spatiotemporal entities— after all, any fact which concerns how things are with some spatiotemporal particular at a specified time can be assigned a place and a time in the same sort of way—but not many, I suspect, would want to take the view that facts have a genuinely spatiotemporal presence in the world. I shall not, however, proceed by attempting to show that EPTs are not spatiotemporal entities. Rather, I shall simply concede to Kim that his EPTs can be assigned both a place and a time so that they may be considered to have some sort of spatiotemporal character. What I shall question is whether having

---

[26] See 'Events as Property Exemplifications', 165, quoted above.

[27] For present purposes, I simply ignore the complications which are raised by attributions of properties to entities which have no clear location.

spatiotemporal character of this sort can be sufficient (along with contingency) for particularity, given that what might be called particular facts—facts like the fact that George III died on 29 January 1820 or the fact that the Taj Mahal was white on 16 June 1994—it would seem, can also be assigned both a place and a time. A defender of EPTs might want to protest that particular facts are not really spatiotemporal entities—that it is not the fact, but rather one or more of its constituents, that has a genuine spatiotemporal presence. But she must then show us why we may not say the same about EPTs.

For those who think, as I do, that EPTs just *are* particular facts, and that no fact can also be a particular, the claim that EPTs are therefore not particulars will seem obvious. The argument above is designed to persuade those who are still inclined to hold out against the view that EPTs are just facts that they must do more than merely point out that EPTs can be assigned a place and a time in order to show this. The spatiotemporal criterion may work well enough to distinguish particulars from *universals*. But the claim that EPTs are not particulars is not, I think, well understood by taking the implied contrast here to be with universality. Those who argue that Kim's events lack particularity do not mean, in making this claim, to group EPTs with entities like redness or the property of being a horse. Those, like Davidson, who have insisted on the particularity of events have intended to contrast that view not so much with the view that events are universals as with the claim that events are entities which have a property which is often referred to in the philosophical literature as 'fine-grainedness'—in particular, with the view that events are in some respects like facts or propositions. Davidson, for example, in 'Events as Particulars' contrasts his own view with that of Chisholm, who regards events as propositional in nature; and Feldman, in 'Identity, Necessity and Events' contrasts 'propositional' and 'structural' views of events with positions according to which events are 'concrete' entities. Lombard also criticizes Kim's view for turning events into 'states of affairs'.[28] But it is not obvious that facts, propositions, or states of affairs are 'universals'. It seems fairly plain, then, that in order to express the sorts of criticisms of Kim's view which such critics have expressed by means of a doubt that Kim's events are genuine

---

[28] *Events*, 56.

particulars, we need to develop a view of particulars which will exclude fact-like entities, as well as traditional 'universals', from the class.

Someone might, of course, hold out for a conception of particularity which permitted fact-like entities to count as a variety of particular. But the sorts of considerations which govern questions about the identity of fact-like entities, as we have already seen, make such entities poor candidates for an ontology which could serve the purposes of someone wanting to formulate token physicalism. The whole point about token physicalism is that it is supposed to provide a way of avoiding reductionism, that it is a form of physicalism which can afford to deny that mental facts simply are physical facts. The conception of particularity we need, then, must exclude particular facts, or the whole *raison d'être* of token physicalism will be lost.

What sort of condition might we employ in order to distinguish particulars from fact-like entities? My suggestion is that what is needed is the secret life requirement, or something very like it. I have already argued that EPTs do not satisfy the requirement—and I think it is reasonably obvious that nothing with any sort of propositional structure could do so. It is admittedly rather odd to speak at all of facts as things which could be identified by means of referring expressions, as is required in order to apply the secret life requirement to facts, for we do not usually *refer* to facts at all; we rather express them by means of those of our sentences which happen to be true. Nevertheless, there do seem to be ways of referring to facts; there are expressions of the form 'the fact that *p*', as well as ordinary definite descriptions and demonstratives—for example, expressions like 'the fact which is expressed by the sentence *S*' or 'that fact I just thought of'. But nothing which could be singled out by any such means as these could possibly satisfy the secret life requirement, as I shall now attempt to show.

It is, of course, intelligible that a fact might be uniquely identified by some means which was not known to be applicable to it by someone who was able, nevertheless, uniquely to identify that fact, i.e. condition (1) of the secret life requirement might be satisfied by a fact. But it seems impossible to imagine how such a state of affairs might arise except by means of a violation of either condition (2) or condition (3). A fact might have as a constituent an object or property which was identifiable by more than one means, thus giving rise to the possibility that someone might fail to recognize that two different expressions referred to the same fact—as might happen, for example, if someone knows that George Eliot wrote *The Mill on the Floss*, does not know that George Eliot and Mary Ann Evans were one and the same person, and so fails to know that the fact that Mary Ann Evans wrote *The Mill on the Floss* is the same fact as the fact that George Eliot wrote *The Mill on the Floss*.[29] But this violates (2), since the person's ignorance clearly depends on her not knowing that 'Mary Ann Evans' refers to George Eliot. Or one can imagine someone failing to know that some relational property of a fact might be used uniquely to identify it—for example, that the fact in question is the most incredible fact known by Mary or the fact which Bill is most upset about. But this violates (3), for all these seem to be relational properties. What does not seem possible is that a fact might genuinely be identifiable by means of quite different *intrinsic* properties of its own. As with EPTs, any multifacetedness which might arise in the case of facts would, I think, always be traceable to the multifacetedness of the *constituents* of the fact; it could never be the case that a fact itself could present more than one face to the world, independently of its constituents being entities which might do so.

Someone with a different view of facts might insist that facts can have the sort of multifacetedness that I have denied them. Someone might think, for example, that the fact that Xanthippe became a widow on some particular day in 399 BC just is the same fact as the fact that Socrates died on that day—though these facts clearly have quite different constituents. But I think that such identities are provably false, given only an assumption I regard as incontrovertible, namely that identical things must exist in all the same possible worlds. For in possible worlds where Xanthippe marries someone else, she may become a widow on some particular day, even though Socrates does not die in that world on that day. The fact that Xanthippe becomes a widow on that day thus 'exists' in possible worlds where Socrates' dying on that day does not. So they cannot

---

[29] Obviously, this depends on a controversial assumption about fact-identity— but if someone wants to adopt a finer-grained view of the identity of facts than is suggested by such an identification, it will be even clearer that they do not have the sort of multifacetedness which I am arguing should be made a necessary condition of particularity.

be the same fact. Additionally, things can be explained by citing the fact that Socrates died on some particular day which are not equally well explained by citing the fact that Xanthippe became a widow on that day. And perhaps most importantly of all, any view of facts which is so coarse-grained that it permits such identities risks sacrificing the modesty which characterizes the view of facts to which I have tried to adhere, since it tries to separate the concept of a fact from the idea of a fact's being that which is expressed by a true sentence. It seems to me self-evident that the sentence 'Xanthippe became a widow' does not express the same thought as the sentence 'Socrates died'. But then, to insist that the fact that Xanthippe became a widow is nevertheless the same fact as the fact that Socrates died must be to separate the fact from the 'what is expressed', and thus to take the first step along the route to an untenable version of the correspondence theory of truth.

I think, then, that it is clear that if the secret life requirement were made a necessary condition of particularity, any entity with a propositional structure ought to fail to qualify. And it also seems clear that the condition needs to be met by any entity about which it makes sense to ask 'Is this thing which I can refer to by means of a mental description or psychologically focused demonstrative perhaps also something which can be described in purely physiological or physical vocabulary?'—so that we ought to make it a necessary condition of the kind of particularity which a token physicalist needs her tokens to possess. What I shall argue in Chapter 8 is that the imposition of this condition serves to disqualify not only Kim's events but also most of those entities which philosophers have referred to as 'token states' from counting as particulars—that they are not the sorts of things on which one could gain the kind of radical diversity of perspective which gives token physicalism sense. Only a whole host of misconceptions surrounding both the concept of a token and the concept of a state have led us to think otherwise.

I hope, then, to have shown that there is an interesting conception of particularity embodied in the secret life requirement, that the tokens in terms of which token physicalism is formulated need to be particulars in this sense, and that Kim's EPTs fail to qualify. In the remainder of the chapter, I shall be considering whether Bennett's events, also property exemplifications of a sort, can avoid the charge of non-particularity.

4. BENNETT: EVENTS AS TROPES

Bennett presents his account of events as a kind of corrective to Kim's. Though he retains the idea that events are property exemplifications, he makes a sharp distinction between metaphysical accounts of the nature of events and semantic discussions concerning the reference of event names.[30] Most of the difficulties which have been thought to attend Kim's account, he believes, stem from confusions in Kim's position on semantic questions about which event names refer to the same event. On Bennett's view, though, this need not—indeed does not—impugn Kim's account of the 'ontological and logical' nature of events.[31] Kim is right, according to Bennett, to think that events are exemplifications—or instances, as he prefers to put it—of properties at times. He is just wrong to think that any description we use to refer to an event must mention the property of which that event is an instance. Indeed, on Bennett's view, it is virtually impossible that an event description should mention this constitutive property. For he believes, *contra* Kim, that the properties of which events are instances are extremely complex—so complex, indeed, that it usually proves unmanageably difficult to say what they are. Any property we might mention in a description which singled out an event would inevitably be only part of the complex property whose instantiation constituted the event in question. Events, according to Bennett, are 'complex tropes',[32] a trope being a case or instance of a property. A complex trope is a case or instance of a correspondingly complex property. The following passage from Bennett's book gives some idea of what Bennett has in mind:

A single event is named by 'Leibniz's coach ride on November 24, 1676', by 'Leibniz's journey on November 24, 1676', and by 'Leibniz's journey between Delft and the Hague'. The event in question was a certain instance—namely, the one that had Leibniz as its subject on November 24, 1676—of a certain complex property. It is not the property of taking a coach ride or of journeying, or of journeying between Delft and the Hague,

---

[30] Bennett uses the term 'name' in a broad sense to mean 'referring expression'. Most of the 'names' with which he is concerned are actually definite descriptions. In what follows, I shall adopt Bennett's broad usage.

[31] *Events and their Names*, 73.

[32] Bennett borrows the term 'trope' from Donald C. Williams, 'The Elements of Being', *Review of Metaphysics*, 7 (1953).

though it includes those. The metaphysical thesis that Leibniz's journey was an instance of property P has not the faintest tendency to imply the semantic thesis that any name of Leibniz's journey must contain a name of P or a predicate that connotes P . . . I shall speak of the property that 'constitutes' a given event *e*, meaning the property P such that *the whole intrinsic truth about e is that it is an instance of P.*[33]

The complexity of the properties whose instances constitute events, on Bennett's view, enables him to avoid some of the difficulties which make Kim's account seem immediately objectionable. For example, there is no longer any insurmountable obstacle to identifying Brutus' stabbing of Caesar with his killing of Caesar, or the swim that Leander took in the Hellespont at *t* with the crossing of the Hellespont that Leander made at *t*, on the grounds that these events are instances of different properties by the subjects concerned. For on Bennett's view, 'Leander's swim in the Hellespont' and 'Leander's crossing of the Hellespont' can both refer to the same complex property instance; to use Bennett's metaphor, they can both 'reach out and grab'[34] the same 'trope'—which will presumably 'include' both the 'swam in the Hellespont' property and the 'crossed the Hellespont' property. But the complexity of Bennett's tropes is also a source of considerable difficulty. For Bennett is not very clear either about the kind of complexity his complex properties are supposed to have, or about which individuals are supposed to have these complex properties. Talk of the 'inclusion' of properties by other, more complex properties might suggest that Bennett has in mind some kind of giant conjunction, perhaps thinned out where there are entailment relations between the conjuncts, 'swam' thus dropping out in favour of 'swam in the Hellespont', etc.—though he nowhere says explicitly that this is the case. And the example of Leibniz's journey, given above, suggests that the complex property in question is supposed to be had by a substance involved in the event, in this case, Leibniz; for it was Leibniz who took the coach trip, did the journeying, etc. But elsewhere, Bennett seems to suggest rather that it is the *event* and not a substance that has the relevant complex property. He talks, for example, of the properties 'being a kick' and 'being an assault' (presumably properties of events) as parts of the complex property whose instantiation constitutes some kicking event.[35] And in other

---

[33] *Events and their Names*, 93.   [34] Ibid.   [35] Ibid. 94.

places, he suggests that the complex properties he has in mind are instantiated neither by substances nor by events, but by spatiotemporal zones: 'It is often more natural to speak of it (the property) as instantiated by *something in the zone*, but I believe that wherever a space-occupying thing x has property P at time T, this is because at a deeper metaphysical level, the zone defined by x and T has a corresponding property P*.'[36]

Perhaps Bennett is indifferent between these views because he assumes that one can translate readily between them. Where Leibniz instantiates some complex property due to his journeying on a particular occasion between Delft and The Hague ('climbed into a coach at 8 a.m. on 24 November 1676, and travelled at 1 m.p.h. for 3 seconds, then at 2 m.p.h. for 2 seconds, . . .', etc.), for example, there will be an event which instantiates some correspondingly complex property ('was a journey by Leibniz in a coach which began with Leibniz's climbing into the coach . . .'), and a space-time zone (presumably the zone which includes and is entirely filled by the whole of the coach journey) which has another complex property—which I dare not begin to try to state. All these complex properties are distinct from one another, grammatically speaking, for they are properties of quite different kinds of entities—but if I am not mistaken, Bennett would not want to regard their 'instantiations' as likewise distinct. One and the same 'trope' could count as the instantiation of all of these complex properties by their respective subjects—object, event, and spatiotemporal region. It is just that 'the whole intrinsic truth' can be told in many ways—as a story about an object, an event, or a zone.

Bennett admits that there will be a good deal of indeterminacy surrounding the question what is to count as the whole intrinsic truth about any event. Is it part of the 'intrinsic truth' about Leibniz's journey to The Hague, for example, that he didn't feel travel-sick? Or are 'negative' properties not to count? What about the fact that a bird flew alongside the coach for part of the time? Bennett acknowledges such difficulties, and accepts that it may not always be determinate which properties are to count as parts of the huge super-property whose instantiation at a time is supposed to constitute some given event: 'Although there are limits to what the . . . property could be, the question of what it is has no

[36] Ibid. 88 n. 2.

determinate answer; in this respect, our language of events contains a lot of slack.'[37] But given that this is so, we might think that there is reason to question the identification of events with the instantiations of complex properties. Does it make sense to say that an event is an instantiation of a complex property, if there is no complex property of which it is definitely the instantiation?

I do not propose at this stage to go further into the question whether Bennett's view of events is generally defensible—though some of what I shall have to say later will have some bearing on the matter. Rather, having articulated this rather general worry, I want to try to adhere to the approach I outlined in the Introduction, and turn to the question of how the view fares in relation to the sorts of theory for which philosophy of mind requires an ontology of events. Interestingly enough, Bennett himself offers an answer to this question—and it is to this that I shall now turn.

5. BENNETT'S ARGUMENT AGAINST ANOMALOUS MONISM

According to Bennett, 'Davidson's philosophy of mind'—by which he means Davidson's particular version of the token identity theory, anomalous monism—'rests on a virtual triviality.'[38] The argument for this depends on his acceptance of a thesis which he calls the Thesis of Universal Nonzonal Fusion, which I shall first try to explain, before moving on to Bennett's deflationary argument.

Bennett makes a distinction between *zonal* and *nonzonal* fusion. Zonal fusion is a straightforwardly mereological notion; an item is the fusion of a lot of smaller items, in this sense, if together they compose or constitute it. A walnut, to give one of Bennett's examples, is the fusion of its shell and its kernel. Events can also be zonally fused, according to Bennett; my greeting and yours, to use Bennett's example again, can be parts of a single exchange. But Bennett also thinks that there can be nonzonal fusion of events. This can occur where two events coincide spatiotemporally; they can be fused, he says 'to make a qualitatively "richer" or "thicker" event'.[39] As an example, he gives the following: 'The spin of the top throughout T is one event, and its synchronous movement across the table is another that coincides with the former, and *the top's whole movement through T* is a third, coinciding with the other two and having them as nonzonal parts.'[40] Bennett also thinks, though he admits he cannot argue for it, that any two zonally coinciding events are nonzonal parts of an event that also coincides with them. This is the Thesis of Universal Nonzonal Fusion. It is a licence to add zonally coinciding events together, wherever they occur, to make new events. Is there any reason to think that we ought not to allow ourselves such licence?

I am inclined to think that Bennett's example represents a particularly favourable case for the advocate of universal nonzonal fusion. Where a top both spins and moves across a table at the same time, there is nothing unnatural about singling out the top's whole movement as an event, or of thinking of its spin and its horizontal motion as 'parts' of this whole movement. Both parts are *movements*, after all, which lends plausibility to the idea that they can be straightforwardly added together. But where zonally coinciding events are of entirely different kinds, the idea of fusion may not be so appealing. Is there an event constituted by the nonzonal fusion of the heating and simultaneous rotating of a metal sphere, for example? Bennett thinks there is—but it seems to me that nothing obviously recognizable as an event would be picked out by such a fusion. There may be even more serious problems for Bennett's view, given that he does not provide any clear restrictions on the kinds of properties whose instantiations at zones constitute events. Is any trope an event? Can we fuse the heating of a metal sphere and the property instance of sphericality which exists at the same zone, for example? If not, one wants to know why not—why some tropes (e.g. a heating instance and a rotation instance) can be nonzonally fused with one another, while others (e.g. a heating instance and a sphericality instance) cannot. If so, some of Bennett's events are very peculiar indeed. Bennett might simply agree—and yet wish to insist that we ought to countenance such fusions when doing philosophy rather than 'the kind of "conceptual analysis" that shades off into mere lexicography'.[41] Let us then tentatively accept the Principle of Universal Nonzonal Fusion for now, with the proviso that some of the fusions thus generated may be 'events' only on some peculiarly philosophical understanding of the term,

---

[40] Ibid. 145.   [41] Ibid. 7.

and see what are the consequences of its acceptance for what Bennett calls 'Davidson's philosophy of mind'.

With the Principle of Universal Nonzonal Fusion in place, Bennett goes on to argue that the idea that all mental events are physical events is a mere triviality. The argument goes as follows. Any event, on Bennett's view, is an instantiation of some (possibly very complex) property—a trope. A mental event is therefore also a trope—what makes it mental must be the fact that it contains an instance of some mental property as a part. But (1) it is virtually undeniable that mental properties are possessed by physical things—so that (2) they are instantiated at the same zones as physical properties. It follows by (3), the Principle of Universal Nonzonal Fusion, that there must be an event which is a fusion of the tropes constituted by the mental property instance, and the physical property instance (or instances) which coincide(s) with it, respectively. Which is to say, according to Bennett, that (4) all mental events are physical. Since (1) is 'a virtual triviality', Bennett can find no significant content in the token identity theory.

There seem to be two big problems with this argument. Firstly, it seems to rely on a very strange view about what it takes to show that a result is trivial. Bennett rests his case for the triviality of (4) on the fact that it is derived from (1), which he takes to be trivial. But (4) is not deduced from (1) alone—it requires the help of the Principle of Universal Nonzonal Fusion, which does not seem to be trivial at all. And surely one would need to show that *both* premisses were trivial (not just that one was trivial and one true) to show that (4) had no substantial content.

But even if Bennett has a reply to this criticism, there seems to be a second inescapable difficulty. The trouble is that (4) does not seem to follow from (2) and (3). What follows from (2) and (3) is that there are some tropes which are the fusions of mental and physical tropes. It does not seem to follow that all tropes which are mental are also physical—just that they can always be *fused* with physical property instances to form new tropes which have both mental and physical properties as parts. Suppose, for example, that I make a decision at *t*. On Bennett's view, this event of decision-making will presumably be a trope—a property instance of the decision-making property. Obviously, I also have lots of other, physical properties at *t*, so that if there is an event (as is implied by the Principle of Universal Nonzonal Fusion) which 'is an instance

of the property that is a conjunction, so to speak, of all the properties instantiated at the zone',[42] it will be an event which has mental
and physical properties as nonzonal parts. But this does not show
that my *decision-making* was a physical event unless we suppose
that the Principle of Universal Nonzonal Fusion is a licence not
only to add tropes together to create new, more complex ones, but
also to *identify* the new trope with the original ones out of whose
conjunction it is formed.

But Bennett is clear, I think, that the fusions which the Principle
of Nonzonal Fusion countenances create new events. In giving the
example of the rotating top which simultaneously moves across
the table, Bennett speaks of the 'third' event which is constituted
by the total movement of the top throughout the time in question,
thus suggesting that he does not think that either the rotation or
the top's movement across the table is to be *identified* with the
top's total movement. I can only think, then, that his argument to
the conclusion that all mental events are physical contains a
straightforward error—and so that his view of events does not,
after all, lead to the immediate trivialization of the token identity
theory.

The question remains, though, whether Bennett's account of
events might be a viable view for a token physicalist to hold. Unlike
Kim's view, there is nothing in Bennett's theory that rules out the
identification of mental with physical events. Indeed, as we have
seen, it actually follows from Bennett's view that there are some
events which are both mental and physical—in the sense that there
are tropes which have mental and physical property instances as
nonzonal parts. But it does not follow that these mixed tropes, as
I shall call them, are the referents of any of the event descriptions
we ordinarily use. For example, it does not follow that my making
a decision at *t* to go swimming on Sunday is a trope which has
instances of physical properties as parts. It does not follow, but it
would seem that it is not ruled out either. We need to know
whether mental event descriptions can pick out mixed tropes in
order to know whether the token identity theory could be true on
Bennett's account of events. How are we to decide?

At this point, there seem to be two ways of proceeding. On the
one hand, one might take the view that it requires a good deal of

---

[42] Ibid. 145–6.

investigation, both philosophical and empirical, to decide whether a decision, or a feeling of pain, or other mental event is a mixed trope—and that we should not expect instant answers. In asking such a question, after all, we are asking about the metaphysical nature of events—to have an answer to this question would be to know whether the token identity theory was true. In order to decide whether physical property instances should be parts of the tropes named by mental event descriptions, therefore, we already need to know the metaphysical truth about mental events.

On the other hand, one might deny that any prior metaphysical investigation needs to be done in order to determine which tropes are picked out by mental event descriptions. As I mentioned earlier, Bennett believes there is a considerable degree of indeterminacy attaching to the question what property instances are to be included in the trope which is picked out by any given event description; but if events are tropes, and if we are to credit ourselves with making any sense at all when we speak about them, there have to be some limits. What sets these limits, in general, would seem to be our understanding of the various concepts which denote what might be called the different *species* of event—*journey, descent, avalanche, picnic, kick, throw*, etc. It is because we know, roughly speaking, what it is to be a journey, a descent, or an avalanche that we have some idea of which property instances ought to be included in a trope description that picks out an event of the right kind. For example, in the case of Leibniz's coach trip from Delft to The Hague, it is our understanding of the concept of a coach trip that gives us a rough-and-ready way of deciding, for any particular property instance, whether it does or does not count as part of the super-property whose instantiation constitutes the coach trip. It is reasonable to suppose, then, that in the case of mental events we should look for guidance in the same place—to the various species concepts under which particular mental events fall.

Below, I shall consider each of these approaches in turn. I shall try to show that in order to make sense of the first approach, we need a non-tropic conception of events; and that to endorse the second, as a means of answering the question whether the token identity theory is true, prevents us from being able even to formulate that theory as the substantive metaphysical claim it is intended to be.

5.1. The First Approach

It is obviously possible to refer successfully to something by means of a definite description even when one's knowledge of the object of reference is very limited. As long as there is some one definite thing that fits the description used, it does not normally matter in the least if I know very little about the thing in question. It does not matter, for example, as far as my ability to refer to mental events is concerned, that I do not know whether or not their ultimate nature is physical. I can usually be confident, in speaking of a particular occurrence of pain, or a decision, or a perception, for example, that I have singled *something* out and be content to wait on philosophy and science to deliver a verdict on whether or not the event in question has a physical nature.

The first approach relies upon our being able to make sense of this idea. It depends upon the thought that the token identity theory answers a substantive metaphysical question—the question whether mental events are identical with physical events—which we can formulate sensibly without being able to answer it. But if events are tropes, it is hard to see how we could ever do this. For tropes are property instances—and so it would seem that in order to know which trope one is speaking about on a particular occasion, one would need to know which property instance was at issue. If I do not know, for example, whether a decision to which I wish to refer by means of some definite description is a trope which has physical properties as parts or not, it would seem that I do not know which trope I have singled out with my words. I can no longer be confident that I have singled something out—and so the question whether *the decision* is a mixed trope does not really make any sense. For if events are tropes, 'the decision' would seem to be a name of nothing in particular until the question of which trope it is is settled.

One might object to this that nothing in the theory that events are tropes prevents reference from being fixed in the usual way. One might try to insist, for example, that 'the decision I made to go swimming on Sunday' still refers to a definite event—an event which is also a trope—and that there is nothing problematic about the suggestion that we cannot be sure, without further metaphysical investigation, which trope it is. But it *is* problematic for anyone wishing to claim a certain kind of ontological primacy for tropes. It is problematic because questions about the identity and individuation of events must still be settled by considerations deriving from the generic concept of *event*, and from what I have called the species concepts that fall under it—*journey, avalanche, walk, wedding*, etc. For example, in order to decide whether some trope, M_1, which is singled out by a mental event description might have physical properties as parts, one needs a way of thinking about M_1 as something other than a trope to begin with—a way of thinking about it which provides an object for thought in the first place and which provides one also with a certain general understanding of the kinds of considerations which would be relevant to any further inquiry into the nature of the object in question. One would need, in other words, to understand M_1 as an *event* before one would ever be able to understand it as a trope, or to decide what kind of trope it might be.

I do not know whether any of this shows that events are not tropes. But it does seem to me to show that the attempt to understand the question raised by the token identity theory as a substantive, metaphysical question, in accordance with the first approach, requires that we be able to understand events in some other way. The underlying problem with tropes, as with Kim's events, seems to be that, ultimately, they are not genuine particulars—we do not point them out, use demonstratives and expect people to know which ones we have in mind, use count nouns to identify them. Bennett, of course, thinks that in a sense we do—because he thinks events are tropes, and so that the linguistic apparatus we use for singling out events serves this very purpose. But as we have seen, and as Bennett himself admits, our event descriptions are very unsatisfactory indeed, understood as devices for referring to specific *tropes*. If you want to pin down a trope, it will not be possible to do it very precisely by using an event description. Tropes are property instances; and at bottom, their individuation remains parasitic on the individuation of the properties of which they are instances. They have, as it were, no natural unity—and no secret life. The unambiguous individuation of a trope would require the enumeration of all the property instances which are its parts—so that when one has said clearly *which* trope one is speaking about, one will already have answered any questions one might have wished to raise in respect of its identity.

For these reasons, then, it seems to me that it is not possible to make sense of the first approach to the question whether mental event descriptions might sometimes 'reach out and grab' the same tropes as physical descriptions, without reverting to a non-tropic conception of events. The question then remains whether Bennett can do anything with the token identity theory by taking the second approach. It is to this question that I now turn.

5.2. *The Second Approach*

The second approach to the question whether mental event descriptions might refer to the same tropes as physical event descriptions, suggests that we ought to be able to decide which tropes are picked out by our various event descriptions by reflection on the sortal concepts contained in them—and that then, having settled on appropriate referents, we should be able readily to answer the question whether the token identity theory is true. Once it is clear which trope is referred to by the name of the mental event, and which is referred to by the name of the physical event, the thought goes, it will immediately be clear whether or not the two names 'reach out and grab' the same trope. Conceptual clarity, therefore, not empirical investigation, is what is wanted in order to settle the question whether the token identity theory is true.

Immediate difficulties become apparent, however, with the attempt to put this suggestion into practice. For the descriptions by means of which we refer to events, and the count nouns and nominal expressions they contain, do not seem to be very helpful when it comes to deciding which property instances are parts of the complex tropes which we have supposedly singled out by their means. Consider, for example, some individual, datable mental event—say, someone's suddenly feeling a pain. If this event is a trope, which trope is it? Presumably a property instance of feeling pain is 'included' in the relevant trope. But what else? Can physical properties be included or not? We need to know this in order to know whether the token identity theory could be true of the havings of pains. But as far as I can see, the concept *feeling of a pain* does not give us an answer to the question one way or another. I do not see why physical property instances should be automatically excluded. But neither does there seem to be any a priori reason to think that they need to be included. It would seem that we would only be justified in giving a positive rather than a negative answer if we already had some other, independent reason for thinking the token identity theory true—an independent reason of the kind which I argued above could only be forthcoming from philosophical and scientific investigation which utilized a non-tropic conception of events.

Perhaps, though, we can be content with this indeterminacy. Might we not simply agree with Bennett that 'our language of events contains a lot of slack',[43] and so conclude that the token identity theory is neither definitely true, nor definitely false? Can we accept, as this second approach suggests, that the question whether some individual mental event is identical with a physical event is really unanswerable, due to the fact that no definite tropes are singled out by the event descriptions which flank the identity sign in the putative identity statement?

I think it is clear that to represent the token identity theory as a theory committed to identities which admit of this sort of indeterminacy would be to misrepresent it. The token identity theorist intends to make true, substantive, empirical claims about the relations which hold between independently identifiable particulars, not claims which might fail to be either definitely true or definitely false, due to what amounts to reference failure. The token identity theorist intends the individual identity statements to which she is committed to be comparable to identity statements like 'Hesperus = Phosphorus' or 'Afla = Ateb';[44] she intends to make an empirical claim, to assert the identity of particulars which are ordinarily approached, as it were, from two different sides. It will be useful to have a name for identity statements which have this character; for not all identity statements are of this kind. In particular, many of

---

[43] *Events and their Names*, 128.

[44] Both these examples are due to Frege. For the first, see his 'On Sense and Meaning', in *Translations from the Philosophical Writings of Gottlob Frege*, ed. and tr. P. Geach and M. Black, 3rd edn. (Oxford, 1980) (though Frege uses 'the Morning Star' and 'the Evening Star' rather than the names 'Hesperus' and 'Phosphorus'). The second is an imaginary case: 'Afla' and 'Ateb' are names given to a single mountain by two separate explorers, each of whom sees the mountain from a different side and learns the name given to it by the local inhabitants on his side of the mountain. Later the explorers meet and are able to work out that the mountain which the first calls 'Afla' and the second calls 'Ateb' are one and the same mountain. For this example, see Frege's 'Letter to Jourdain', letter VIII/12, in *Wissenschaftlicher Briefwechsel*, ed. G. Gabriel *et al.* (Hamburg, 1976); tr. as *Philosophical and Mathematical Correspondence* by H. Kaal, abridged by B. McGuinness (Oxford, 1980), 128.

the identity statements which one meets with in philosophy, such as 'Brutus' stabbing of Caesar = Brutus' killing of Caesar' or 'the statue = the lump of clay', do not assert identities between objects approached in this way from different epistemological standpoints. It is not as though Brutus' stabbing of Caesar was observed by one person and his killing of Caesar by another, so that the question then arises whether the two observers saw the same event. At this level, all the facts about the relations between stabbing and killing are already settled—Brutus killed Caesar by stabbing him. The identity statement which relates the stabbing and the killing is therefore not intended to be *empirically* informative—everything of empirical relevance is already known, prior to the settling of the identity question. Under these circumstances, the relevant identity statement has to be understood as the expression of a philosophical theory; it does not answer the only kind of identity question one might have occasion to raise in an everyday context. I call identity statements which are intended to be empirically informative *two-route identity statements*, because in such cases, the two expressions whose referents are alleged to be identical are associated with different epistemological points of view—with what might be reasonably, if somewhat metaphorically, called different *routes* to their referents. In the case of Hesperus and Phosphorus, for example, the observation of a star in the evening is one route to the planet Venus; and the observation of a star in the morning is another—and the question can then arise whether these routes both lead to the same planet.

I think it is important not to let the philosophical context in which the token identity theory is normally discussed obscure the fact that the identity statements between mental and physical events to which it is committed ought nevertheless to be understood as two-route identity statements. What the token identity theorist supposes is that introspection or folk-psychological interpretation provides one kind of 'route' to the identification of certain events ('mental' events); and that neurophysiological investigation provides another, as yet under-exploited, route to the identification of those very same events. The token identity theorist needs a view of events, therefore, on which events can be definitely identified—singled out as particulars—from both these points of view.

But it is highly doubtful whether the second approach can really accommodate this need. It seems as though what Bennett will have to say, if he takes the second approach, is something like this: Event descriptions like 'S's feeling of a pain at *t*' do not definitely pick out any particular tropes. There are limits to what the tropes singled out by such phrases might be—but there is no definite answer to the question whether the trope should have any physical property instances as parts. At least, this is what he must say if I am right to think that the issue cannot be settled purely conceptually, by anything which is contained in the concept *feeling of a pain*. And so, on Bennett's account, it will be genuinely indeterminate whether or not events like feelings of pains are physical events. And this prevents us from understanding the token identity theory as a substantive metaphysical theory with consequences for two-route identity questions about identifiable particulars. The question is turned for Bennett, on this second approach, into a quasi-conceptual question which, due to the vagueness in our event language, has no definite answer.

In effect, the second approach denies that the singular terms which Bennett calls 'event names' really function as singular terms at all, on the grounds that they do not serve to single out any definite 'tropes'. But this is a bit like insisting that the referring expressions which we use to single out substantial objects do not really refer to any definite objects, on the grounds that no substantial object can be identified with any definite parcel of matter. Both lines of reasoning begin with a certain conception of the objects to which some category of singular term must refer, if they refer at all—events are conceived of as tropes, in the first case, substantial objects as parcels of matter, in the second. It is then argued, on the grounds that the singular terms in question are patently hopeless, conceived of as devices for referring to definite items of the specified kind, that the putative singular terms are not really singular terms at all. But what seems to be wrong with the argument, in both cases, is the starting-point. One might equally say that since it is clear that the singular terms in question *are* patently hopeless, understood as devices for referring to definite items of the specified kind, it must have been wrong to assume that these items were the referents of the singular terms in the first place. Substantial objects, that is to say, are not identical with parcels of matter; and events are not tropes.

The individual identity statements to which any token identity theorist must be committed are thus misrepresented if they are represented as statements which have no determinate truth value. It is not true that the event descriptions which flank the identity sign in such statements necessarily fail to single out determinately any definite individuals. They may fail to single out determinately any definite *tropes*, but no general failure, or indeterminacy, of reference follows from this. Any such description which satisfies the usual requirements on unique identification will single out some definite event, about which identity questions can then arise. And once again, these events will be *particulars*, things which satisfy the secret life requirement, not complex tropes which can only be singled out by means of a complete enumeration of the properties 'included' in the complex.

It seems to me, therefore, that Bennett's view of events leaves us without a way of making sense of token physicalism. To proceed in accordance with the first approach, I have argued, we need a non-tropic conception of events. To proceed in accordance with the second prevents us from understanding the identities to which the token identity theory is committed as informative, two-route identities. On neither reading do we have an account of events which could help with the provision of an ontology for the philosophy of mind.

2

Events as Changes

IN my dictionary, the word 'event' is explicated as follows: 'that which happens: result: any incidence or occurrence'.[1] Neither of the accounts of events I have so far considered has made very much of the fact that events *happen*; indeed, since neither Kim nor Bennett places any weight at all on the distinction between events and states, one must presume that both are quite prepared to countenance as events things that do not have the character of happenings at all. Of course, it is not necessarily incumbent upon a philosophical theory of events to incorporate all that is included in the ordinary-language concept—the purposes for which the theory is intended might demand that some ordinary-language considerations be overridden—but since we have found neither of the theories of events so far considered to be adequate for the purposes of characterizing token physicalism, perhaps it would be sensible to wonder whether what is wanted is an account that adheres more closely to the dictionary definition. Indeed, in the light of the fact that many of the problems encountered in the attempt to use Kim's and Bennett's accounts of events to formulate token physicalism were traceable to a failure, on the part of these theories, to respect the particularity of events, it may already have come to seem obvious that what is wanted is an account which takes the ordinary truth that events are happenings rather more seriously. To go along this route is obviously to begin looking for an account of events which will fail to be at the same time an account of *states*; for states are not happenings. But in my view, this may be no bad thing. Indeed, I shall attempt, in what follows, to make some headway in elucidating the category of event by drawing some *contrasts* between happenings and states.

[1] *Chambers's Twentieth Century Dictionary* (Edinburgh, 1983).

1. HAPPENINGS

What is it, exactly, for something to be a *happening*? The absence of any discussion of the concept from the literature perhaps suggests that it has been felt to be a mere synonym for *event*, without elucidatory value. But that does not seem quite right. The concept of a happening has at least one important feature not shared by the concept of event and that is its association with the corresponding verb, 'to happen'.[2] And perhaps it would not be altogether foolish to think that this association might enable us to get some purchase on the idea of an event which was not so obviously available before the verb-related substantive was clearly in view.

We might, for instance, try to make a start in constructing an event–state distinction by saying that events *happen*, whereas states do not—perhaps we might say instead that states *obtain*. Of course, this is *only* a start, and as yet the concepts of *happening* and *obtaining* must be admitted to be just as foggy as the original *event* and *state*. But at least two strategies for making the ideas of happening and obtaining rather more precise, and for distinguishing them one from another, now suggest themselves.

The first, which I shall call *the temporal strategy*, is based on the perception that things which happen bear a rather different relationship to time from things which obtain, and attempts to elucidate the event–state distinction by describing and explaining these different relationships. The second, which I shall call *the dynamic strategy*, tries to trade rather on the thought that happening, but not obtaining, necessarily involves *change*.

These strategies have sometimes been combined, and sensibly so, for it seems to me that there is truth and insight in the foundations of both. Barry Taylor's account of events, for example, combines a careful examination of the contrasting temporal features of events and states with the idea that events are to be distinguished from states of affairs in virtue of their being changes.[3] But I want to separate the strategies here, because it seems to me that it is a complicated matter to extract what is true from each. I shall postpone discussion of the temporal strategy until the next chapter; in

---

[2] Though of course the noun 'event' is not entirely without verbal associations, being etymologically derived from the Latin *evenire*. This point was made to me by Jennifer Hornsby.

[3] Taylor, *Modes of Occurrence*.

this chapter, I shall be concerned with the dynamic strategy and the associated thesis that events are changes.

Lawrence Lombard has perhaps developed the idea that events are changes in more detail than any other writer.[4] I have therefore made his book the main focus of this chapter. But it will quickly become apparent that I regard the concept of change which is developed by Lombard as too narrow to support a general theory of events. His account excludes too many things which would ordinarily be accounted events, and which a good philosophical theory of events ought to be able to encompass. I have therefore tried to move beyond criticism of Lombard's own specific proposals, to consider whether a better and broader account of change might improve the chances of the dynamic strategy. My answer will eventually be negative, to the extent that it suggests that the concept of change is not quite what is wanted to explicate the idea of a happening. I shall try to show both that there are events which do not involve change of any kind, and also that there are states which are, in a sense, dynamic. But I want to concede right at the outset that there are important connections between the concept of event and the idea of change. The dynamic strategy has tremendous appeal, and I shall try to show that the counter-examples demand the reinterpretation and supplementation of the strategy, rather than its outright rejection.

2. EVENTS AS CHANGES IN OBJECTS

The starting-point for Lombard's account of events is what Lombard calls 'the only simple, straightforward and intuitive criterion that attempts to give necessary and sufficient conditions for its being the case that some object has changed',[5] a criterion which he calls the *Ancient Criterion of Change* (ACC). The Ancient Criterion of Change is spelt out by Lombard as follows:

An object, x, changes if and only if

    (i) there is a property, P,
    (ii) there is an object, x,
    (iii) there are distinct times, t and t', and
    (iv) x has P at t and fails to have P at t' (or *vice versa*).

---

[4] In *Events: A Metaphysical Study.*   [5] Ibid. 79.

Every event, according to Lombard, is a change on the Ancient Criterion and the concept of an event is thereby tied very closely to the idea not simply of change, but of change *in an object*.[6]

Whether or not it is plausible to regard all events as changes in objects obviously depends, among other things, on how broadly Lombard proposes to interpret the term 'object'. For at first blush, there certainly seem to be events that are not changes in ordinary, physical objects. There are events such as weddings and wars and picnics which certainly *involve* changes in ordinary physical objects, but do not seem to be *identical* with such changes, nor indeed with sums of such changes, since presumably many of the numerous changes which might be thought to be involved in an event like a picnic might individually have failed to occur without affecting the identity of that event.[7] And indeed, not only the concept of event, but also the concept of change, appear to have application outside the realm of physical objects. Arguably, there are changes in such 'objects' as the weather and the British economy, for example, its beginning to rain at noon on Tuesday, and the rate of inflation's rising in January; and there are changes at places which, however, do not seem to be ascribable to any particular objects, e.g. the implementation of new working-practices in some factory.

---

[6] Though not everything which is a change on the Ancient Criterion is allowed to count as an event. One important exclusion is relational change. Lombard defines relational change as follows:

An object x, in going from having to lacking a property, P, at an interval of time, t, changes relationally if and only if

(i) x, in going from having to lacking P at t, changes (according to ACC), and

(ii) it is not possible that x goes from having to lacking P at t while there is no object, y (distinct from x and any of x's parts), and no property, P', such that y, by going from having to lacking P', changes at t. (*Events*, 97)

This definition is designed to reflect the thought that a change whose occurrence depends essentially, in a non-causal way, on events occurring in objects other than the object to which the change is ascribed cannot be a genuine alteration in that object. Xanthippe's becoming a widow thus does not count as an event, because Socrates (or at least some husband of Xanthippe) has to die in order for such a change to occur.

[7] For example, *S* might in fact have eaten a sausage roll on the Sunday School picnic; but if we wish to allow that *S* might not have eaten the sausage roll at that same picnic, it will not be possible to identify the picnic with any fusion of events that has the sausage-roll-eating as a constituent. This argument for the non-identity of such events as these with the sums of the numerous events of which they might be thought to be composed is parallel to the well-known modal arguments against the identification of substances with the sums of their parts.

Lombard calls events of all these varieties *subjectless* events, but it
will be useful, for my purposes, to distinguish between those which
can be regarded as changes in a single object, on a broad interpretation of the concept of an object, and those, like picnics and
weddings, which cannot. I shall call events of this latter kind
composite events, since they involve changes in many objects, and
I shall call events which can be regarded as changes in objects only
on a broad construal of the concept of an object *broad-object*
events. And perhaps there are also events such as standings still and
sayings (of) nothing which, though they do not seem to be
subjectless, do not involve change, at least not in any very obvious
way (I shall call these *changeless* events). How is an account based
on the idea of change in an object to incorporate such difficult cases
as these?

  Unfortunately, Lombard himself does not take up this challenge.
He does not attempt to cater for awkward cases, but rather takes a
narrow interpretation of the Ancient Criterion as his baseline and
accepts what he takes to be the consequences of that interpretation.
With respect to the question of subjectless events, for instance,
Lombard simply bites the bullet and denies that happenings such as
these are events at all.[8] On his view, changes which are ascribed
only to matter or to pluralities of objects, or which can be ascribed
to no particular object at all, are not events. This leads to some
important exclusions. Lombard considers the hypothetical situation in which a rise in world temperature leads to the melting of all
the world's snow, and maintains that in such a case there would be
no event which was the melting of all the world's snow, because the
world's snow does not constitute an object, on his view.[9] Neither
can there be an event which is Smith's and Jones's greeting each
other (since Smith and Jones are two objects, not one); or any
events which are fallings of snow or boilings of water or meltings of
gold (though there can be fallings of snowflakes and increases in the
kinetic energy of the particles of which gold and water are composed); or events which are rises in the rate of inflation or changes

---

  [8] Davidson also suggests that he is attracted by this suggestion; see 'The
Individuation of Events', 173–4: 'most events are understood as changes in a more
or less permanent object or substance. It even seems likely to me that the concept of
an event depends in every case on the idea of a change in a substance, despite the fact
that for some events it is not easy to say what substance it is that undergoes the
change.'
  [9] *Events*, 124.

in the weather or shifts in the popularity of the government.[10] Only unitary, full-blooded, bona-fide objects, on Lombard's view, can be the subjects of events. I shall call this *the restrictive conception of an object*, or the RCO, for short, and I shall call the conception of events to which it gives rise *the restrictive conception of an event*, or RCE. In Section 3 below, I shall argue that there is nothing in Lombard's account of change that forces us to interpret the ACC in accordance with the RCO, and so that we are free, if we wish, to adopt a broader view of the kinds of things that might constitute changes in objects.

3. IS THERE A MOTIVATION FOR THE RCO?

Lombard admits that a direct argument for the claim that all events have subjects (in the restrictive sense) is 'notably lacking' in his discussion.[11] However, he does claim that the concepts deployed in the construction of his theory make it impossible that there should be subjectless events, and also says that he does not know how to get a grip on the concept of an event without seeing it as bound up with the concept of change; nor how to get a grip on the concept of change without seeing change as something undergone by objects (in the restrictive sense).[12] I have already given reasons for thinking that this latter claim is odd, since we seem to be able to make sense of the concept of change in connection with such 'objects' as the weather and the economy. But perhaps Lombard has reason to believe that the details of his account of change make a nonsense of such applications. Perhaps, then, we ought to look more closely at those details and their implications for the RCO.

Lombard's account of change draws on two main conceptual resources, both closely related to one another. The first is the distinction between *static* and *dynamic* properties.[13] Static properties are those whose possession by an object carries no implication that the object either has changed, is changing, or will change; Lombard gives as examples the properties of being blue, weighing ten pounds, and being located at place p_1. Dynamic properties, by

---

[10] Ibid. 240–1, where Lombard makes it clear that changes in what might be called 'mere heaps' (water, gold, snow, etc.) and in pluralities of objects, or in such dubious entities as the rate of inflation and the weather, are not allowed to count as events.   [11] Ibid. 241.   [12] Ibid. 242.   [13] Ibid. 104–6.

contrast, imply change in the objects to which they are ascribed; Lombard gives as examples 'being a presently shrinking thing' and 'being a thing that is turning green'. Lombard believes that the concept of a dynamic property provides the resources for extracting what truth there is in Kim's view that events are exemplifications of properties at times. For on Lombard's view, events are exemplifyings of *dynamic* properties by objects.[14]

Lombard appears to think that this aspect of his account demands that the ACC be interpreted in accordance with the RCO. Thus, he writes: 'I suppose I could be said to have argued that there are no subjectless events in so far as I have suggested that events are changes, that changes are exemplifyings, and that there can be no exemplifyings unless there are things that exemplify.'[15] But the phrase 'things that exemplify' seems no more to dictate the RCO than did the original 'object', mentioned in the Ancient Criterion. There seems no obvious reason why places, the weather, the economy, all the world's snow, etc. should not be thought of as things that exemplify dynamic properties. Composite events, like weddings and wars, remain a little problematic, as do standings still and sayings (of) nothing; it is particularly hard to see how these changeless events might be exemplifyings of dynamic properties. But Lombard is surely not forced, merely by his use of the concept of a dynamic property, to banish broad-object events from his ontology.

The second main resource exploited by Lombard in his account of change is the concept of a *quality space*.[16] This concept is designed to capture the idea of change in a single respect, and to reflect the associated idea that when an object changes, it does not merely come to lack a property it earlier had. For example, when an object ceases to be red, it does not simply lose its redness. Rather, it comes to have a new property which will be associated, in an important way, with the property it no longer has—that is to say, it will come to have another colour property.[17] The nature of this association is spelled out by Lombard's definition of a quality

[14] Lombard makes a distinction between *exemplification* and *exemplifying*, but the difference is unimportant for my purposes and I shall not discuss it here.

[15] Ibid. 242.

[16] Ibid. 113–14.

[17] The 'degenerate' property of colourlessness must be allowed to count as a colour property, for these purposes.

space. Quality spaces are sets (S) of simple, static properties, {P_0, $P_1, \ldots, P_n, \ldots$}, which meet the following two conditions:

(1) If at any time, t, any object, x, has $P_i \epsilon S$, then at t, for any $j \neq i$, it is not the case that x has $P_j \epsilon S$.

(2) If any object, x, which has $P_i \epsilon S$ at any time, t, fails to have P_i at a time $t'(t \neq t')$ (and still exists), then x changes in S (or in respect 'S'), that is, by t', x has, for some $j \neq i$, $P_j \epsilon S$.[18]

(1) ensures that properties belonging to the same quality space cannot both be possessed simultaneously by an object (e.g. an object cannot be both red and blue all over). (2) incorporates the demand that when an object changes by losing a property, it must come to possess another property belonging to the same quality space.

Armed with these definitions, Lombard then proceeds to offer the following elucidation of the concept of *event*: 'An *event* is a "movement" by an object from the having of one to the having of another property, and where those properties belong to the same quality space, and where those properties are such that the object's successive havings of them implies that the object changes non-relationally . . . An event is a movement by an object through some portion of a quality space.'[19] This definition appears to build somewhat on the simpler formulation given by the ACC. It incorporates the idea of movement through a quality space into the concept of an event, where the ACC speaks only of the loss or gain of properties. Could it be here, in the concept of a quality space, that the motivation for the RCO is to be found?

Here again, unfortunately, we seem to draw a blank. It is hard to see that there are any grounds for denying that such 'objects' as the weather and the rate of inflation can move through quality spaces.

---

[18] Ibid. 113.

[19] Ibid. 114. There is a striking resemblance between this formulation and some remarks made by Aristotle about the concept of *kinesis* in *Physics*, book 5, tr. R. P. Hardie and R. K. Gaye, *The Complete Works of Aristotle*, 2 vols., 1: ed. Jonathan Barnes (Princeton, 1984), 379: 'We have, then, the following factors: that which directly causes motion, and that which is in motion; further that in which motion takes place, namely time, and (distinct from these three) *that from which and that to which it proceeds (for every motion proceeds from something and to something), that which is directly in motion being distinct from that to which it is in motion: for instance, wood, hot and cold - the first is that which is in motion, the second is that to which the motion proceeds, and the third is that from which it proceeds'* (224^a34- $^b4$; my italics).

If the weather changes from being sunny to being dull, one after-
noon, why should we not say that 'being sunny' and 'being dull' are
static properties of the weather which belong to the same quality
space? Sunniness and dullness seem to be mutually exclusive and,
perhaps together with one or two other possibilities (e.g. 'being
intermittently sunny'), are exhaustive of ways the weather might be
in that particular respect (the sunny-or-dull respect, as opposed, for
example, to the windy-or-calm respect). Similarly, the various possible percentage figures that might represent the rate of inflation
seem to define a quality space, since each rate is exclusive of all
other rates, and since the rate must have some particular value at
any given time. Once again, composite events present a problem, as
do changeless events; but there certainly does not seem to be
anything internal to the concept of a quality space that could
motivate the RCO and the consequent exclusion of broad-object
events.

Lombard seems, then, to be wrong when he claims that the
concepts deployed in his theory of events entail the RCE. It appears
that we might, without too much difficulty, incorporate at least
broad-object events into the account, by rejecting the RCO and
operating instead with a wider conception of the objects in which
events may be said to be the changes. In this way, perhaps, we
might be able to found a theory of events on the idea of change,
without having to accept all the exclusions that Lombard himself
concedes. Whether or not this is an opportunity we ought to
welcome is doubtless a contentious question. In my view, we certainly ought to take a view which is broader than Lombard's in at
least *some* respects; it seems to me absurd, for example, to deny
that there can be events which are changes in masses of matter.
Whether or not economic events, such as changes in the rate of
inflation, ought to count as events is perhaps more controversial.
Hornsby argues that such things are events, on the grounds that any
such event, *e*, 'is the sort of thing we might be able to learn the
cause of: an economist might be able to cite features of *e* which
bring it within the scope of intelligible, more or less projectible
generalisations'.[20] I am inclined to agree with Hornsby that such

[20] J. Hornsby, 'Physicalism, Events and Part–Whole Relations', in E. LePore and
B. P. McLaughlin (eds.), *Actions and Events: Perspectives on the Philosophy of
Donald Davidson* (Oxford, 1985), 453; repr. in *Simple Mindedness: A Defence of
Naive Naturalism in the Philosophy of Mind* (Cambridge, Mass. 1997).

things ought to be accounted events, though for rather different reasons which will not really become apparent until the next chapter. But if anyone thinks that a change in the value of some variable cannot really be accounted an *event*—perhaps because it can be given no very precise location—I shall not quarrel; nothing in what I have to say depends crucially upon this point.

I suspect that there may be less controversy about the contention that composite events ought to find a place in a good philosophical theory of events. It is natural to say, I think, that such things as picnics, weddings, and wars are all events. Our everyday concept of *event*, at any rate, suggests that this is the case; we might ask about the date of a wedding, without any appearance of oddity, for example, by asking 'When is the big event?'; or speak of the Gulf War as the most significant military event of the second half of the twentieth century. We cite such events as the causes and effects of others and they seem to be things which happen. But composite events do not seem to be changes in objects, even broadly construed. How might these be accommodated by the dynamic strategist?

The obvious move for the dynamic strategist to make here is to say that though composite events are not themselves changes in objects, they are composed of such changes. Picnics, for example, might be said to be composed of various runnings, playings, eatings, etc., and wars of various movements of troops and artillery, killings, bombings, and so on. If the dynamic strategist is to make a place for composite events in this way, then, her overall thesis will have to be a disjunctive one: events either *are* changes in objects (more or less broadly construed) or are ultimately composed of changes in such objects. I want to turn, now, to consider the second half of this disjunction.

4. COMPOSITE EVENTS AND THE COMPOSITION RELATION

What is it for one event to be composed from others? Clearly, any concept of composition which is to apply to events will have to be rather different from that which we apply to physical objects and their parts. In her paper 'Physicalism, Events and Part–Whole Relations', Jennifer Hornsby has argued that the concept of composition we employ in the physical-object case depends on what she terms 'the spatial ideology'; where continuants are concerned, we can trade on the relation which continuants bear to space: 'The claim about *parthood* for continuants is available because, for continuants, it is arguably a sufficient condition of x's being a part of y (at some time) that x occupy some part of the volume of space that y occupies (at that time). The notion of part that is pressed into service, we might say, relies only on the spatial ideology . . .'.[21] But as Hornsby points out, this same conception of parthood, the spatial conception, cannot be what is required to make sense of the composition relation for *events*. For it does *not* seem, in general, where x and y are events, to be a sufficient condition of x's being a part of y that x merely occupy some part of the volume of space that y occupies. Indeed, the notion of 'occupation' seems inappropriate to deal with the spatial features of events, as Lombard himself is concerned to point out.[22] The concept of 'occupation' seems closely bound up with the concept of matter, and with the idea that matter excludes other matter from the space which it fills, but events are not made of matter, and their occurrence at a place does not prevent other events from occurring there simultaneously. Locatability, it would seem, needs to be understood without reference to the idea of occupation, as far as events are concerned. Many people, Lombard amongst them, have urged that event location ought to be regarded as parasitic on the location of the object in which the event in question is a change (the *subject* of the event, in Lombard's terminology), and that we ought not to try to pin down the location of an event to any region more definite than the location of its subject.[23] But if an account of event composition is not able to draw on anything richer than *this* conception of

[21] J. Hornsby, 'Physicalism. Events and Part-Whole Relations', 455.

[22] *Events*, 70. P. M. S. Hacker also makes the point: 'The rising of an arm needs space, but does not occupy space, only the arm that rises does that. A car fills a space, but the event of its rolling into the garage does not; rather it occurs at a place. A small wedding gets no larger by getting the little gathering of family and friends to spread out, and a large wedding gets no smaller, only stuffier, by being crammed into a little chapel' ('Events and Objects in Space and Time', *Mind*, 91 (1982), 10).

[23] Since any change in a part of an object is a change in the whole of that object, Lombard suggests that in order to avoid the unwelcome suggestion that all events might have the same spatial location (the universe), we should insist that the spatial location of an event be the location of the *smallest* object a change in which constitutes that event (*Events*, 123).

event location, it will run into difficulties with events which are changes in non-spatial objects, like changes in the public mood or the economy; and will also lack the resources to explain why, for example, we would not want to count the yellowing of a leaf on a tree as part of the tree's growing, even though the leaf is a spatial part of the tree.

If composition is to play an important role in any theory of events, then, a concept of composition and parthood rather differ ent from that with which we are familiar in our dealings with continuants will have to be brought into play. For space and time alone will not serve to delimit events—it would seem that in attempting to decide on the parts of events we also need to take account of what might loosely be called 'relevance considerations'. For example, let us say that the Gulf War began on 15 January 1991 and ended on 28 February. Let us suppose, further, that we can manage roughly to delimit the spatial region within which the war might be said to have occurred.[24] It is clear that the specification of such spatiotemporal limits, even supposing it to be possible, still leaves us a long way from a satisfactory account of the composition of the war. For many events falling within those spatiotemporal boundaries will not be parts of the war, e.g. the various domestic activities of people living in the region, the movements of Kuwaiti insects, the closing, at night, of desert flowers, changes in the weather, etc. Clearly, we do have some sort of pretheoretical grip on the relation of parthood for events which enables us to rule these out, and to rule other events—troop movements, bombing raids, deaths, etc.—very definitely in. What I have above called 'relevance considerations' are the factors of which we take account in making these decisions.[25]

[24] It should be noted that this will be no easy task. There is room for dispute about both the temporal and spatial bounds of an event such as the Gulf War. Some would perhaps insist that the war began back in August 1990, when Iraq invaded Kuwait; others would suggest it did not really begin until January 1991. Neither are there very clear spatial limitations on the events which might be thought to compose the war. One's first thought might perhaps be that the war has at least a vague location, namely the Gulf, and so that no events occurring outside the Gulf could be allowed to count. But what about the flight of a B52 from its base in Gloucester? This would seem to be an event that is part of the war, and yet it is not confined to a Gulf location.

[25] The term 'relevance' needs to be treated with care, since it is not in general true that any event which is relevant to the war must count as one of its parts. For example, changes in the weather can clearly have a major effect on the course of a

It seems clear that each event sortal brings with it its own bundle of relevance considerations. The concept 'war', for example, suggests that we need to exclude most civilian activity, events in the plant and animal kingdoms, and geological and meteorological events, and demands that we include all offensive and defensive operations. The concept 'wedding' requires the inclusion of all parts of the ceremony itself, but not all events in the church need count; we might perhaps be able to exclude a spider's spinning of its web in the roof of the church. But there will be numerous difficulties and vaguenesses—will the eating of breakfast by some army officer count as a part of the Gulf War? Should training and exercises be included? The death of some cormorant as a result of the oil-slick? A flight by some bomber that never deposits its load, but returns to base due to mechanical difficulties? Event sortals, it seems, do not necessarily provide us with resources sufficient to enable us to make definite decisions about such questions.

Of course, the dynamic strategist may be free simply to accept that there are no definite answers here. It is not clear that the existence of this kind of vagueness presents her with any difficulties. For the fact that we are unable to be definite about which events are parts of which others does not necessarily show that the composition relation is out of place. After all, the fact that we might have difficulties determining which water droplets are parts of some cloud does not show that the cloud is not composed of water droplets. It may be sufficient for the dynamic strategist if she is able to insist that each sortal that is genuinely an *event* sortal necessarily determines, via associated relevance considerations, that at least some changes be definitely included amongst the parts of each event (i.e. that having changes as parts is a *necessary* condition of eventhood for composite events); and perhaps also that it is sufficient for something's being a composite event that it have changes amongst its definite parts (that having changes as parts is a *sufficient* condition of eventhood for composite events).

In what follows, I want to argue against both these suggestions—directly against the first, by means of a counter-example; and indirectly against the second, for while I think it is true that it is a sufficient condition of something's being an event that it be com-

war, and in that sense be relevant to it, though it does not seem right to count such changes amongst its parts.

posed of changes, I believe the reason for this cannot be understood independently of considerations that take one well beyond the dynamic strategy.

5. ARE THERE CHANGELESS EVENTS?

Is it a necessary condition on composite events that they have changes as components? Consider the concept of a *vigil*, taking that word in the sense where it designates a silent mass demonstration organized, for example, in protest at a war, or in memory of those killed in a war or accident. 'Vigil', in this sense, seems to me to be a noun entirely on a par with 'wedding', 'funeral', 'picnic', etc.; one can take part in a vigil, go to or on a vigil, hold a vigil, etc. If a demonstration is an event, surely a vigil, which can be a kind of demonstration, must be an event too. But it seems most unhappy to say that a vigil is composed of changes. The whole idea is that everyone should be still and silent. Obviously, there *will* be changes occurring at the region of the vigil during the time at which the vigil takes place—metabolic changes in the participants and breathing, for example—but these do not seem to be parts of the vigil; the relevance considerations associated with the concept of a vigil would surely exclude them. There might, of course, be changes that were not irrelevant—e.g. flickerings of candles, makings of speeches (assuming that makings of speeches could be regarded as composed of changes in the speaker)—but these do not seem at all essential to the vigil. If nobody remembered to bring a candle, and nobody decided to make a speech, it surely would not endanger in the least the vigil's status as an event.

It might be argued, I suppose, that certain mental changes must occur at a vigil. A determined dynamic strategist might insist that mental activity is to be regarded as a succession of mental changes—and so that the contemplation which occurs at the vigil is the source of the change which turns the vigil into an event. But this just seems wrong. If human beings were capable of sustained meditation on a single thought, and began that meditation just before the official beginning of the vigil, carrying it through until just after the official end, so that their thoughts underwent no change at all during the vigil itself, that would not make the vigil any less an event. It seems, then, that there can be events which neither are changes, nor are composed of changes.

I suppose it might now be said that one counter-example does not necessarily make a case. Perhaps the dynamic strategist could just deny that vigils are events—though she then faces the daunting task of deciding what they are. Or perhaps there are other ways of attempting to show that a vigil is, after all, a kind of change. Perhaps it could be said, for instance, that a vigil is a change at a place. But even if a workable conception of change at a place could be developed, there remain changeless events which could not be readily accounted for by this manœuvre. I mentioned earlier that such events as standings still and sayings of nothing (perhaps events which might be thought to be parts of vigils) do not seem to involve change. If I deliberately refrain from responding to your question, for example, it seems wrong to say that any *change* has thereby occurred in me. I may have been silent before and in saying nothing, I simply remain silent. To the extent that such events can be intentional actions, though, it is arguable that we ought not to exclude them from the class of events.

It must be conceded, though, that the class of changeless events is extremely small. Most events certainly do involve change—and in view of this fact, one might feel that it would be a mistake simply to reject the dynamic strategy on the basis of a few awkward examples. Equally, though, awkward cases can be revealing, and I should like to set out here a few thoughts about how the awkward cases might be accommodated, together with some rough indications of how one might manage to respect the obvious connections between events and change, without simply building change into one's definition of an event.

A full account of my view of the relation between events and change will not be possible until after the discussion of verbal aspect in the next chapter, but perhaps it will help to note here that though the concept of *happening* does involve the suggestion of a certain dynamism, the kind of dynamism in question might not need to be motion in the kinetic sense, or metaphysical change, but might rather be a matter of what could perhaps be called 'narrative motion'. A standing still, for instance, can move a story on to the next stage in just the same way as a walk or a run (e.g. 'Peter stood stock still, listening. Then he began to run . . .').[26] Mostly, of course, it is changes, or events involving changes, which move things on in this way—so that we usually have no reason to report the occurrence of changeless events (or perhaps more accurately, no reason to talk in ways which can be construed as implying the occurrence of such changeless events). It is this which explains the close connection between events and change, and the appeal of the dynamic strategy. Where we wish to talk about things which have not changed, stative vocabulary is usually more appropriate. But just occasionally, we do have reason to use the language of happening even in the absence of change. Sometimes, as it were, we use our language to carve out events from a part of space and time where things remain unaltered. Usually, there is nothing to command our attention in such dreary scenes, but from time to time, an aspect of an unchanging situation can have a significance which warrants the use of the language of events. Where we have a reason for singling out some point in time during the obtaining of some unchanging situation on which our attention is to be newly focused, as it were, we fulfil the pre-conditions of event talk—as where, for example, we consider a saying of nothing, though itself merely a continuation of a silence that has persisted, perhaps, for many hours, as a *response* to a question.[27] This seems to be what is crucial to the concept of an event—the idea of a point in time at which something of new significance begins to unfold—and this is usually, and unsurprisingly, a time at which some change occurs—but it need not be. In taking the concept of change as definitive of the concept of an event, then, it might be said that the dynamic strategist mistakes an extremely common means of fulfilment of this pre-condition of event talk for the pre-condition itself.

I shall have more to say in the following chapter about how the temporal strategy might help us to understand the relation between events and change. I want to move, now, to consider a second

---

[26] Note that there need be no implication here that the standing still represents any change in Peter's circumstances. He might have been standing around for hours. The language merely makes it clear that his standing still is something in which we are newly interested.

[27] It is true, of course, that the asking of the question in a case such as this is itself a change and that it is the occurrence of this change which makes the new perspective on the respondent's silence appropriate. But 'the respondent's saying of nothing' does not refer to this change.

objection to the view that the distinction between events and states
is to be explicated in terms of change and the absence of it.

6. STATES AND CHANGE

A little earlier, I raised the question whether it might be a sufficient
condition of something's being an event that it be composed of
changes. A difficulty for this thesis might perhaps be thought to
arise from the fact that certain *states* are very intimately connected
with lower-level change. For example, temperature and pressure
states in gases bear an important relation to movements (changes in
position) of the molecules of the gases; and states of equilibria in
certain chemical systems might involve the constant passage of
molecules between their liquid and gaseous states. Such states as
these cause trouble for the unrefined suggestion that states differ
from events in being essentially non-dynamic. For it now seems that
some states necessarily involve change no less than events. How is
the dynamic strategist to deal with this difficulty?

One attractive and obvious suggestion is that the relation between states and the changes to which they are related is different
from the relation between events and their parts—that it is a
relation of *dependence* rather than of *composition*. This would
enable the dynamic strategist to hold on to her disjunctive thesis, to
say that states neither *are* changes, nor are composed of changes,
while admitting that they may depend on changes for their existence in various complicated ways. In one way, it seems to me that
this reply is perfectly correct; indeed, I am very doubtful whether
we can really make sense of the composition relation with respect
to states. But to make this reply, it seems to me, is already to own
that the dynamic strategy cannot by itself bear all the weight of the
event–state distinction. For the reply relocates the source of that
distinction in the composition and dependence relations. What we
now need to know is what it is, exactly, about the nature of states
which prevents their being composed of changes; and it is not
implausible to think that this must be a question for the temporal
strategy.

In order to explain this, I should like to pre-empt a little the
discussion of the next chapter and to introduce here the concept of
temporal shape. It is often observed that in merely giving the

temporal dimensions of an existent thing—in specifying the beginning- and end-points of its existence—one does not thereby determine its temporal character. For vastly more important than these temporal reference points, in determining the ontological category of any item, is the *way* in which that item fills the relevant period of time—whether it *persists through* the time, or *occurs during* the time, or *obtains throughout* the time, etc. Continuants, for example, persist *through* time and exist, as wholes, at every moment of their existence, whereas events occur *at* times or *during* periods of time, and are unlike continuants in having temporal parts. The differences which are indicated by these contrasting verbs and prepositions I call differences of temporal shape.

Now, it seems to me not implausible to hold that the composition relation can only intelligibly relate items which have the same temporal shape. Composing larger things out of smaller ones, after all, is an easily comprehensible operation in the realm of continuants, where our grip on the idea of composition is firmest, and not, one might think, the kind of operation which could produce wholes which were radically different, with respect to their most important ontological properties, from the parts which go to make them up. Bodies, for example, are composed of limbs, organs, skin, hair, blood, etc., all of which persist through time and are like the bodies they compose in lacking temporal parts. But events, on this view of the composition relation, cannot compose substances. There have, of course, been attempts to argue that substances can—or perhaps ought—to be viewed as composed of time-slices, which in their turn are to be construed as event-like entities; but on the account I am proposing here, such attempts are simply doomed to failure. If the time-slices have temporal parts, then the items which are formed from adding them together will also have temporal parts, and so will not be continuants, but rather four-dimensional space-time worms. Quinean rabbit-stages, and the like, that is to say, could never be added together to form a *rabbit*.[28]

I think it is here, in the concept of temporal shape, that we may find the resources to explain why it is that states cannot be composed of events. For states do not have temporal parts. It is sometimes claimed (and I think often implied by the persistent tendency

---

[28] For this idea see e.g. W. V. O. Quine, 'Speaking of Objects', *Ontological Relativity and Other Essays* (New York, 1969).

of philosophers to lump events, states, and processes together and to treat them as a single category) that states do have temporal parts,[29] but a little reflection suggests that this is simply wrong. Some water's being at 90°C, for instance, seems to be a state which exists, as it were, in full, at all times at which the water is at that temperature; it is not incomplete in any way at any moment at which the water is at that temperature, in the way in which a football match, say, is incomplete at half-time. States, unlike events, do not unfold; they do not occur. I suggest, then, that states are like continuants in lacking temporal parts. And if this is right, we have a principled reason for insisting that events cannot *compose* states. They cannot compose states because their temporal shape is radically different; because nothing that has temporal parts can compose something that does not.

It seems to me, then, that the dynamic strategy alone does not quite get to the heart of the event–state distinction. Firstly, the class of events is larger than the class of items singled out by the dynamic strategist's disjunctive thesis (that events either are changes or are composed of changes). And secondly, if we are to be able to understand why the dynamic quality of certain states does not threaten to undermine the event–state distinction, we will need to move beyond the dynamic strategy to consider the differing relations which events and states bear to time. In the next chapter, therefore, I want to move to consider the temporal strategy and how it might be used to develop a workable account of the differences between events, states, and processes.

---

[29] e.g. by Peter Simons in *Parts: A Study in Ontology* (Oxford, 1987), 129: 'Occurrents comprise what are variously called events, processes, happenings, occurrences *and states*. They are, like continuants, in time, but unlike continuants they have temporal parts' (my italics).

3

The Temporal Strategy: Time and Aspect

THUS far, I have considered a number of contemporary views about the nature of events and have argued that none really answers to the purpose of the philosopher in search of an ontology for the mind. In so far as such a philosopher needs an ontology of events, I have suggested, what she needs is an ontology of genuine mental *particulars* and this some of the most prominent contemporary theories of events fail to provide. In Chapter 2, I considered whether it might be more promising to try to develop a theory of events by contrasting events with states, but eventually concluded that the dynamic strategy, which attempts to draw this distinction by adverting to the close connection between events and change, would not succeed unless it could be incorporated into a broader picture which took note of the differences between the ways in which events and states respectively relate to time.

In this chapter, I want to begin by trying to build on the suggestion, adumbrated at the end of Chapter 2, that what is common and peculiar to events, and what distinguishes them from states, is a certain kind of 'temporal shape'—to exploit what I called at the beginning of Chapter 2 the 'temporal strategy'. The temporal strategy seems to me promising as far as the events needed by the philosophy of mind are concerned, for the following reason. There is room for dispute about whether or not, and in what sense, mental phenomena are physical, whether they are spatially located, and whether they have subjects, and if so, what those subjects might be. All these are substantive questions in the philosophy of mind, and some of the difficulties we encountered earlier with various theories of events derived from the fact that the theories themselves dictated an answer to one or more of these questions, and so could not coherently be used as a neutral starting-point for their formulation. But there is no controversy about the temporality of mental phenomena—about the fact that they take place in, or persist through, time. In so far as the temporal strategy builds on an aspect of mentality that is an undisputed feature of the metaphysics of mind, then, we have grounds for hope that it might deliver a characterization of events and states sufficiently free of controversial metaphysical consequences to provide the ontological framework for which we have been looking.

The temporal strategy might also seem hopeful for a second reason. For besides *event* and *state*, there is a third category often mentioned (though seldom discussed) in connection with the ontology of mind—the category of *process*. Since there has been so little explicit discussion of processes in the philosophy of mind, it is hard to know what philosophers have meant to include in this category, but 'doing mental arithmetic', 'weighing up the pros and cons', 'working out what to do next' could all comfortably fill the frame '. . . is a kind of mental process', without any violence being done to ordinary usage. On the other hand, these might also seem to be kinds of mental *event*. Davidson, for example, recognizes no event–process distinction, and it seems clear that doings of mental arithmetic, weighings up of the pros and cons, and workings out of what to do next would all count as events on his view. Davidson's framework provides no semantic reason for treating doings of mental arithmetic any differently from the butterings of toast and the flyings of spaceships which he explicitly treats.[1] Consider, for instance, the sentence

Jones did mental arithmetic in the classroom during lunchtime.

According to Davidson's views about the semantics of adverbially qualified sentences, this sentence goes over into logical notation as follows:

$(\exists x)$(Did mental arithmetic (Jones, x) and In (the classroom, x) and During (lunchtime, x)).

In other words, the sentence requires an analysis which delivers ontological commitment to events of doing mental arithmetic, just as the sentence 'Jones buttered the toast in the bathroom, with a knife, at midnight' commits us to toast-buttering events, and it is

---

[1] See 'The Logical Form of Action Sentences', in Nicholas Rescher (ed.), *The Logic of Decision and Action* (Pittsburgh, 1967); repr. in Davidson, *Essays on Actions and Events*.

not clear how processes are to get in on the Davidsonian act at all. We face the question, then, whether there is really any difference between events and processes, and if so, how it is to be explained. Might 'event' and 'process' be just two words for the same thing? Or could processes perhaps be a subset of the class of events—or might they be composed from events? There is obviously a need to be clearer about what exactly it is, if anything, that distinguishes events from processes; and it is at least conceivable that the temporal strategy might be able to shed some light on the matter.

Any attempt to explain the difference between events and states—and perhaps between both of these and processes—in terms of the different relations which entities of each of these kinds bear to time will have to draw on a rich conception of temporal character. For example, it would be clearly mistaken to suppose that states are merely long events—that simple duration is the key to understanding the temporal differences between the two categories. It is true that, usually, events tend to be relatively short-lived, lasting for minutes or hours, rather than days and weeks, while states are generally rather more permanent and long-lasting (e.g. someone's knowing that Beijing is the capital of China is a state that will probably last for most of his or her life). But these facts about the relative duration of events and states are contingent, not necessary truths. There can be long events—perhaps the Hundred Years War would count as an example—and also short-lived states, e.g. a liquid's being at boiling-point on an occasion where it reaches boiling-point only for a few seconds and then cools rapidly again. It is not duration, but something else, which marks the crucial difference between the two categories.

In this chapter, I shall try to shed some light on the differences between events, processes, and states by drawing on the phenomenon of verb *aspect*. Though some insight is gained into the category of *state* by this discussion, the main focus of this chapter will be the event–process distinction. I shall try to show how the invocation of aspect can permit us to regard the distinction between events and processes as akin, in some respects, to the familiar distinction between substantial objects and the matter of which they are made. I shall then move on, in Chapter 4, to discuss in more detail the category of *state*.

I suggested in the last chapter that certain important ontological distinctions might depend upon the way things fill time, rather than on the amount of time they fill. I also suggested that one could glean information about these distinctions by looking at the different verbs and prepositions we use to talk about the relations which events and states respectively bear to time (e.g. events *happen in* time, states *persist through* time, etc.). But there is also another resource to be tapped. There are important differences between the kinds of verbs which are associated with states and those which seem to imply the occurrence of events, especially where psychological phenomena are concerned. The features of human nature and experience which have usually been classified as mental are, on the whole, associated either with verbs, or else with nouns closely related to verbs (e.g. 'belief', 'desire'); and there seem to be major differences between the behaviour of those verbs which indicate the occurrence of events ('recognize', 'notice', 'spot', etc.) and of those which rather suggest the presence of more or less permanent psychological states ('know', 'believe', 'fear', etc.). This suggests that perhaps there is insight to be gained from an examination of the different behaviour of these verbs. There is a great deal of temporal information packed into verb use, and it seems reasonable to suppose that an investigation of the way in which this information is conveyed ought to play a major part in the temporal strategy. I want to begin this chapter, therefore, by considering some of the attempts which have been made to elucidate these important temporal distinctions between verb types.

1. VENDLER AND KENNY

In a paper entitled 'Verbs and Times',[2] Vendler distinguishes between four kinds of verb and verb phrase: *verbs of activity*, of *accomplishment*, of *achievement*, and *stative verbs*, on the basis of what he refers to as their differing *time schemata*. Verbs of the first two kinds are alike in possessing continuous tenses, but differ in other ways. Vendler gives 'run' and 'push a cart' as examples of activity verbs, and 'run a mile' and 'draw a circle' as examples of accomplishments, and begins by enlarging on the distinction as follows:

[2] Z. Vendler, 'Verbs and Times', *Philosophical Review*, 66 (1957). The views put forward in this paper form the basis of ch. 4 of Vendler's book *Linguistics in Philosophy*.

If I say that someone is running or pushing a cart, my statement does not imply any assumption as to how long that running or pushing will go on; he might stop the next moment or he might keep running or pushing for half an hour. On the other hand, if I say of a person that he is running a mile or of someone else that he is drawing a circle, then I do claim that the first one will keep running till he has covered the mile and that the second will keep drawing till he has drawn the circle.[3]

It is not altogether clear, though, that this is a very satisfactory way of drawing the distinction. In order for it to be true of someone that she is running a mile, it does not really seem to be true that she needs to complete the mile—whether or not it can be truly said of somebody that she is running a mile seems to have more to do with intention than eventual success. And neither does it seem obviously right to say, as Vendler does, that it does not make sense to talk of finishing running, though one can finish running a mile. Surely one *can* finish running (e.g. one might pull up exhausted and say that one has finished running for the day).

But other things that Vendler says about the distinction do seem to be true. Vendler points out that if someone stops running a mile then she did not run a mile; though if she stops running, then she did run. Also, Vendler associates the question 'For how long did he φ?' with activity verbs (e.g. 'For how long did he run?', but not 'For how long did he run a mile?') and the question 'How long did it take to φ?' with accomplishment verbs (e.g. 'How long did it take to run a mile?' but not 'How long did it take to run?'), and this, too, seems to be accurate.

Neither achievement verbs nor stative verbs admit of continuous tenses, according to Vendler. Achievement verbs are distinguished from stative verbs by the fact that achievement verbs can be predicated only for moments of time, while states, broadly speaking, endure for shorter or longer periods. Thus, in 'I recognized him immediately' we have a verb of achievement, while 'I knew it all along' contains a stative verb. A simple test distinguishes achievements from states: in the case of the former, the question 'At what time . . .?' makes sense; in the case of the latter, 'For how long . . .?' is usually more appropriate. For example, 'At what time did you realize that you'd left the oven on?' is a comprehensible question, but 'For how long did you realize that you'd left the oven on?' is

---

[3] 'Verbs and Times', 145.

TABLE 3.1. *A summary of Vendler's typology*

With continuous tenses		Without continuous tenses	
Activities	Accomplishments	Achievements	States
Run	Run a mile	Recognize	Know
Eat	Eat an apple	Find	Believe
Pick potatoes	Pick a potato	Reach the hilltop	Love

not; and 'At what time did you love him?' would need to be construed as asking for a period of time ('Oh, all through my second year') before we can make sense of it. 'For how long did you love him?', on the other hand, is straightforward. Table 3.1 summarizes Vendler's typology.

Vendler notes that it is only verbs which admit of continuous tenses that can be used to respond to the question 'What are you doing?' One can be running a mile, or picking potatoes, but one cannot be recognizing or knowing or believing anything. In the latter cases, the appropriate questions are of the form 'Do/Did you φ?', rather than 'Are/Were you φ-ing?' Vendler concludes from this that only verbs found in continuous forms designate processes going on in time:

This difference suggests that running, writing, and the like are processes going on in time, i.e., roughly, that they consist of successive phases following one another in time. Indeed, the man who is running lifts up his right leg at one moment, drops it the next, then lifts his other leg, drops it, and so on. But although it can be true of a subject that he knows something at a given moment or for a certain period, knowing and its kin are not processes going on in time.[4]

Vendler is clearly right to insist that verbs which cannot take continuous tenses do not correspond to processes. But it is important to be clear that the reason why achievement verbs are not usually found in continuous-tense form is quite different from the corresponding reason in the stative case. Roughly, achievement verbs do not take continuous tenses because they relate to things which can happen instantaneously—things that one can have done,

---

[4] 'Verbs and Times', 144.

or will do—but not normally things that one can be in the process of doing, for the simple reason that they are normally over too quickly for it to be possible for anyone to 'catch one in the act', as it were, of doing them. When one recognizes someone, or finds something, it happens (at least usually) in a flash—thus these are not things that one can 'be doing'.[5] But states are different. It is not because knowing is instantaneous that one cannot be knowing or believing. It is because states do not *take up* time at all; they have no temporal parts.

Anthony Kenny arrived independently at a typology of verbs rather similar to that developed by Vendler, in his book *Action, Emotion and Will*. While Vendler distinguishes four categories of verb, Kenny makes use of only three, dividing verb types into *activities*, *performances*, and *states*. Broadly speaking, the main difference between the two typologies is that Kenny does not distinguish, as Vendler does, between accomplishments and achievements. Kenny labels all verbs that do not admit of continuous tenses 'static verbs', and gives as examples 'knowing' and 'being happy', which would count as stative verbs also under Vendler's system. This criterion for static verbs can make it appear as though Kenny simply fails to recognize the existence of a class of non-static verbs—Vendler's verbs of achievement—within the class of verbs not admitting of continuous tenses, but some of Kenny's examples make it clear that this is not the case. Rather, he includes Vendler's verbs of achievement, 'recognize', 'discover', 'notice', and the like, within his class of performance verbs, thus indicating that the basis of his disagreement with Vendler is rather over the question whether or not these verbs have genuine continuous tenses.

It is undeniable that it is possible, even if not usual, to find most of Vendler's achievement verbs in continuous-tense form; consider, for example, 'I am discovering for the first time what everyone saw in him' or 'He was slowly recognizing that I had been right all along'. Discovering and recognizing are not always instantaneous—and where they are conceived of as unfolding in a period of time, use of a continuous-tense form may become appropriate. This

---

[5] 'Usually' because there are some exceptions—see below. These verbs also have a stative usage. The question 'Do you recognize . . . ?' is asking not whether some rather short-lived event has occurred but rather about a present state of familiarity in the respondent. 'Do you find him attractive?' exhibits 'find' in a similarly stative usage.

is a point made by Alexander Mourelatos, in a paper that is intended as a critique and elaboration of the views of Vendler and Kenny.[6] One of Mourelatos's main aims in the paper is to argue that Vendler and Kenny are mistaken in supposing that the distinctions they are seeking to capture and explore are basically distinctions between verbs (and verb phrases) conceived of as lexical types. Rather, he argues, the relevant typology ought to be one which classifies whole predications into kinds. In the next section, I want to discuss, and in some respects to endorse, Mourelatos's view.

2. TYPES OF VERB VERSUS TYPES OF PREDICATION

Mourelatos notes that not just some, but many verbs fall into more than one of Vendler's and Kenny's categories, a phenomenon he calls 'multivalence', which he deems sufficiently widespread to 'make it quite wrong for us to talk in terms of exceptional or catachrestic uses of certain verbs'.[7] In certain cases (the verbs 'know' and 'understand', for example), where one kind of usage is overwhelmingly predominant (in this case, the stative usage), it might be sufficient to remark idiosyncratic contexts and leave it at that, but, as Mourelatos argues convincingly, very many verbs have no special affinity for one or other of the Vendler–Kenny verb categories. 'Run', for example, can function either as an activity verb ('I ran for hours') or as an accomplishment verb ('I ran to the shop'), as indeed Vendler recognizes, but the distinction between these contexts does not hinge, as Vendler implies, on the presence or absence of a stated end. 'I was running to the shop', no less than 'I was running', describes an activity, not an accomplishment, according to Mourelatos:

The generic activity of running can be further differentiated into a species (one among indefinitely many) of running-a-mile without losing its character as an activity. In other words, regardless of whether a mile is or fails to be run, any substretch of running-a-mile activity divides homogeneously into sub-stretches of the same. There is, after all, a qualitative distinction between the activity of running a mile and the activity of running the hundred-meter dash or the Marathon.[8]

---

[6] Mourelatos, 'Events, Processes and States'.   [7] Ibid. 419.   [8] Ibid. 420.

It looks, then, as though 'run-to-the-shop', as well as 'run' can be an activity verb, and the basis for the distinction between Vendler's first two categories (and between Kenny's activities and performances) collapses.

In the light of these difficulties for Vendler's and Kenny's analyses, Mourelatos argues that what is wanted to deal with the phenomena which interested Kenny and Vendler is a threefold distinction, at the level not of verb types, but of types of predication. Kenny's activity–performance–state trichotomy, adapted to act as a distinction among types of predication rather than types of verb, suggests itself as suitable, but, as Mourelatos points out, this will not do if we are looking for a quite general typology of predication. Activities and performances are normally things people, or perhaps animals do; it is not clear how Kenny's trichotomy would accommodate sentences not involving agency of any kind. What is needed, Mourelatos argues, is a 'topic-neutral' typology to correspond to Kenny's trichotomy; and the relevant categories, on his view, are *event*, *process*, and *state*.

There are other refinements in Mourelatos's account, for example, his distinction within the class of event predications between 'developments' and 'punctual occurrences'. For now, though, it will be sufficient to reproduce here his own schematic representation of his preferred typology (see Fig. 3.1), together with a few examples.

'Situation' is simply the generic term used by Mourelatos to encompass all the kinds of predication with which he is concerned. 'Occurrences' include both processes and events. Here are his examples of predications from each of the four categories.

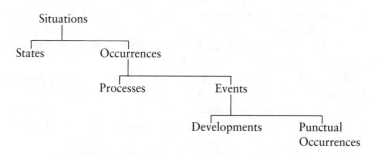

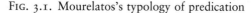

FIG. 3.1. Mourelatos's typology of predication

State: The air smells of jasmine.
Process: It's snowing.
Development: The sun went down.
Punctual Occurrence: The cable snapped. He blinked. The pebble hit the water.

It is easy to get an intuitive feel for the distinctions between these various categories of predication just by looking at Mourelatos's examples. But it is not quite so easy to provide a set of criteria which will serve as infallible guide-lines in the categorization of predications as predications of event, state, or process. Indeed, as Mourelatos points out, no simple grammatical or syntactic test may suffice. An interplay of factors may be involved, including the verb's meaning, its tense, the nature of the verb's subject and object, and of the qualifying adverbials, if any. But something on which Mourelatos places great emphasis in his account of the event–process–state distinction is the phenomenon of verb aspect, so I shall take some time to explain what is meant by this term.

3. ASPECT

Verb aspect is a phenomenon more familiar to linguists than to many philosophers, being more clearly marked in other languages than it is in English. For example, corresponding to the two English sentences 'I was writing a book' and 'I wrote a book', Russian has 'Ja pisal knigu' and 'Ja napisal knigu' respectively, where *pisat'* and *napisat'* are distinct verbs.[9] This phenomenon is widespread in Slavonic languages, where most verbs occur in two forms, called the *imperfective* and *perfective* respectively. It is now recognized by linguists that many of the features of English and other languages which were traditionally assigned by grammarians to tense are aspectual distinctions.

There seem to be two ways of thinking about aspect in English. The first way ties decisions about whether a predication has perfective or imperfective aspect to the presence or absence of an *aspectual marker*—that is to say, a grammatical or syntactic fea-

---

[9] This example is taken from A. Galton, *The Logic of Aspect* (Oxford, 1984), 1.

ture—in the case of English, the presence of a continuous-tense form. It will then be easy to decide which aspect a predication has; where a continuous-tense form is present, the predication will have imperfective aspect; otherwise, it will be perfective. But if we make the distinction in this way, it is obvious that we will need to invoke features other than aspect in order to locate predications within the Mourelatos typology. For example, 'I was running a mile every day at that time' will be technically imperfective, but it cannot be straightforwardly accounted a process predication, since what the imperfective encodes here is not a single activity going on in time, but rather the repetition of a kind of event. Likewise, 'He sang for hours' will be technically perfective, but it is natural to think that it really ought to fall into the 'process' category; 'for hours' is the kind of adverbial which Vendler associates with his activity predications, and the translation into Russian of the sentence would use a marker for imperfective aspect. Mourelatos suggests that he thinks of aspect in this first way as only one of the features relevant to categorizing a predication; he mentions it as one of six features which might help to determine the place of a predication in his typology.[10]

The other way of thinking about aspect is to see the aspect of a predication as something which is itself to be determined by a rather complicated interplay of factors. Thus, one might regard 'He sang for hours' as having imperfective aspect, even though it lacks the continuous-tense form. This seems to be Galton's view; he writes that '*almost any* element of a sentence can contribute to aspectual character'.[11]

It does not seem to me to matter much which of these ways of looking at aspect is chosen, as long as usage remains consistent. I shall take over Mourelatos's usage, whereby the aspect of an English predication is determined simply by whether or not its main verb is in a continuous tense. The question we now need to ask is what relevance the presence of a continuous-tense form has for a predication, and how it is connected with the event–process–state trichotomy.

It is certain that many interesting connotative differences can be encoded through aspect. R. L. Allen uses the terms 'inclusive' and 'intrusive' to describe the perfective–imperfective contrast, and in

---

[10] 'Events, Processes and States', 421.   [11] *The Logic of Aspect*, 70.

many ways, these terms are more suggestive.[12] Allen describes
aspect as a speaker's 'way of looking' at a predication, and argues
that a speaker's choice of aspect depends on whether the event in
question is to be looked at 'from the inside' or 'from the outside'.
The two sentences

   (1) Your teacher told me that you weren't doing well in
       mathematics, and
   (2) Your teacher was telling me that you weren't doing well in
       mathematics,

for example, differ only in the way in which the occasion of the
teacher's imparting of the unwelcome information is presented to
the listener. In the first case, the aspect is inclusive (perfective); that
is to say, the event is presented as a complete whole which is now
to be viewed in its entirety from the perspective of the present. The
second sentence, by contrast, seems to invite the listener back into
the past to a time at which the event in question was still occurring,
when it was still, as we might say, perhaps suggestively, 'in the
process' of happening; the aspect is intrusive (imperfective) and the
event is viewed 'from the inside'. In many ways, intrusive aspect is
a more intimate aspect; several linguists have noted the use made by
writers of intrusive aspect to present an event as though the reader
were living through it (e.g. 'Suddenly the bullets were flying past his
head').

   But is it really true that aspect is really no more than a speaker's
'way of looking' at a predication? Might there not be some *seman-
tically* significant differences between perfective and imperfective
aspects—in which case one might think that talk of 'ways of looking' at a predication understates the contrast here? Let us take as an
example the perfective–imperfective pair

   (1) I was writing a novel yesterday.
   (2) I wrote a novel yesterday.

Are there any differences between (1) and (2) which might be of
semantic importance?

   We might note, to begin with, that while (2) implies (1), the
reverse is not true. If I was writing a novel yesterday, I did not

---

[12] In R. L. Allen, *The Verb System of Present-Day American English* (The Hague,
1966), 218–19.

necessarily finish it, so it does not follow that I wrote a novel yesterday. But if I wrote a novel yesterday, it does follow that I must have been writing it yesterday. Second, there are the points about adverbial modification which Vendler notes, in attempting to draw his contrast between activities and accomplishments; I might say, for example, that I was writing a novel *for hours* yesterday, but not that I wrote a novel for hours. Similarly, if I say that I wrote a novel yesterday, I could add 'and it took me eight hours'; whereas one would not add any comment about how long the writing *took* to the sentence 'I was writing a novel yesterday', though we might ask how long it *went on for*. And thirdly, the two sentences behave differently in connection with *tense*. This is pointed out by Galton. (1) has a present-tense equivalent—as Galton puts it, 'I am writing a novel' assigns to the present moment what 'I was writing a novel' assigns to the past. But 'I write a novel', which is, grammatically speaking, the present-tense form of (2), does not assign to the present moment what (2) assigns to the past. Indeed, in so far as we can understand this sentence in isolation at all (that is to say, unqualified by an adverbial such as 'every year'), it would seem that we need to understand it as meaning the same as its imperfective counterpart, 'I am writing a novel'. In Galton's words, 'Roughly speaking, we may say that perfective aspect is logically incompatible with present tense meaning'.[13]

If we are satisfied, then, that there is something of semantic significance about the perfective–imperfective contrast, how does it relate to Mourelatos's typology? Clearly, it bears on the event–process distinction. Normally, we might say, an imperfective predication can be assigned to the process category; and normally, too, where it occurs with the right kind of verb, perfective aspect indicates that a predication ought to be classified as an event predication—unless adverbial modification (as for example in, 'He sang for

---

[13] *The Logic of Aspect*, 3. 'Roughly speaking', presumably, because there seem to be special cases which provide exceptions to the general rule, e.g. performatives. For example, 'I name this ship' has present-tense meaning, though its aspectual character seems to be perfective. However, Galton is at pains to point out that it remains true that sentences such as 'I name this ship' do not assign to the present what sentences like 'I named this ship' assign to the past—the reason being that the present-tense sentence is not a *report* at all—and so does not, in the relevant sense, assign anything to the present. An utterance of 'I name this ship' just *is* an act of naming; it does not report it. Thus 'I named this ship' is not a past-tensed version of 'I name this ship', but rather a *report of my utterance*, at some past time, of the sentence 'I name this ship' (*The Logic of Aspect*, 13–14).

hours') suggests otherwise. The relevance of aspect for state predications is less clear. Mourelatos does not give a precise criterion for differentiating between states and occurrences; he is more concerned with establishing the legitimacy of the category of event, and hence with the means for distinguishing event from process predications. Clearly, the Kenny–Vendler criterion for stative verbs, which makes the admissibility of continuous tenses the crucial test, is not really suitable where the typology is of predications, rather than of verbs considered as lexical types. A fuller understanding of the nature of stative predications will demand a closer look at factors other than aspect and this will have to await the discussion of the next chapter. The distinction between event and process predications, however, *is* largely analysable in aspectual terms, and I want to go on now to discuss Mourelatos's suggestions about the relevance of this distinction for the ontological questions with which I am primarily concerned.

4. NOMINALIZATION TRANSCRIPTIONS: EVENTS AND PROCESSES

One of the most interesting arguments in Mourelatos's paper is designed to show that the distinction between count nouns and mass nouns has a striking parallel in the domain of verbs. Mourelatos begins by referring to arguments by Geoffrey Leech and others that the distinction between count and mass nouns sometimes has a role to play in the determination of the category of certain predications: those where the predication has an object whose classification as count or mass noun affects the character of the predication as a whole.[14] Leech argues, for example, that in the sentence 'He played a Mozart sonata', where the object is a count noun ('a Mozart sonata'), the predication as a whole is turned thereby into an event predication, whereas in 'He played a little Mozart', where the object is a mass term ('a little Mozart'), we have instead a process predication. This claim is supported, I think, despite the absence of imperfective aspect, by the following observations:

---

[14] G. N. Leech, *Towards a Semantic Description of English* (Bloomington, Ind., 1969).

1. There is an entailment not only from 'I played a little Mozart' to 'I was playing a little Mozart' but also from 'I was playing a little Mozart' to 'I played a little Mozart' (contrast the novel-writing case above).
2. If I played a little Mozart, one would ask *for how long* I played, not *how long it took*.
3. 'I am playing a little Mozart' seems to assign to the present moment what 'I played a little Mozart' assigns to the past.

Mourelatos, though, thinks the connection between the count–mass contrast and the event–process distinction runs deeper than this. He introduces the concept of a *nominalization transcription* to make the point. Most predications can be given a nominalized form, in which the verb is transformed into a kind of noun. For example, corresponding to 'Jones brushed his teeth' there is the nominalized sentence 'There was a brushing of (his) teeth by Jones'. Mourelatos argues that the character of the appropriate nominalization can give an indication of the nature of the original predication. The nominalized transcriptions of event predications, he claims, are normally *count-quantified*. In some cases, where the number of occurrences is mentioned in the original sentence (e.g. 'Jones changed his clothes three times'), this will mean that the occurrences are explicitly counted in the nominalization (e.g. 'There were three changings of (his) clothes by Jones'); more ordinarily, the number of occurrences will be one, and the fact that the nominalization is count-quantified will be signalled by the appearance of an indefinite article (e.g. in the previous example, 'There was a brushing of his teeth by Jones').

The nominalizations of process predications, however, do not share this feature, according to Mourelatos. He gives two examples. The first, 'John pushed the cart for hours', becomes 'For hours there was pushing of the cart by John'. The second, 'Jones was painting the Nativity', is rendered 'There was (some) painting of the Nativity by Jones'. In neither case does an indefinite article seem appropriate. As Mourelatos puts it:

The pushing and the painting in these contexts do not have the terminus or closure that would allow us to speak of *a* pushing or *a* painting—we are not told that the cart was pushed some place, or that the Nativity did get painted. The parallel with simple nouns for these transcriptions is not in sentences of the form 'There is at least one K'; it is rather in sentences of the same form as 'There is snow on the roof', or 'There is gold in this mountain'.[15]

The suggestion is, then, that process predications stand to event predications in something like the way that mass nouns stand to count nouns. But can we go further? Just as the differential behaviour of mass nouns and count nouns might lead us to want to make an ontological distinction between masses and individuals, might not the distinction between event and process predications point to an ontological distinction? And if so, how exactly do we move, in this case, from grammar to ontology?

There are at least two very pressing questions here. First, does every event predication demand the occurrence of at least one event for its truth?[16] For example, if the average number of children per British household fell last year, was there an event which was its falling?[17] There is undoubtedly something odd, I think, about any such supposition. One can give no spatial location to such an event (other than perhaps saying that it occurred 'in Britain'—but this does not seem to be the location of the fall in the average number of children in the same way as it is the location of the numerous other events which occur in Britain. It does not occur anywhere in particular in Britain—even if the fall is more marked in some regions than others). And perhaps more importantly, there are also problems about providing it with temporal coordinates. We can say that the fall happened last year, but not that it happened at any particular time in the year—nor even, I think, that it lasted the whole year. The idea that such an event could 'last' or 'take time' seems wrong—and there is something strange also about the idea that such an event has temporal parts. I shall call events which might cause worries of this kind *non-paradigmatic events*. I shall not attempt to define this concept precisely, since it seems to me probable that there is no sharp dividing-line between respectable events and those whose status as real occurrences we might be inclined to doubt. But as a rough guide-line, perhaps we might say that any event which does not seem to have a definite time of occurrence is likely to cause us unease—and will therefore count, for my purposes, as non-paradigmatic.

---

[15] 'Events, Processes and States', 427.

[16] A parallel question also arises for processes—but I consider only events here, since the same considerations apply to both.

[17] I owe this example to Paul Snowdon.

And second, there is a question about how we are to understand the event–process distinction itself. For if we base the event–process distinction on an account of the difference between event and process *predications*, it renders untenable a certain kind of tempting view about events and processes. For example, consider the two sentences

(1) Smith pushed the cart to the top of the hill.
(2) Smith pushed the cart for hours.

(1) would be an event predication, on Mourelatos's view; the aspect is perfective and the nominalization transcription would be:

(1*) There was a pushing of the cart to the top of the hill by Smith,

the presence of the indefinite article indicating an event predication. (2), on the other hand, would be a process predication; the aspect here is imperfective and the nominalization transcription would be:

(2*) There was pushing of the cart by Smith for hours.

But suppose what actually happened was that Smith pushed the cart for hours in order to get to the top of the hill, where he finally arrived. Both (1) and (2) might be used to say what Smith did, to describe, as we might want to say, what happened 'in the world'. But (1), we might suppose, indicates the occurrence of an event, (2) the occurrence of a process. It is tempting to suppose that Smith's pushing of the cart for hours *just was* his pushing of the cart to the top of the hill; but how can this be, if 'Smith's pushing of the cart for hours' refers to a process and 'Smith's pushing of the cart to the top of the hill' refers to an event? Perhaps we might conclude that 'event' and 'process' are really just two ways of looking at the same thing. But if so, is it possible to continue to conceive of the event–process distinction as a genuinely *ontological*—rather than a purely grammatical—distinction?

Despite the appeal of this thought, I believe that a grammatically rooted event–process distinction can be defended against the charge of ontological profligacy. In Section 6, I shall attempt such a defence. But before doing so, I want to say something about the first question I mentioned—the question whether every event predication corresponds to an event—in particular, whether non-paradigmatic events should be allowed to count.

5. NON-PARADIGMATIC EVENTS

I am inclined to think that whether or not non-paradigmatic events ought to be counted as events rather depends on the purposes for which one's theory of events is required. A theory which postulates events to provide a semantics for adverbially qualified sentences, for example, will probably need the category of *event* to be grammatically based; for adverbial modification is not confined to predications which correspond to events of a paradigmatic kind. If the theory is to be a *general* semantic theory, therefore, there might be good reason to make the class of events as inclusive as possible. But we are looking for an account of events which might serve for the formulation of a number of theories in the philosophy of mind. Should we want to countenance non-paradigmatic events, given this purpose?

One might think that it is possible simply to remain indifferent about this matter. For it is natural to suppose that neither mental events, nor the kinds of physical events which are involved in the statement of the relevant class of theories, are in any danger of being non-paradigmatic. Mental events, even if token physicalism is false, it might be argued, can at least be located where the bearers of the relevant mental predicates are located; and they seem to have definite times of occurrence. Sudden rememberings, the occurrences of mental images, the makings of conscious decisions, the thinkings of definite thoughts, and actions, are all events which seem to take place in time in a straightforward sense. But caution is needed here. For there do seem to be event predications involving predicates which would standardly be regarded as 'mental', which might give more grounds for doubt. Consider, for example, the question 'Did you remember to lock the back door?' and the answer 'Yes, I remembered'. Now, it is certainly arguable that it may be true of me that I remembered to lock the back door, without its also being true of me that I ever thought consciously about locking it at any stage, without there ever having occurred to me the thought 'Oh, I must lock the back door'. It may just have been part of my dreary, habitual round of nightly duties—I did it unthinkingly, as I always do it. In such a case as this, there would seem to be no definite answer to the question when I remembered to lock the back door; it was not a clockable event, like my suddenly remembering that I am supposed to be at the dentist's. We might think, then, that such remembering events are a bit like fallings in the average number of children per household—mere ontological shadows, as it were, of the nominalized versions of certain predications, not to be taken at face value. What ought the token physicalist to say about such 'events' as this?

There seem to be at least four possible views one might take about such cases:

1. The mental attribution is, strictly speaking, false—it is not really true that I remembered to lock the back door, if there was no special time at which I remembered to do so.

2. The mental attribution is true, but does not require the occurrence of a mental event for its truth—some other account of the semantics of a sentence of this kind can be given.

3. The mental attribution is true and does require the occurrence of a mental event for its truth; it is just that the event in question is not a conscious occurrence, but an unconscious one.

4. The mental attribution does require the occurrence of a mental event for its truth—but this event can be non-paradigmatic. There is no need to conceive of it as having occurred at any definite time at all—even unconsciously. Rather, we need to shake ourselves free of an unduly restrictive conception of what constitutes a 'real' event.

I do not intend to choose here between these four positions; nothing I have to say in what follows will depend upon making such a choice. But I do want to point out that any choice one might make will have consequences for the scope and perhaps for the plausibility of certain theories about mental events, including token physicalism. If one is inclined to choose position (1), for example, the theory that all mental events are identical with (or constituted by) physical events will extend only to those events which are conscious and clockable—those which afford no room for scepticism about their occurrence. One might think that this is the most plausible version of the theory—that such events are identical with physical events occurring in the brain is a highly attractive view, while one might be less sure about mental events our evidence for the occurrence of which is quasi-theoretical, rather than introspective. At the other end of the scale, position (4) is hard to make cohere with token physicalism at all. For if a mental event can be said to have occurred merely in virtue of the fact that some event predication is true, whether or not it can be supposed to have occurred at any particular time, it seems difficult to square this with the view that all mental events are identical with, or constituted by, physical events. For it is natural to think that the neural events with which, on most conceptions of what token physicalism amounts to, mental events are supposed to be identical, or out of which they are constituted, must take place at particular times—that they are paradigmatic events. But it does not seem to make sense to say both that an event has a definite time of occurrence and that it has no such definite time of occurrence.

The token physicalist, therefore, might have good reason to reject (4). But any of the other three views, it seems to me, is consistent with the theory. (3) might be held, for example, by someone who believed that folk-psychological explanation demonstrates a quasi-theoretical commitment to a number of non-introspectible mental *states*—and who did not see why we should not also be theoretically committed by folk psychology to non-introspectible events. The question whether every event predication corresponds to an event, therefore, seems to remain an open one—a token physicalist can simply define the class as widely or as narrowly as required to give the sense she wishes to the claim that all mental events are identical with, or constituted by, physical events. If a narrower class is chosen, an account of event predication *alone* will not be enough to explicate the category of event—something will need to be said about what distinguishes 'real' events from those which are merely the 'ontological shadows' of nominalizations. But even if one chooses to opt for some narrow definition which excludes non-paradigmatic events, like falls in the average number of children per household, it still seems to me that at least the *necessary* conditions of eventhood should be sought in the temporal features of event predication. I shall try to make good this claim in Section 7. I turn, now, to the event–process distinction.

6. EVENT AND PROCESS AS ONTOLOGICAL CATEGORIES

An example may be the best way of making persuasive the case for an ontological distinction between events and processes. Consider the present humming of my computer. I might think or speak about this humming; I might say, for instance, that the humming of my computer is distracting me. Now, this humming is undoubtedly something which is taking place in time—it is an entity which has temporal parts, and thus is somewhat event-like in nature. But there are good reasons for thinking that it is nevertheless not an event. I might describe the humming, for example, as persistent, or continuous—but it does not really seem to make sense to describe an *event* as persistent or continuous. And the humming might *stop*, but do events really *stop*? They come to an end, but that is different. These are small and subtle differences, but they are real enough. And they seem to me to show that when I speak of the present humming of my computer, I am not referring to any individual event. Rather, I am referring to a continuous activity, something which is *going on through time*, a process.

Against this argument for a distinction, though, one might bring the following, forceful reasoning. There seems to be nothing in the nature of time itself, as it were, or in the nature of change, which dictates that happenings should divide themselves into two categories, events and processes. Looking back over any given period of time, for example, it is not instantly obvious that happenings of two entirely distinct varieties were occurring throughout. All we seem to have, when we view the world from this kind of temporal standpoint, is a succession of events, longer or shorter, more or less spatially dispersed chunks of which can be (perhaps only inexactly) picked out by event names and event descriptions. All we *really* have, it might be said, are events succeeding other events in time— and different ways of looking at those events—from the 'intrusive' or from the 'inclusive' point of view, to use Allen's terminology. The event–process distinction arises as a result of the existence of these different viewpoints, and to this extent, is just a by-product of grammar.

But this way of looking at things is, I think, unduly dismissive of the importance of grammatical distinctions for ontology. Just because we can conceive of a point of view from which 'intrusive' aspect is redundant—a kind of 'God's-eye view' of the history of the world, say—does not mean that the referring terms which are associated with our use of intrusive aspect in the time-bound circumstances in which we actually live our lives can only refer to the very same entities as are available from the 'God's-eye' perspective.

We do possess referring expressions deriving from imperfective contexts, as well as ones deriving from perfective predications; and there are reasons for wanting to insist that the referents of these expressions must be genuinely distinct, even where the entities they single out appear to coincide both spatially and temporally, as did Smith's pushing of the cart for hours and Smith's pushing of the cart to the top of the hill. For processes have properties which it would be inappropriate to ascribe to events, and vice versa. For example, as I have already noted, the humming of my computer in the *process* sense can be *persistent*; but it does not really make sense to think of an event as persistent. And events, it is natural to say, *take* time, while the same does not seem to be true of processes. Smith's pushing of the cart to the top of the hill, for example, took four hours; but his pushing of the cart for hours did not *take* four hours, though it lasted for four hours. Arguments from Leibniz's Law, then, can be straightforwardly brought to bear against any proposals for the identification of processes with events.

It can be harder to grasp the distinction between processes and events than it is to understand the distinction between masses and individuals, which can be regarded as parallel in some respects. For one has to overcome, in this case, not only the natural inclination to assume that the dimensions along which language may carve the world are simple, linear, spatial and temporal axes, but also confusions generated by the fact that the same gerundial nominal is used to refer both to the event and to the corresponding process. Thus, looking at our difficulty with Smith, for example, one is inclined to think that after all, there can only have been one *pushing*. But this inclination stems from an accident of our language, which has in this case no lexical difference to correspond with the grammatical distinction between event and process. To help with this, I want to introduce the following notation: 'ϕ-ings$_E$' are events and 'ϕ-ings$_P$' are processes. ϕ-ings$_E$ are countable; when Smith pushed the cart to the top of the hill, there was exactly one pushing$_E$ of the cart to the top of the hill, and if he does it again the next day, there will have been two. Pushings$_P$, on the other hand, are not countable. 'Pushing', in this sense, is an activity of which there can be more or less, but not one or two. The complicated truth about Smith and his pushing is therefore this: that while it is true that, in a sense, there was only one pushing (one pushing$_E$), there was also, alongside this pushing$_E$, some pushing$_P$. And the pushing$_E$ and the pushing$_P$ are items of different ontological types and for the reasons given above cannot be identified with one another. It is a familiar (though still not sufficiently uncontroversial) point that in refusing to identify continuants, like statues, horses, and human beings, with the lumps of matter of which they are composed, we do not 'double count'. In insisting on the distinctness of spatiotemporally coinciding events and processes, I am merely making a parallel claim in respect of entities with temporal parts.

I now want to go on to say a little more about the concept of temporal shape, to see how it might be used to talk about the differences between events, states, and processes, and to discuss, finally, whether an account of events based on temporal shape might be a plausible rival to the accounts of events I considered in Chapters 1 and 2—in particular, to the view that events are changes.

7. TEMPORAL SHAPE

How do the distinctions between event and process predications link up with the concept of 'temporal shape' which I introduced at the end of Chapter 2? There, I suggested that the question whether or not an entity has temporal parts counts as a question about its temporal shape. But if the difference between events and processes is itself to count as a difference of temporal shape, we need to add to these observations. For both events and processes, on the account I have offered, have temporal parts, and so both can be said to 'happen', to 'occur', to 'take place'. How might we extend our conception of the features of an entity which contribute to its temporal shape, so as to account for the event–process distinction?

One thing which helps a little is the difference we have already noted between entities which take time and those which can be said to go on for a time. The humming of my computer, for example, does not take two hours—it only goes on for two hours. But these features of events and processes do not seem to be completely reliable as guides to the distinction. Though many events certainly take time—buildings of houses and runnings of miles, for example—there seem to be other events where this form of words is not appropriate—not only instantaneous (or very short-lived) events, but also events which do have temporal duration. Of a picnic, for example, I think one would ask how long it lasted, not how long it took; and the nominalization transcriptions of certain predications which otherwise seem to be perfective also cause problems. Consider, for instance, the sentence 'I went to the fair'. This would seem to be perfective: one would, I think, produce 'There was a going to the fair by me' and not 'There was going to the fair by me' as its nominalization transcription; if I went to the fair twice, then there were two goings to the fair by me, etc. But in normal circumstances, I think it would be inappropriate to ask how long it took to go to the fair—though one might ask how long it took to *get* there. 'How long did you go for?' seems more natural—but this was the form we associated above with processes.

Though it is generally true that events take time, while processes last for a time or go on for a time, then, I do not think we can rest entirely content with this account. It may be more hopeful, I think, to look to differences in certain temporally sensitive *adjectives* which it is appropriate to apply to events and processes respectively. A process like the humming of my computer, for example, can be persistent, continuous, ongoing, constant, incessant, perpetual, unremitting, sporadic, intermittent, irregular, steady. But none of these adjectives can be comfortably applied to an event—at least, where such an adjective is so applied, it must be given a different sense. This is related to the fact that the aspectual features of event predications make certain kinds of adverbial modification inappropriate; for example, if Smith pushed the cart to the top of the hill, we cannot say that he pushed it to the top of the hill constantly (unless we mean that he did it many times over); though we can say that he pushed it for hours constantly. Processes are things which, as it were, go on throughout periods of time—and so we can sensibly ask how they went on through that time—whether they went on constantly, or intermittently, etc. But events simply happen—there is a 'when', and a 'how long' to be asked, but it does not make sense to ask a certain kind of 'how' question, the kind which asks for the distribution of the happening in time.

I suggest, then, that the receptivity of an entity to such temporally sensitive adjectival modification ought to be accounted a feature of its temporal shape. Putting all that we have said so far together, then, we can say, roughly, that those features of a temporal entity which determine its temporal shape are those which determine which of the following may be said of it:

1. Whether it persists, occurs, goes on, continues, happens, obtains.
2. Whether it takes time, lasts for a time, goes on for a time, persists for a time, occurs at a time.
3. Whether certain temporally sensitive adjectives may be applied to it—these include 'intermittent', 'continuous', 'persistent', etc.

Of course, this is *only* rough; in particular, much more might be said about other kinds of adjectives which might serve to indicate differences of temporal shape—those to do, for example, with *change*, which might be thought to distinguish persisting physical objects from events and processes. But since the considerations alluded to in (1) will suffice to make this distinction, I will not pursue the matter here.

On the basis of this rough outline, then, we can now say this:

1. *Physical objects, their parts, and the masses of matter which constitute them* all share a temporal shape—they persist through time, last for a time, and may change; none occurs or happens. This is related to the point, raised at the end of Chapter 2, that the part–whole relation depends on identity of temporal shape between part and whole.

2. *Events and processes* have many features of their temporal shapes in common; both occur, both have temporal parts. But subtle differences of temporal shape which are related to the aspectual distinctions discussed above also exist; processes, but not events, can be persistent, intermittent, etc. Processes, then, if we are sticking to the principle that only entities which share a temporal shape can be related by the part–whole relation, ought not to be regarded as *parts* of events (and vice versa).

3. *States* seem to have many temporal features in common with physical objects. They persist through time (at least usually) and have no temporal parts. That states, but not physical objects, can be said to obtain seems to me to be related not to a temporal difference, but rather to the special relation between the obtaining of a state and the holding of certain *truths*; e.g. if the state of my believing that *p* 'obtains', that is because I believe that *p*. I conclude, therefore, that states share a temporal shape with physical objects.

Having given a rough indication of how the concept of temporal shape might be elaborated, I now want to argue that the best hope for a 'metaphysical theory of events' may lie with the concept of temporal shape.

It is, I think, a hopeful feature of the concept of temporal shape that it can be used to explain what unites those events which are described by means of nominals derived from event predications (capsizings, runnings, pushings, etc.) with those which are referred to rather by means of nouns independent of verbs (funerals, picnics, vigils, etc.). For despite the differences between them, all these kinds of events *occur*. The idea of occurrence, of something which happens in time, which consists of temporal parts succeeding one another, is common to all. Compared to the accounts offered by Kim, Bennett, and Lombard, an account of events based on the concept of temporal shape would, admittedly, be a 'thin' account; it will perhaps be felt that to say that what events have in common is that they occur is not to say very much. Certainly, it does not say anything very rich about the 'metaphysical nature' of events. But perhaps it may be that no such rich account is really possible. The only characteristics of events which seem both sufficiently general to enable us to include all those things we might want incorporated into the category, and yet sufficiently specific to enable us to distinguish events from other entities, like physical objects, processes, and states, seem to be temporal characteristics. These features are common to vigils and weddings and pushings$_E$ of carts and settings$_E$ of the sun; and either jointly or individually seem to enable us to distinguish between these entities and things which are not events, like the sky's being blue at t and the humming$_P$ of my computer. To say this is not, admittedly, to say a great deal, but perhaps this may seem less unsatisfactory and surprising if one reflects on what a general account of *continuants* might look like; would we be able to say anything more than that they persist through time and have spatial, but no temporal, parts?[18] I suggest that when dealing with such large categories as 'event' and 'continuant' we might be foolish to expect any very rich account to be forthcoming.

An account of events based on the idea of a common temporal shape might also enable us better to understand the close but non-necessary connection between events and change. Most things

[18] It is not obviously true that all continuants are made of matter (for one might want to class, for example, holes, rainbows, shadows, as continuants of a kind).

which can be said to occur either are changes or involve change of one kind or another—for it is quite natural that we should only have reason to single out entities which consist of a succession of temporal parts where the succession is in some way pertinent, noticeable, or causally significant—and, by and large, it is successions of temporal parts such that successive parts differ from one another in various respects that matter to us in these ways. But this is not always true. Sometimes, a succession of resembling temporal 'slices' of a thing, person, or area can have event-like significance—as, for example, when a vigil is held, or a person responds by pointedly saying nothing at all. These can merit the status of occurrences because we can interpret the succession of resembling 'slices' in such cases as an *action* or a *demonstration*— something which deserves to be focused on *as* a succession, as something which occurs. But we need to beware of conflating such changeless events with states. States differ from events most fundamentally not in being 'unchanges', not in being constituted by successions of resembling time-slices, but rather in failing to have temporal parts at all.

I would like to suggest, then, that temporal shape is the key to understanding the category of event and also to making sense of the event–process and event–state distinctions. In the next part of this book, I want to move on to discuss in more detail the concept of a state—a concept which, I believe, has been grossly misused in philosophy of mind. Aspect alone, as I mentioned earlier, seems unlikely to provide any general account of states, although there are some generalizations one can make ('stative' verbs are rarely found with imperfective aspect, for example). But clearly, more needs to be said. I shall begin the next chapter, therefore, with a discussion of states and the expressions by means of which we refer to them and otherwise demonstrate our commitment to their existence.

II

States, Causation, and Causal Explanation

4

States and the Type–Token Distinction

WHAT are states? Do we need to refer to them, and if so, why do we need to do so? Is it all right to admit them straightforwardly into our ontology, or do we need to treat them with caution? What role do they play in causal explanation? These are some of the questions I hope to address in the next two chapters. My eventual aim will be to argue that a misunderstanding of the nature of states and of the role played by states in causal explanation has lent illusory support to much past and current thinking in philosophy of mind. In particular, I shall argue that eliminative materialism and many versions of both physicalism and functionalism are often shored up by a conception of statehood that cannot be sustained, and that the current debate about the efficacy of mental content is seriously distorted by the understanding of states that informs the usual formulation of the problem. But in this chapter, I want to attempt only a preliminary task: to pave the way for a discussion of the causal-explanatory role of states by trying to categorize and clarify the language we use to talk about them.

Sometimes, I think, during the course of this chapter, it will seem as though I am embarked on no more than exercises in grammar— but I ask the reader to bear with me. It is not as fashionable now as once it was to trace philosophical mistakes to linguistic confusions, but sometimes there is no avoiding the conclusion that this is their source. I believe the availability in English of the concept of a *state* has had significant and unfortunate effects on the shape of a number of philosophical debates—and the task of explaining how this has happened cannot proceed without a thorough examination of the range of constructions and turns of phrase which have been supposed by philosophers to legitimize the category.

It is not easy to say what, precisely, this range includes. If philosophers' examples are anything to go by, states have no special affinity for any particular kind of linguistic form. Expressions belonging to a wide variety of linguistic categories have been commandeered by philosophers to serve to provide examples of things they have called 'states'. Abstract nouns of various kinds (e.g. 'solidity', 'depression', 'knowledge') have been said to designate states, as have several sorts of complex nominal phrase ('being green', 'the chameleon's being green', 'the traffic-light's remaining red at *t*'); nominalized adjectives, sometimes of an artificial kind ('greenness', 'chairhood'); nominals referring to arrangements or distributions of objects in space ('the arrangement of cars after the car accident');[1] and of course there is also a range of expressions incorporating the word 'state' itself, as when we speak of 'states of the brain' or 'states of belief and desire'. Are some of these expressions equivalent to others? Is there a clear sense in which all refer to entities of the same sort? Is it possible to find any order amongst this chaotic mixture of grammatical constructions?

A brief examination of the motley collection of expressions just surveyed suggests that there are at least two distinctions which might prove useful in the attempt to sort out our stative language. One is the type–token distinction. This distinction is frequently invoked in connection with states and one might reasonably think that it could be of some help to us here. For example, we might say that, whereas 'solidity' is a type of state, a state that can be possessed by any number of things, we can also refer to 'token' states of solidity which can be said to exist wherever solidity is possessed by an individual thing—for example, we can refer to 'the solidity of that brick'.[2] I shall return in Sections 4 and 5 to the use of the type–token distinction in connection with states. The second distinction which suggests itself as relevant is a distinction between two different sorts of nominal expression which have been used by philosophers to refer to items they have called 'states'. As well as a wide variety of abstract nouns like 'solidity', 'marriage', 'belief', we also

---

[1] This last example is cited as an instance of a state by F. F. Schmitt in 'Events', *Erkenntnis*, 20 (1983), 281.

[2] The things I am here calling 'token states' are referred to by Bennett in *Events and their Names*, 15, as 'abstract particulars'. P. F. Strawson also 'notes their existence' in 'Particular and General', *Proceedings of the Aristotelian Society*, 54 (1953–4); repr. in Strawson, *Logico-Linguistic Papers* (London, 1971), 34: 'The simplest, though not the only recipe, for forming the names of members of this class is as follows: in the formula "the . . . of . . ." fill the first gap with the property-name in question and the second gap with the definite designation of a suitable individual. Thus we may speak of *the wisdom of Socrates* as an instance of wisdom; of *the redness of Smith's face* as an instance of redness; and we may also speak of *Jones' present mental state* as an instance of anger.'

find nominal expressions like 'being solid' (which can also be made individual in their application by means of an attributive tie; we can talk, for example, of 'that brick's being solid' or 'Kate's knowing that Helena is the capital of Montana'). This distinction is noted by Chomsky in a paper entitled 'Remarks on Nominalization'; he calls the former 'derived' and the latter 'gerundive' nominals. For the purposes of this chapter, I shall follow him in this usage.[3]

What are we to say about this second distinction? There are clearly interesting and important differences between derived and gerundive nominals. But perhaps we should begin by noting a similarity. It is quite plausible to suppose that both sorts of expression are basically derived—though in different ways—from certain kinds of predicational structures. Both 'solidity' and 'being solid', for example, are expressions which it is plausible to think of as second-level nominals derived ultimately from the adjective 'solid' and the constructions in which it figures. In this respect, then, states appear to be closely related to properties—indeed, we need to ask at this point whether there is really any difference between state types and properties, between state tokens and property instances. For if there is not, it is reasonable to think that we might be able to effect some simplifications that could help us in the discussions to come.

1. STATES AND PROPERTIES

Are state types just properties by another name? In many cases, it certainly seems to be a matter of indifference whether we say that a particular noun names a property or a type of state. There is probably almost as much variation in the kinds of nouns and nominals which philosophers have used in order to refer to properties as there is in the language they have employed to talk about states, but derived nominals like 'solidity', and gerundive constructions like 'being solid', have certainly been among the most favoured devices.[4] It does not seem to be true, though, that the

---

[3] N. Chomsky, 'Remarks on Nominalization', in D. Davidson and G. Harman (eds.), *The Logic of Grammar* (Encino, Calif., 1975), 188.

[4] Gerundive nominals seem to need to be prefaced by the phrase 'the property of . . .' before they can be said to refer to properties. For properties ought to be things which an individual can be said to have—and a thing cannot have being solid, though it can have the property of being solid.

concept of a state type and the concept of a property are simply coextensive. For one thing, some derived nominals seem to name states *rather* than properties. Strawson suggests, for example, in one place, that anger is really a state, not a property or quality; and though he gives no account of what the difference between states and properties might amount to, I think he is right to suggest that anger is not a property.[5] The property that a human being has when she is angry is surely the property of being angry, not anger; 'anger' does not seem to be a noun of the right kind to refer to the property itself. This might suggest that gerundive nominals (perhaps preceded, as suggested in note 4, by the phrase 'the property of . . .') are better suited to refer to properties than derived ones, but this is not true in general. Other derived nominals fit the '. . . is a property' schema perfectly well; there is nothing strange, for example, about the claim that solidity is a property, as well as a type of state. This confirms an observation made by Chomsky in the paper referred to earlier, namely that derived nominals are a very mixed bunch, bearing what Chomsky calls 'varied semantic relations to the base forms'.[6] In particular, only some of them, it seems, bear the relation to that form which consists in naming the property which the predicate ascribes.

Which derived nominals can be regarded as making reference to properties? On the whole, it seems to me that genuine property names are normally derived from adjectives by the addition of certain endings. In particular, the suffixes 'ity' (e.g. 'solidity', 'ferocity', 'limpidity'), 'ness' (e.g. 'redness', 'coolness', 'hardness'[7]), and sometimes 'hood' (e.g. 'manhood'), effect a kind of reflexive focusing; they function to turn adjectives into the names of the properties they attribute to things. Nouns like 'anger', 'sorrow', and 'pain', on the other hand, though clearly associated with stative predicates, do not merely name the properties for which those predicates may be supposed to stand. A thing may *have* (or *possess*) the property of solidity or coolness; but one does not have the property of anger or sorrow. These nouns seem to name not prop-

---

[5] 'Particular and General', 33.

[6] 'Remarks on Nominalization', 189. The 'base forms' here are first-order predications based on the predicate with which the derived nominal is associated.

[7] Although it seems to me that not all nouns formed using 'ness' are of the same kind. Redness is the property that something has when it is red, but happiness is not (or need not be) the property someone has when she is happy. Happiness can be a condition (like anger) as well as a property.

erties but rather what might loosely be termed *conditions*; they do not seem to belong at all in the same ontological category as solidity and redness. But note that the 'state of ...' locution of which philosophers are fond accommodates nouns of both kinds comfortably—as well as gerundive phrases like 'being red'.

The discussion up to this point might make it seem as though the class of properties ought simply to be regarded as a subclass of the class of state types, state type being regarded as an overarching category, encompassing the referents of all the various different sorts of stative nominals, derived and gerundive. However, quite apart from the worry that classifying all these things together might be dangerously indiscriminate, we also need to recognize that we would not normally be prepared to grant that all nouns and nominals which fall into one or other of these grammatical categories are the names of state types. We seem to demand a certain 'intrinsicness' of those features, properties, and conditions of objects which we are prepared to call states.[8] 'Being cold', for instance, seems to be a reasonable candidate—it sounds all right to say that my being cold might be a state of me, or one which I am 'in'—but 'being late', 'being important', 'being French' do not. It would doubtless be a complicated task, and one which I shall not attempt here, to spell out precisely what this thought about intrinsicness might amount to; but it is clear, anyway, that semantics as well as syntax plays a role in our decisions about what is to count as a state.

The relationship between properties and state types, then, is not a simple one. The class of properties is not identical with the class of state types—nor does either class include the other. And the class of state types which we have characterized so far seems to contain entities of significantly different kinds—pain along with being in pain, anger along with being angry, etc. None of these is obviously out of place in the frame '... is a type of state', but one might reasonably wonder whether the grammatical diversity here can

---

[8] A similar point is made by David Armstrong in *Belief, Truth and Knowledge* (London, 1973), 12: 'although states of objects are non-relational properties of objects, not all non-relational properties of objects are states of these objects'. Armstrong suggests that states, in addition to being non-relational, must also be properties which it is intelligible to suppose the object possessing the property might lack (so as to exclude, for example, the state of being a horse); and also properties which do not necessarily involve processes (so as to exclude, for example, states of running).

really be tolerated by any genuine ontological category. At the very least, more needs to be said about it. I want to turn now, therefore, to consider what the differences might be between these different varieties of noun and nominal.

2. NOMINALIZATION TRANSCRIPTIONS: STATES

It may be useful to begin by considering some ordinary first-order predications which do not themselves involve any reference to states, but whose truth might be thought to entail or to depend upon the existence or 'obtaining' of some state or other—the 'base forms' of which Chomsky speaks. These predications seem to fall into two main categories. First, there are those which involve verbs of the kind classified as 'stative' by Vendler and Kenny, e.g. 'He knew all along what we had done', 'I believed in God for years', 'She feared a Conservative victory', 'The corpse lay on the ground'. Second, there are those which involve a combination of some part of the verb 'to be', and an adjective, participle, or other attributive phrase, e.g. 'The pillar box is red', 'John was angry', 'I am in pain'. The fact that verbs and adjectives alike may serve as the basis for the formulation of state terminology is pointed out by Vendler, who refers to states as 'that puzzling type in which the role of verb melts into that of predicate, and actions fade into qualities and relations'.[9] Having given some examples of stative verbs, including *having, possessing, desiring, wanting,* and *liking,* Vendler continues:

In connection with the last group, an obvious idea emerges. From the point of view of time schemata, being married, being present or absent, healthy or ill, and so on, also behave like states. But then we can take one more step and realise that this is true of all qualities. Indeed, something is hard, hot or yellow for a time, yet to be yellow, for instance, does not mean that a process of yellowing is going on. Similarly, although hardening is a process . . . being hard is a state. Now perhaps we understand why desiring, knowing, loving, and so on, that is, the so-called 'immanent operations' of traditional philosophy, can be and have been looked upon as qualities.[10]

---

[9] *Linguistics in Philosophy,* 109.
[10] Ibid.

How are these first-order predications associated with the existence of states? It will be useful here to invoke again the idea of a
nominalization transcription. Just as a predication involving an
event or process verb, such as 'Smith sang the "Internationale"' or
'Jones ran alongside the ice-cream van', can be transformed to yield
explicit quantification over events or processes, e.g. 'There was a
singing of the "Internationale" by Smith' or 'There was running
alongside the ice-cream van by Jones', so stative predications can be
transformed to yield sentences which appear to refer explicitly to
states. But in the stative case, there are many different ways in
which a noun or nominal expression can be related to a first-level
predication. First, with adjectival predications, there is usually a
choice between nominalizing the whole predication to yield a gerundive expression and nominalizing only the adjective to produce
some sort of derived nominal. For example, 'Jones is cold' can be
nominalized to give either:

(1) There is Jones's being cold (whole predication nominalized),
    or
(2) There is Jones's coldness (adjective only nominalized)

—and this gives rise, correspondingly, to two alternative forms of
stative nominal: the gerundive form 'being cold', and the simple
property noun 'coldness'. In addition, some adjectival predications
are associated, more or less closely, with stative nouns that do not
fall into either of these categories—e.g. 'anger', 'indignation', 'bore-
dom'. And secondly, predications based on the stative verbs sometimes yield nominal expressions other than the gerunds which are
always available. This is a notable feature of the propositional
attitude verbs: 'believe' and 'desire', for example, yield 'belief' and
'desire', as well as the gerundive nouns 'believing' and 'desiring'.
But these nouns are significantly different from all the other varieties of stative noun: from gerunds, from property nouns like 'coldness', and also from nouns like 'anger' and 'sorrow'—for they are
count-quantifiable. One can have *a* belief or three lifelong desires or
a great many hopes, for example—whereas one would not usually
speak of a believing or many coldnesses or six angers.[11] Mourelatos

[11] Though there are exceptions to these generalizations. It is possible to read some
nominalizations involving the noun 'belief' as mass-quantified (e.g. 'I had belief in
him'); and possible also to think of contexts in which one might find 'coldness' and
'anger' used with an indefinite article. To speak of more than one coldness or anger,
though, would be highly unusual.

notes that the gerundive nominals produced by transcription of stative predications are mass-quantified: 'How do the nominalisation transcriptions work in the case of state predication? Count-quantified transcriptions do not seem to work at all. We cannot transform "John hates liars" into *"There is *a* hating by John of liars"; nor can we transform "Helen dominates her husband" into *"There is *a* dominating by Helen of her husband".'[12] But the phenomenon is not restricted to gerundive expressions; it is true of nearly all the nouns which philosophers have classified, explicitly or implicitly, as stative that they fail to accept count-quantification. It needs to be noted, then, that the propositional attitude nouns are very unusual amongst the nouns usually classed by philosophers as stative nouns in this respect. They are anomalous. And perhaps this should give us grounds for wondering whether beliefs and desires are really well characterized as states at all. For now, I simply raise the issue; I shall return to it in more detail later in the chapter.

We have seen, then, that the category of *state* masks one difference which might conceivably have ontological significance: the distinction between things like beliefs and desires which fall under count nouns, and those like anger, indignation, etc. which are referred to by mass terms. But it also masks a second, arguably even more significant difference—one which corresponds to the grammatical distinction between gerundive and derived nominals. Roughly speaking, the difference is this: gerundive nominals like 'Jones's being angry' or 'the water's being cold' are in effect nominalizations of whole sentences, not merely of the adjectives or verbs which occur within them.[13] They correspond to whole propositions, not to sub-propositional units of any sort. And this makes it natural to think that if they can be said to have referents at all, their referents are really facts, or states of affairs. Indeed, it is notable that when philosophers write about facts or states of af-

---

[12] 'Events, Processes and States', 428. Note that it need not damage Mourelatos's suggestion that count-quantified transcriptions do not work for states to point out that one might be able to make sense of, for example, 'John hated liars three times in his life' or 'Helen dominated her husband more than once'. For as Mourelatos notes, what is really being counted here are stages or junctures of John's life, in the first case, and occasions on which Helen dominated her husband in the second—not the hatings and dominatings themselves.

[13] See Chomsky, 'Remarks on Nominalization', for a convincing presentation of the case for the view that gerundive nominals are transformations of sentential structures.

fairs, they frequently use gerundive expressions. Armstrong, for example, defines a state of affairs as 'a particular's possessing a property'[14] and Austin gives 'the cat's having mange' as an example of a fact in his paper 'Unfair to Facts'.[15] Gerundive nominals in general seem less secure in their status as nouns than other kinds of noun; and this is surely related to their suitability for referring to facts. They are, as it were, only half-way through the process of conversion from verb to noun; to adapt a metaphor used by Vendler, there is a verb 'alive and kicking' inside them.[16] And it is not surprising that this sense of incompleteness should be associated with verb-derived nominals which refer to facts—for such nominals, one might think, *need* somehow to combine the functions of verb and noun if they are to be capable both of indicating the content of the fact and, simultaneously, of designating it.

A number of notable features of the behaviour of gerundive nominals bear out the suggestion that their referents differ in kind from the referents of derived nominals and the possessive constructions based on them. In various ways, expressions of the latter kind are more abstract, more remote from the realm of concrete instantiations, than the gerundive variety. For example, *being angry* is a way of being for a person but *anger* is not; *being angry* is a phrase which preserves, for 'angry', a kind of adjectival submissiveness that is all but lost in the derived nominal. There remains, in the gerundive form, the suggestion of a substance, a subject which is qualified; whereas 'anger' is a noun which has achieved a significant degree of independence from the associated adjective and works much better as a subject expression than the gerundive nominal. Indeed, we could probably go further and say that gerundive nominals never really appear as genuine subject expressions at all. Of course, we can produce grammatically acceptable (if clumsy) English sentences which combine gerundive nominals with predicative expressions: e.g. 'Jones's being angry was inexplicable' or 'Smith's thinking that I was lying was uncharitable'. But such sentences cannot be treated as straightforward ascriptions of

[14] D. M. Armstrong, *Nominalism and Realism*, vol. i of *Universals and Scientific Realism*, 2 vols. (Cambridge, 1978), 114.

[15] J. L. Austin, 'Unfair to Facts', in Austin, *Philosophical Papers*, 2nd edn. (Oxford, 1970), 166.

[16] *Linguistics in Philosophy*, 131.

properties to entities. For we could not transfer the adjectives to attributive position; we could not speak, for example, of 'Jones's inexplicable being angry' or 'Smith's uncharitable thinking that I was lying'. We should rather have to use adverbial modification (i.e. 'Jones's inexplicably being angry' or 'Smith's uncharitably thinking that I was lying') which provides evidence of what we might call, following Vendler's metaphor, the 'aliveness' of the verb inside the nominal, at any rate on the plausible assumption that the appropriateness of an adverb is evidence for the presence of a verb. And the aliveness of the verb in these gerundive nominals, in turn, supports the suggestion that their referents are facts—things' being thus and so—essentially structured entities—not particulars in the sense developed in Chapter 1.

Another difference between derived and gerundive nominals is the comparative comfort with which we can combine the former with demonstrative adjectives. 'This anger', 'that pain', 'this belief that p', for example, are much easier to accept than 'this being angry', 'that being in pain', 'this believing that p'. This suggests that gerundive nominals do not single out the sorts of things that it makes sense to make the objects of demonstrative thoughts—and as I suggested in Chapter 1, this is true of structured entities like facts. There are also revealing differences between the attributions we might be prepared to make using the two sorts of nominal in particular cases. Suppose, for example, that Jones becomes angry in response to a situation that I concede justifies—indeed requires—some kind of angry reaction, but that Jones is angrier than he ought to be, or angry in the wrong sort of way—violent when it would have been better to stay icily calm, for example. In such a situation, I might judge that Jones's anger had been counter-productive or unforgivable, say, while conceding that his being angry had been quite justifiable. His being angry is just a fact, a state of affairs whose existence consists entirely in the truth of the first-level predication 'Jones was angry'—and if I accept that anger of *some* sort was an appropriate reaction in this case, then I shall not want to complain about this state of affairs. What I am complaining about—Jones's anger—is not a state of affairs but something which is more like a particular in the sense defined in Chapter 1—a bearer of properties, something with a (no doubt rather limited) number of specific characteristics of its own. I hesitate to say simply that it *is* a particular in my sense—for it is not clear to me whether someone's anger could satisfy the secret life requirement. I am inclined to think that probably it could not—that the only alternative means of singling out a state like Jones's anger would have to trade either on different ways of singling out Jones or anger, or on relational properties (e.g. Jones's anger might be the most emotional state he has ever been in), and thus that such states are not particulars in the sense defined by Chapter 1. But neither is Jones's anger a fact. Evidently, its existence is dependent upon the fact of Jones's being angry—and so there is a clear sense in which it is a second-level entity—unlike, for example, Jones's liver or Jones's house. But it is not itself a fact.

I think, then, we have to accept that the philosopher's category of state is not a truly unitary category. It has been used to encompass both states of affairs—entities which are referred to by means of what are, in effect, nominalizations of whole sentences (as with 'Jones's being angry'); and entities which are the referents of derived nominals which are much more like singular terms ('Jones's anger', 'solidity', 'Smith's belief that Beijing is the capital of China'). Obviously, these latter expressions are different in many respects from more standard examples of proper names and definite descriptions—and indeed different from one another—but we ought not to let these contrasts obscure a divide which is far more significant that any of these dissimilarities: the divide between facts and things. To avoid further confusion, I propose to reserve the term 'states of affairs' for the fact-like entities to which gerundive nominals may be supposed to refer. Later, I shall try to show why the difference between states of affairs and other sorts of state is of so much importance. Next, I want to discuss some interesting features of the 'state of . . .' locution itself, with particular reference to the use of the concept of a state in philosophy of mind.

3. THE 'STATE OF . . .' LOCUTION

The 'state of . . .' locution seems to have two clearly distinct uses. First, any of the kinds of stative nominal already mentioned can be prefixed by the expression 'state of'; we can speak, for example, of states of greenness, depression, knowing that p, or whatever. The second kind of use occurs where the expression 'state of . . .' is completed not by terms which refer to the state types themselves, but rather to the things which are said to be 'in' them. Thus, for example, one can speak of the state of a room, or the state of the nation, or of one's state of health—meaning thereby to talk of the overall condition of whatever is in question.

The motivation for the view that states ought to be thought of as arrangements and distributions of objects in space may stem, at least partly, from this conception of a state as the overall condition of an object. For it is very natural, in giving consideration to the question how such a state might be represented in thought, to suppose that supervenience might have a part to play. The idea that the way a thing is depends upon the configuration of its ultimate constituents might suggest that the best we could do in giving a complete description of the state of that object would be to describe this configuration. In the case of the room, for example, the thought perhaps goes something like this: the 'overall state' of a room supervenes on facts about the objects in it, and in turn, the facts about the objects in it supervene on facts about their ultimate atomic parts. It would be in principle possible to give a complete description of the room by describing the position of every particle in it—and all other facts about the room would then be fixed by the facts about the arrangement and distribution of these particles. This arrangement and distribution can therefore be regarded as the 'state' of the room.

Is there anything wrong with this view? Perhaps there is nothing to object to in the thought that arrangements and distributions of objects in space are in principle capable of being described, and that the resulting descriptions might be called 'state descriptions'. But we need to enter some very significant cautions. The first is that these arrangements and distributions would not themselves be spatial entities—it is the objects themselves which have position in space, from which descriptions of their arrangements and distributions would be merely an abstraction. The second is that while this seems attractive as an account of states of rooms, it does not seem so attractive as an account of states of health or of nations, which ought perhaps to make us a little sceptical of its capacity to deliver any very general understanding of the nature of states. The third, and perhaps most important, is that we ought not to confuse states in this sense with the referents of the stative nominals I considered earlier in the chapter. There is nothing in the view that we may talk, if we wish, of the arrangements and distributions of objects in space as 'states' of rooms, gardens, etc. to imply that expressions like 'the room's being cold' or 'the garden's being untidy' must *refer* to these or any other arrangements and distributions. For all that has been said so far, these two concepts of what it is to be a state remain entirely distinct.

Where it is used in the first way, the 'state of . . .' locution seems, as William S. Robinson points out, to be 'little more than a stylistic variant on ordinary predication', and he continues: 'we can say that Jones is dressed, is sick, is depressed or is cold; we can also say that Jones is in a dressed state (or state of being dressed); is in a sick state (or state of being ill); is in a depressed state; or is in a cold state (or a state in which she is cold)'.[17] But the 'state of . . .' form of expression, even if it is only a stylistic variant on ordinary predication, has nevertheless been very powerful, as stylistic variants go. For it has several features which have enabled philosophers to formulate various theses concerning states which might not have seemed nearly so attractive had they had to restrict themselves to other modes of expression.

The identity theory of mind is a good example of a theory which can be made to seem more palatable by means of the introduction of the 'state of . . .' locution into its explicit formulation. One important feature of that frame is that it readily accepts a great many different kinds of expression. We can talk comfortably, for example, of states of redness, red, being red, or even of the state of the object which *is* red, depending on what suits our purposes at the time. This makes it possible for it to sound as though one is proposing identities between things of the same ontological type, even when the grammatical form of what is put into the 'state of . . .' frame on one side of the identity statement is completely different from what is put into the frame on the other side. Thus, for example, that a state of belief should be identical with an unspecified 'state of the brain' sounds reasonable enough—for we can assure ourselves that both are *states* after all. But to speak of a 'state of the brain' is to use the 'state of . . .' location in a second, and quite different, sense from the way in which it is used in speaking of states of belief.

Of course, it might be said that talk of 'states of the brain' (or 'brain states') is just an inevitable consequence of lack of

---

[17] W. S. Robinson, 'States and Beliefs', *Mind*, 99 (1990), 33.

physiological knowledge—that it serves as a kind of dummy phrase, standing in for the particular stative expressions which we will eventually be able to supply. But what sorts of expressions will these be? It seems highly unlikely that anything simple based on a single derived or gerundive nominal is ever going to serve (e.g. 'excitation of cells $N_1 \ldots N_n$', 'o.1 per cent concentration of sodium ions being present in region R'); it strains credulity that the connections between the brain and mentality are going to turn out to be so simple. If we have ambitions to identify our psychological states with 'states of the brain', huge conjunctions of derived or gerundive nominals—or perhaps a mixture of the two—are presumably going to be required to describe the relevant condition of the brain in physiological language. But what do such conjunctions single out? Do they single out things which are even in the same ontological category as the 'mental states' with which they are alleged to be identical? If we call both 'states', of course, we may be deluded into thinking that there is an easier route to an affirmative answer to this question than is in fact the case. In Chapter 8, I shall present the case for a negative one.

Talking of states of belief, desire and so on, rather than simply of beliefs and desires, also helps to conceal a difficulty once regarded as the main obstacle to the identity theory; that we can ascribe properties to propositional attitudes and other so-called 'mental states' which might make one uneasy about the proposal to identify them with physically describable states. One might, for example, describe someone's belief that God exists as ungrounded or true or profound or dogmatic, and none of these properties, one might think, could possibly be possessed by any physical state. Early identity theorists and their opponents were much preoccupied with this problem.[18] Some tried to get around the difficulty by arguing that it was a serious methodological mistake to argue against an empirical theory like the token identity theory on the basis of what

---

[18] See e.g. J. Cornman, 'The Identity of Mind and Body', *Journal of Philosophy*, 59 (1962), 490: 'we can talk about intense, unbearable, nagging or throbbing pains. And yellow, dim, fading or circular after-images. And dogmatic, false, profound or unconscious beliefs. On the other hand, we can also discuss publicly observable, spatially located, swift, irreversible physical processes. Thus, if the identity theory is correct, it seems that we should sometimes be able to say truthfully that physical processes such as brain processes are dim or fading or nagging or false, and that mental phenomena such as after-images are publicly observable or physical or spatially located or swift.'

it does and does not currently make sense to say, since the sort of empirical results that would show mental and physical states and processes to be identical would also bring about changes in our ways of speaking.[19] Others, like Smart and Nagel, suggested that the use of gerundive nominals to formulate the relevant identity statements enables one to avoid the difficulty.[20] But the 'state of . . .' idiom also provides a way of escape. It would be unnatural to say of a *state* of belief (or a 'belief state') that it was, for example, true or false or profound or dogmatic. The problems associated with Leibniz's Law which arise so starkly for beliefs do not, therefore, make themselves felt so readily if one talks rather of identifying states of belief with states of the brain.

Another significant feature of the 'state of . . .' idiom is the fact that 'state' is a count-quantifiable noun. Count-quantifiability lends a certain feeling of ontological respectability to the nouns it characterizes. The widespread tendency amongst philosophers to introduce the 'state of . . .' locution may be partly due to the fact that it provides a way of transforming some of the odd noun phrases which result from the nominalization transcriptions of stative predications into more ordinary ones. To talk, not of 'my pen's being green', but rather of 'The state of being green which my pen "has" (or "is in")', for example, confers a suggestion of substantive backbone on a nominal expression which otherwise might not sound very much like a referring expression at all—substantive backbone which perhaps helps to prop up the continuing trade in relations such as identity and constitution, in the attempt to provide an account of the interconnections and dependencies between various states. As already noted, most stative nouns are only mass-quantifiable—so talk of 'states' in the plural ought really to be like

[19] Philosophers who have tried this tack include Jerome Shaffer, 'Could Mental States be Brain Processes?', *Journal of Philosophy*, 58 (1961), and Richard Rorty in 'Mind–Body Identity, Privacy and Categories', *Review of Metaphysics*, 19 (1965).

[20] See T. Nagel, 'Physicalism', *Philosophical Review*, 74 (1965), 343: 'nothing obliges us to identify a sensation or a pain or a thought with anything physical, and this disposes of numerous objections. For although I may have a visual sense impression whose attributes of form and color correspond closely to those which characterise the "Mona Lisa", my *having* the sense impression does not possess those attributes, and it is therefore no cause for worry that nothing in my brain looks like the "Mona Lisa".' J. J. C. Smart also suggests a similar tactic in 'Sensations and Brain Processes', *Philosophical Review*, 68 (1959); repr. with slight revisions in C. V. Borst (ed.), *The Mind–Brain Identity Theory* (London, 1970), 61.

talk of 'substances' in the plural—a form of expression which quantifies over things which are masses, not individuals. But the uses of the noun 'state' are too varied for this implication always to be clear—and it is very easy to be lulled into speaking and thinking of states as though they were particular entities.

It is likely to be objected at this point that states *can* sometimes be particular entities; that there is simply an ambiguity in the noun. The distinction between states in the mass sense and states in the individual sense, it might be said, has always been quite clear in the philosophical literature—it is the distinction between type states and token states. But I believe the concept of a token state is much less clear than it is normally taken to be. If it were not for the fact that the claim is open to misunderstanding, indeed, I think I should put my point by saying that there simply are no such things as token states. To explain why, though, I shall need to spend quite some time discussing the type–token distinction. I shall begin, therefore, in Section 4, by trying to explain what I take the type–token distinction proper to be, before going on to discuss in Section 5 some misuses of it which I believe to have had significant and unfortunate consequences for philosophy of mind.

4. THE TYPE–TOKEN DISTINCTION

The original explication of the type–token distinction—at any rate, the first that introduces the distinction under that name—occurs in the work of C. S. Peirce. Peirce's distinction is part of his theory of signs. Primarily, he uses the type–token distinction as a device for explaining two ways in which one might individuate meaningful entities, especially *words*; and it is probably still true that notwithstanding its widespread use in philosophy of mind, many people are still introduced to the distinction by way of the context in which Peirce originally developed it—as part of an introduction to the categorization of linguistic entities, such as words and sentences. The following, fairly extensive quote from Peirce's 'Apology for Pragmatism' will serve to summarize his account of the type–token distinction:

A common mode of estimating the amount of matter in an MS. or printed book is to count the number of words. There will ordinarily be about twenty *the's* on a page, and of course they count as twenty words. In another sense of the word 'word', however, there is but one word 'the' in the English language; and it is impossible that this word should lie visibly on a page or be heard in any voice, for the reason that it is not a Single thing or Single event. It does not exist; it only determines things that do exist. Such a definitely significant Form I propose to term a *Type*. A Single event which happens once and whose identity is limited to that one happening or a Single object or thing which is in some single place at any one instant of time, such event or thing being significant only as occurring just when and where it does, such as this or that word on a single line of a single page of a single copy of a book, I will venture to call a *Token*.[21]

Some of what Peirce says here about types and tokens seems specific to the semiotic context in which he develops the distinction—such as, for example, the claim that a type is a 'definitely significant Form' or that a token is 'significant only as occurring just when and where it does'. The talk of significance, at any rate, is easiest to make sense of where the types and tokens in question are entities of a sort which can possess meaning. But it is natural to think that the distinction need not be restricted in its application to semiology. Building by analogy on Peirce's example, one might suggest the following pairs of examples as further illustrations of the type–token distinction at work in contexts which have nothing particular to do with the theory of signs:

(1*a*) the Union Jack (considered as a general emblematic form),
(1*b*) particular Union Jacks made out of fabric, paper, etc. which instantiate this general emblematic form;

(2*a*) the waltz (considered as a dance form),
(2*b*) particular waltzes danced on particular occasions by individual people;

(3*a*) the whale (the species),
(3*b*) particular, individual whales which are members of the species;

(4*a*) *Wide Sargasso Sea* (the book written by Jean Rhys),
(4*b*) individual copies of *Wide Sargasso Sea*;

(5*a*) the hexagon (considered as an abstract mathematical shape),

---

[21] In his *Collected Papers*, iv: *The Simplest Mathematics*, ed. C. C. Hartshorne and P. Weiss (Cambridge, Mass., 1933), 423.

(5*b*) individual hexagons drawn on blackboards, on paper, carved out of wood, etc.

Though I am not here concerned primarily with the exegesis of Peirce, I am inclined to think that Peirce would have recognized all these as illustrations of his type–token distinction. In particular, all these examples can be associated in the same way as Peirce's own with two different ways in which one might set about performing a counting task. Imagine, for example, that I am asked to count the number of flags on a page of a picture-book on which are drawn two Union Jacks, one Stars and Stripes, and three Hammer and Sickles. If I am counting types of flag, then I shall say that there are three flags on the page; if I am counting tokens, then I shall give the answer six. Similarly, if I am asked to count the number of dances that are going on in a room where one couple is waltzing, while ten are doing the tango, I may answer either two or eleven, depending on whether I am counting type or token dances. All the other cases can be associated in an exactly analogous way with two different ways of executing a counting task.

The type–token distinction which is exemplified by these cases is obviously associated with an ambiguity that exists in a whole host of count nouns—'word', 'flag', 'dance', 'animal', 'book', 'shape', etc.—nouns which are used as parts of expressions which can refer to or quantify over either types or tokens. The expression 'this animal', for example, is type–token ambiguous—if I say, 'This animal will be extinct in five years', I am clearly referring to the type, the Giant Panda, perhaps; whereas if I say 'Get this animal out of my house', I am—probably, anyway—referring to some token creature. Likewise, the quantificational expression 'How many animals . . .?' is type–token ambiguous, so that, for example, the question 'How many animals are in this forest?' admits of more than one correct answer, depending on whether it is the species or the individual creatures which are to be counted.

Type–token ambiguity of this sort is extremely common; indeed, I have been unable to think of a count noun that never allows for it under any circumstances. It is true that some count nouns are not naturally ambiguous when preceded by the question 'How many . . . ?'—consider 'person', 'stream', 'mountain'—but these nouns reveal an ambiguity in certain other contexts. What appears to be lacking in these cases is any obvious classificatory scheme in terms of which to render the request for a count of types comprehensible.[22] Because we do not make everyday use of any particular scheme for typing mountains, for example, it is hard to make sense of the question 'How many mountains . . . ?', except as a request for a token count. But other contexts seem to allow for a type reading of a kind: consider the question 'Which mountains do you like?' Here, I might reasonably reply, 'Oh, rugged, glaciated ones, mostly', rather than giving a list of individual mountains—thus indicating that I have understood the question to be asking about mountain types, not tokens. Or one might speak of 'the mountain', meaning to refer not to any individual peak, but rather to a type of geographical landform. This latter construction, indeed—the combination of definite article and count noun—seems to provide a foolproof way of giving any count noun a type reading. 'The mountain', 'the valley', 'the flag', 'the motel', 'the bird', etc. are all phrases which permit—and in certain contexts demand—interpretation as type designators—as, for example, one might say that the motel is a firmly entrenched feature of American life or that the bird is an evolutionary triumph.

It is reasonably clear, I think, that the type–token distinction which emerges from this consideration of the ambiguities of count nouns should be regarded as a relative, logical, not an absolute, metaphysical, distinction. That something counts as a type relative to some range of tokens ought not, on this understanding, to rule out its categorization as a token relative to further more general types; and neither should the classification of something as a token of some type or other mean that it cannot count as a type relative to further tokens. Tokens, therefore, need not always be individuals of a spatiotemporal or any other variety. To see how this can happen, consider the count noun 'oxide'. 'Oxide' is a perfectly good count noun—there are many oxides and 'the oxide' would seem to be a perfectly good name for a type of chemical compound. One might say, for example, though I have no idea whether it is true,

---

[22] Of course, even those nouns which do yield two natural readings of a 'How many . . . ?' question may not be associated with an utterly unequivocal means of performing the count of types; thus, for example, though we know of an easily operable and reasonably clear system for typing words, we might have to request some elucidation—is the word 'pen' to count twice, for instance, when it refers to a writing implement and when it refers to a pound for containing animals? This reveals a further ambiguity within the count noun, which can be used to quantify over type words considered either as lexical or as semantic types.

that the oxide is a particularly stable type of compound. But in so far as tokens of this type exist, they are not spatiotemporal particulars. For it is important to realize that on the understanding of the type–token distinction which I have been developing, little piles or masses of various oxides do not count as tokens of the type 'oxide'. One would not, merely by knowing what an oxide was, have a grasp of any rules for individuating such piles or masses. What one would have to know is rather that copper oxide, for example, counts as one oxide and magnesium oxide as another. These are the things which fall under the count noun 'oxide' and which are severally quantified over by the plural form 'oxides'—and which, as it were, are counted by the count noun. If one had three oxides on the work-bench in front of one, one would not, or at least would not necessarily, have three separate piles—one would have three different chemical compounds. But copper oxide is not an individual in any ordinary sense—and indeed is itself a type relative to the compounds Cu_2O and CuO. It is a token *and* a type, a dual classification which is made perfectly comprehensible by the recognition that the type–token distinction is a relative and not an absolute distinction.

It may already be obvious that my characterization of the type–token distinction does not square well with the suggestion that the distinction can be used to differentiate between any general property or condition, e.g. solidity, anger, or believing that p, and those entities philosophers sometimes call their 'cases' or 'instances' or 'exemplifications', those things which are referred to by genitive expressions associating the property in question with something particular which has the property, e.g. 'the solidity of that brick', 'Jones's anger', 'Smith's believing that p'. To begin with, we can note that though the types named in $(1a)$–$(5a)$ are associated closely with properties, they are not themselves properties. For example, the whale is not a property, although it is closely associated with the property of being a whale. The influence of nominalism may, I think, have made philosophers shy of recognizing the category of types as such—to admit such entities as the whale and the hexagon to our ontology might seem extravagantly Platonic—but one need incur no commitment to the ultimate irreducibility of talk of types by conceding that apparent reference to them has a place in our language which is somewhat different from the place occupied by property terms. After all, the type–token distinction, as characterized by Peirce, is a distinction the need for which arises out of *ambiguity*—out of the fact that a linguistic expression such as 'the world "the"' can function in two different ways to refer to two quite different kinds of entity; and the association of the type–token distinction with ambiguity is lost if we are prepared to treat properties—the terms for which are not similarly ambiguous—as types. If we extend usage in this way, we may easily lose sight of the fact that the type–token distinction proper is primarily a logical, and only secondarily an ontological, distinction—it clearly has some important connections with the universal–particular distinction, but it is not identical with it.

One might wonder, though, whether there is anything much to be gained, apart perhaps from clarity, by insisting on the restriction of the term 'type' to the narrow limits which are set by its connection with the ambiguity of certain count nouns. Each type proper, after all, is uniquely associated with a particular property—the whale with the property of being a whale, the Union Jack with the property of being a Union Jack, and so on—and so one might think that only a certain carping exactitude could motivate a refusal to extend the type–token terminology to the relation between these properties and the individuals which have them. We could, for example, surely allow ourselves enough licence to say that 'being a whale' was a type of which individual whales were the tokens, if it were useful to do so; it is hard to see what harm could come of it. But even if we were to sanction the severance of the tight connection with count noun ambiguity that this extension of usage would involve, we have certainly not yet sanctioned the inclusion of properties and their instances in the class of type–token pairs. For a start, we might decide that the distinction between properties whose specification involves the use of a count noun and those which do not is important. If we understand what being a whale involves, for example—what it is to be a whale—then we understand where one whale ends and the next begins; we understand a property which is connected with the individuation of the tokens that fall under it.[23] But solidity, anger, and believing that *p* are

[23] One could, I suppose, refer artificially to the property of being a whale by speaking of 'whalehood', or some such thing—so perhaps the *explicit* use of a count noun is not needed. But it remains true that 'whalehood' is a property which is connected with individuation—one could not understand what whalehood involved, it seems to me, without knowing how whales were to be individuated. 'Hood' seems, in general, to be a suffix which sits comfortably only with count nouns.

different. While solid things could be said, in a loose sense, to be of the type 'solid', for example, we are not given, by an understanding of the predicate '. . . is solid' alone, any means of going about a count of solid things. And what is more, it is not, in any case, solid things—bricks, blocks of ice, lumps of metal—that are being alleged to stand in the token to type relation to the property of solidity, but something else entirely—cases or instances of the property of solidity. The tokens described by (1*b*)–(5*b*) above all fall under everyday count nouns like 'waltz' or 'book', but those we are considering have to be referred to by means of genitive nominals or by artificial expressions containing the rather general and abstract philosophers' count nouns 'instance', 'exemplification', and 'case'. The relationship between properties and their instances, then, seems not to be of the type–token variety.

Of course, we could call the distinction between properties and their instances a type–token distinction if we liked. But if we were to do so, we would need to cease to apply that terminology to other relationships—those exemplified by 1–5 above, for instance. To continue to apply type–token terminology in both sorts of case is likely to suggest that the relation between a property or state type and what are called its 'instances' or 'exemplifications' is not significantly different from that between a type proper (like 'whale') and the things that fall under that type (individual whales). But clearly, there is all the difference in the world between these two relations. Tokens in the sense which I prefer have certain properties (e.g. 'being a whale') which are the basis for their classification into types. But instances or exemplifications of properties, as usually understood, do not *have* the properties of which they are the instances. Being an instance of a property and having that property are utterly different. And there are other dangers in this usage, too. We tend to think of tokens as individuals—the very word is soaked with connotations of particularity and concreteness—and so the supposition that property instances are related to properties as tokens to types makes compelling certain models and pictures of their ontological status, their role in causality, and their relationships to one another. But it may be that the entities to which we refer by means of the complex genitive constructions which philosophers have associated with property instances are not particular or concrete, at least, not on an understanding of these terms which can make sense of the associated models and pictures. I shall say more about this in Chapter 7.

It is in philosophy of mind, of course, that the type–token distinction really earns its keep. In the final section of this chapter, I want to cast some doubt on the propriety of some usages which have become common there, and to provide some justification for my claim that my complaints about the misuse of the type–token distinction are not mere technical quibbles. For the purposes of the arguments to come, it will be useful to have a name for the combination of an expression for a type together with an indication of the set of tokens which falls under it, such as are found in examples 1–5 above. I shall call such a combination a *type–token pair*. I want to look at two putative type-token pairs which have been important in philosophy of mind. The first, I shall argue, is simply misclassified as a case of the type–token distinction. A better case can be made for the second, but some significant qualifications need to be made, qualifications which will be of some importance in the arguments of later chapters.

5. TOKEN STATES IN PHILOSOPHY OF MIND

The two putative type–token pairs I want to consider are these:

(6a) pain in general,
(6b) individual pains had by individual persons—e.g. individual headaches, toothaches, twinges, cramps, etc.

(7a) the belief that *p*,
(7b) individual cases or instances of the belief that *p*—e.g. my belief that *p*, John's belief that *p*.

It would not, I think, be difficult to obtain the agreement of quite a large number of philosophers that these pairs exemplify the type–token distinction. I begin with the first.

My complaint about (6) is very simple. It is clear that in so far as individual headaches, and so on, are pains, they are, in one sense, tokens relative to the type 'pain' or 'being a pain'—just as whales are tokens of the type 'whale' or flags tokens of the type 'flag'. But they are not tokens relative to pain in general. As it occurs in the phrase 'pain in general', 'pain' is a mass noun, not a count noun—

and individual pains are no more the tokens of pain in this sense than individual lambs are tokens of the meat which is referred to by the noun 'lamb'. Lamb in this latter sense does not have tokens, for there is no relevant plural—and neither does pain.

The need to distinguish between pain in general and individual pains is, of course, not in question. Originally, the necessity for such a distinction arose out of the perception that the kinds of identity statement which physicalistic philosophers were offering as examples of the sorts of claims to which they wished to commit themselves were too strong—that they seemed unlikely to square with the neurophysiological facts, given such phenomena as variable realization and plasticity. Instead, therefore, it was suggested, physicalists should restrict themselves to making claims only about the physical status of psychological particulars—about the identity of each individual pain, or perhaps each individual occurrence of a feeling of pain, with a physical event, for example, rather than about the identity of pain in general with any physical phenomenon. I am not denying that this distinction is important and needs to be made—but it is mass–count, not type–token, ambiguity that needs to be invoked in order to make it. Using the type–token distinction to do the job instead, in my view, has been a remarkably damaging mistake.

The assertion that something or other is a type invites completion. 'Type of what?' is a tempting question—and when it is alleged that pain is a type, the reply 'type of state' comes all too naturally. Of course, there is a quite innocuous sense in which pain *is* a type of state—it is a condition that a human being or other animal can be in. But here 'type' just means 'sort' or 'kind'—and its use does not imply the existence of any set of particular token pain states falling under the type. All it implies is the existence of a range of such conditions—anger, misery, depression, happiness, etc.—of which it is one. These might, indeed, be called token states in a sense, for the count noun 'state' is a noun under which such conditions as these can be brought—but these are not the sorts of things that philosophers usually have in mind when they speak of token states. It is usually supposed that token states are individual entities, not general conditions like anger that anyone can have or 'be in'. But the claim that pain is a type of state involves no commitment whatever to the existence of any such individual entities.

To see this, compare the claim that pain is a type of state with the grammatically similar claim that water is a type of substance.[24] Now it is evident that the claim that water is a type of substance does not commit us to the existence of a set of token substances, where these are conceived of as particulars distinct from the substances—water, oil, copper sulphate, etc.—themselves. In the case of the noun 'substance', indeed, we are not even tempted by the idea that there are token substances, in this sense. Though 'substance' is a count noun, we readily recognize that the plural form, 'substances', quantifies not over individuals but over things which are referred to by mass nouns—water, copper oxide, and so on. These are the things to which the claim that water is a type of substance commits us—a range of substance types, not a set of spatiotemporal particulars. And similarly, the innocuous claim that pain is a type of state does not commit us to the existence of any set of individual token states—only to the existence of a range of state types. But once we are in the business of using the type–token distinction to differentiate between pain in general and particular pains, it is easy to be misled into replacing the innocent reading of the term 'type' which occurs in the claim that pain is a type of state with a philosophically charged reading according to which the existence of types implies the existence of tokens. And all of a sudden, we find ourselves committed to a new set of entities—token states of pain. But why should we believe that there are any such things as these? Let us not multiply entities beyond necessity. There are certainly facts about pain which relate to particular people and which we could refer to by means of gerundive nominals—e.g. my being in pain—and there are individual pains, like headaches and toothaches, and there is the phenomenon of pain in general. But why should we add to all these a further mysterious class of entities: token pain states? No natural-language category refers to them, no philosophical purpose is served by introducing them. My claim is that, in view of these facts, we should say that there simply are no such things.

In making this claim, I need to avert a misunderstanding that might arise in the rather special case of pain. 'Pain' is rare among our terms for varieties of state because, unlike, for instance, anger,

---

[24] I intend the term 'substance' here to be read in the everyday sense in which milk, oil, blood, etc. are substances—not the philosophical sense which ranges over, for example, human beings, animals, and plants.

depression, misery, and happiness, it can be a count as well as a mass noun. I do not want to deny the significance of the count noun sense of this word—and in this sense, I am not averse to saying that there are token pains. What I wish to deny is that we should reframe the sorts of things we say about these entities using a relatively well-understood, everyday count noun in the obscure, and in my view illegitimate, language of token states. One motivation for this reframing is presumably generalization—we cannot speak naturally of angers or happinesses—whereas there is nothing grammatically uncomfortable about token states of anger or happiness. But grammatical acceptability conceals philosophical unacceptability, if the account of the type–token distinction which I have offered above is along the right sort of lines. For we need to ask: what are the types of which these 'token' states are the tokens? 'Anger' cannot be the type of which token states of anger are the tokens, for 'anger' is not a count noun, but a mass noun. Unlike 'whale', 'flag', 'dance', and so on, it is not ambiguous in the slightest. So the type–token distinction that I have characterized above cannot be used here. Of course, as I mentioned above, it would be possible to insist on an alternative understanding of the type–token distinction which admitted these examples. But I have already briefly indicated the dangers of this approach—and will discuss them further in the chapters to come.

I shall turn now to the second of the putative type–token pairs I want to consider in this section, namely:

(7a) the belief that *p*,
(7b) individual cases or instances of the belief that *p*—e.g. my belief that *p*.

Is (7) a genuine type–token pair? Certainly it has features which make it comparable to examples 1–5 above. 'Belief', for example, is a count noun, just like 'flag' or 'book', and it seems possible to regard my belief that *p* as simply one among many other beliefs that *p*—each person that believes that *p* generating one token belief—just as each individual flag is one of many flags. But there are differences as well as similarities. In particular, one important feature of the propositional attitude nouns 'belief', 'desire', and so on is that their overwhelmingly most usual employment is as part of expressions which refer to or quantify over the entities that philosophers have thought of as belief (and other propositional attitude) *types*—that is to say, over beliefs, desires, etc., which are abstract things, differing from one another only in their content. Thus, for example, the belief that p is one belief; the belief that q is another. We do not always need to suppose, in order to use this count noun, in order to speak intelligibly of beliefs in the plural, that anyone possesses the beliefs in question. We can talk about beliefs in the abstract, as things individuated by their contents, examine sets of beliefs for consistency, decide whether or not they are true, etc. It is not normal—though it is possible—to use the count noun 'belief' in such a way that it ranges over what are called 'token' beliefs—my belief that p, for instance, as opposed to yours. I might say, for example, that my belief that God exists is firmer than yours—but such examples are comparatively rare. The apparatus of pluralization, quantification, demonstration, and identification which is normally associated with the need to talk about the collection of tokens which falls under any given count noun and to distinguish between them, identify them one with another, count them, point them out, etc., when used in association with the propositional attitude count nouns 'belief', 'desire', and so on, is nearly always put to work in connection not with the so-called 'tokens', but rather with a class of entities which deserve the designation 'abstract', if anything does, which are distinguished from one another only by differences in their content. It is here that our need for these distinctions is greatest, for it is primarily the differences between propositional attitudes which are indicated by their different contents that are of most interest to us—not the differences between attitudes in the same mode and with the same content but which belong to different subjects. Hence, phrases such as 'the beliefs that p' sound exceptionally odd—we do not usually have any occasion to quantify in this way over distinct propositional attitudes with the same content.

It is also notable that even when the possessive constructions which are supposed by many philosophers to indicate reference to token propositional attitude states are present, often sense can only be made of what is said by interpreting these phrases as referring rather to so-called type beliefs—as, for example, if I were to say that I was pleased that you shared my belief. And there are other cases where it is at the very least not obvious that it is 'tokens' rather than types that are in question—as, for example, if I were to allege that your belief that p was not true. The only cases where use

of this possessive construction really does seem unequivocally intended to single out entities which are clearly distinct from any type
concern the attribution of properties which relate to subject-relative
matters—how firmly a particular belief is held, for example, or how
good a particular subject's reasons for believing something are—as,
for example, if I were to say that your belief that p was well thought
out, though mine was not. Only in this rather limited range of cases
do we seem to have a use for distinguishing beliefs held by one
person from beliefs held by another, as opposed to beliefs with one
content from beliefs with another. Not every occurrence of locu-
tions such as 'my belief that p', 'John's belief that p', etc., then, can
be interpreted as implying reference to anything distinct from what
is referred to by the locution 'the belief that p'.

   Still, it might be said, once the concession has been made that it
is at least sometimes possible to use a noun like 'belief' so as to
range over entities of which, for instance, my belief that p and your
belief that p can be two distinct examples, a commitment to token
beliefs is with us. In a sense, this is true; it needs to be conceded that
the count noun 'belief' can indeed be used in these two different
ways—to refer to and quantify over distinct abstractly
characterizable beliefs with different contents, and to refer to and
quantify over distinct subject-relative beliefs with different subject-
relative properties. And it seems to me that this really is a genuine
type–token distinction. Subject-relative beliefs can be ranged into
types according to their contents—and 'the belief that . . .' seems to
be the most natural way we have of referring to the types under
which they are thereby brought. But it should be recalled, at this
point, I think, that the type–token distinction thus exemplified is a
relative, and not an absolute distinction. Nothing is implied about
the metaphysical nature of token beliefs by the admission that they
are tokens. And this is a significant reminder, because the talk of
token propositional attitude states which abounds in the philosophical literature often carries implications which go beyond
anything that would be sanctioned by this merely relative
understanding of the term 'token'. Token propositional attitude
states, for example, are regularly ranked alongside mental events
and processes as particulars of which philosophy in general, and
philosophy of mind specifically, are obliged to give an account.
But this view of token propositional attitude states is a metaphysical view which needs to be argued for; it is not established merely

by the fact that we can give a sense to the idea that some expressions involving the nouns 'belief', 'desire', etc. can be regarded as making reference to entities that are tokens relative to others—any more than the fact that there are token substances, in this relative sense, implies that copper oxide and magnesium oxide are individuals.

The reason why these points about the type–token distinction seem to me to be so significant is that they raise important questions about the shape of many of the theories and debates current in philosophy of mind. Questions about the relation of mentality to the physical world are still often treated as though they were primarily questions about the status of *entities*—a treatment which has been largely made possible by the thought that the category of token state is available to capture the huge tracts of psychological life which are non-occurrent, whose particularity is not phenomenologically guaranteed. But with the type–token distinction properly elucidated, it becomes clear that not all those entities which stand to certain others in the purely logical relation of token to type need possess the metaphysical characteristics which would make them suitable for capture in this sort of particularist model of the mind. I have not yet shown, of course, that they do not possess the requisite metaphysical characteristics; all I am claiming is that the question needs to be asked.

And there is a point to be made, too, about physicalism. The type–token distinction has come to figure large, not just in the formulation of detailed arguments in the philosophy of mind but also in the official histories which are told of developments in the subject over the last forty years or so. Type physicalism, we are often told—the kind of physicalism which insists on the existence of identities between mental and physical properties—is widely (though not universally) regarded these days as a theory which makes claims that are too strong to be plausible. Today, perfectly respectable physicalists can allow that there is no realistic prospect of mapping the predicates peculiar to so-called folk psychology onto physical ones. The thought has become commonplace that as long as all the 'tokens'—all the particular entities we need to countenance—are physical, we can help ourselves to as many non-physical concepts, categories, properties, and so on as we like. Commitment to token identity or constitution claims has thus come to be seen by many as a sufficient condition for the only sort of physicalism that has any chance of being true. But it is also—because it is thought to be a very moderate version of the view—often supposed to be a necessary condition, too. That all tokens should be physical has come to be regarded as the touchstone of minimal physicalist commitment.[25]

But in this context, the designation of something as a token becomes a matter of great moment. That something is a token now implies that it is an individual of a sort that needs neat incorporation, by means of an identity or perhaps a constitution claim, into the physicalist world-picture. And so once we have invented for ourselves the category of token state, token physicalism becomes a doctrine with considerable consequences. It turns out that in order to be physicalists, we have to be committed to the existence of identity or constitution relations between such things as token states of belief and desire, and perhaps also of other sorts of token state—anger, misery, etc.—and 'token states of the brain'. But then, as many philosophers have realized, we have to be committed a priori to the view that folk psychology will be, as it were, borne out by neurophysiology—that things will turn out, neurophysiologically speaking, in such a way as to permit the necessary one–one mappings. Many of those who think that such general a priori commitments are absurd have embraced eliminative materialism. But might not dispensing altogether with the category of token state be a conservative and wholly reasonable alternative to the eliminativist's radical denial of mentality?

I shall return to these themes in Chapters 8 and 9. In the next chapter, I want to examine the way in which the concept of a state connects with out thinking about causality and causal explanation. For the role played by reference, or what is often construed as reference to states in causal explanation, is one of the main reasons why philosophers have felt the need to invoke 'token' states. Not seeing how anything universal, like a state type or a property, could be involved in local, causal interactions, philosophers have turned to token states instead. But I shall be trying to argue that they are not needed; and more than that, that their introduction obscures, rather than clarifies, the workings of the causal explanations whose underpinnings they are supposed to illuminate.

---

[25] See e.g. D. Papineau, *Philosophical Naturalism* (Oxford: Blackwell, 1993) for a view of this sort.

5

Particulars, Facts, and Causal Explanations

EVENTS, processes, and token states owe a great deal of the prominence they have attained in contemporary philosophy to the fact that they appear to be essential to the ontology of causation. They are not, of course, the only categories of entity which are found associated in ordinary language with the relations of causation and causal explanation. First, a number of different sorts of non-particular entity, including facts, properties, and the entities I have been calling 'conditions', are often spoken of as though they were causes and effects (e.g. 'The fact that the lorry was so heavy caused the bridge to give way', 'Acidity caused the litmus to turn red', 'Your headaches are due to tension'). Second, entities in the category of substance, or thing,[1] are frequently attributed causal efficacy by means of a variety of idioms (e.g. 'The elephant caused the damage', 'You made me jump', 'The stone broke the window'). But philosophers often appear to find irresistible the conviction that entities in these two broad classes cannot literally be regarded as relata of the causal relation. Entities in the first class are often deemed unsuitable to count as genuine causal relata by virtue of their non-particularity, it being thought metaphysically impossible that anything abstract or universal should have real causal influence of any kind.[2] Here, for example, is Keith Campbell, voicing a widely held view: 'If you are burned by a hot wire it is, after all, not heat in general, or wires in general, or the other characteristics of

---

[1] D. H. Mellor (*The Facts of Causation* (London, 1995), 119–20), uses the term 'thing' to cover the sorts of particular entity I have in mind—and in some ways it is better than the term 'substance', for it is more inclusive. It is important, for instance, that entities like rainbows, holes, subatomic particles, and galaxies, none of which seems well described as a substance, can figure as the causes cited by singular causal claims. I shall therefore follow Mellor in this usage.

[2] Though of course the characterization of facts as 'abstract' is controversial. The abstract–concrete distinction is unclear, no doubt, but some views of facts would be in obvious conflict with the spirit of the suggestion that facts are abstract entities.

this wire, but *the heat of this wire* which does the burning.'[3] On the other hand, entities in the second class are thought to be, in a sense, *too* particular[4] to stand in straightforward causal relations, one to another. Once again, Keith Campbell makes the point explicit: 'It is the heat of this stove, here and now, that burns you, on the finger, here and now. The causal agent is a state, or event, or process, always particular and always qualitative. It is not the stove, the whole stove, that burns you; not even the whole stove here now. For its solidity, iron structure, enamel surface and smoothness have nothing to do with it. It is the *temperature* that does the damage.'[5] Evan Fales makes the same sort of claim, though for somewhat different reasons, in his book *Causation and Universals*.[6] Fales claims that there are both 'phenomenological' and 'systematic' grounds for taking events, rather than things (which he calls 'particulars'), to be the relata of the causal relation. The phenomenological grounds are said to be 'straightforward': 'When an object affects one in some way—say by striking one—it is never merely the object as such which one perceives as producing the effect. What is perceived is that certain of the object's qualities, and not others, are involved.'[7] And of the 'systematic' grounds for taking events to be the relata of the causal relation, Fales writes:

> If those relata were particulars, it would not be possible to formulate causal laws, for the universality of laws is achieved by specifying, not a list of particulars, but the properties they must satisfy, the kinds of things they are. And if we say that the particular must be of a certain kind, the claim that causes or effects are particulars becomes indistinguishable from the one which takes causal relations to relate individuals 'in virtue of' certain of their properties. But the latter phrase can reasonably be understood as expressing what are events or states of affairs.[8]

[3] K. Campbell, *Abstract Particulars* (Oxford, 1990), 4. See also T. Honderich in 'Causes and *If p, even if x, still q*', *Philosophy*, 57 (1982), 292: 'It is not the general property of weighing a pound, which is other or more than this teapot weighing a pound, that is flattening the napkin . . . what is flattening the napkin is *this teapot's weight*, an individual property of this teapot . . .'.

[4] Here I draw on the concept of particularity outlined in Ch. 1, according to which it is the mark of a genuine particular that it is the bearer of numerous different properties and is not itself to be identified with an exemplification or instantiation of any of those properties.

[5] Campbell, *Abstract Particulars*, 22–3.

[6] E. H. Fales, *Causation and Universals* (London, 1990), 53–5.

[7] Ibid. 54.

[8] Ibid. 54–5.

And Fales also notes a temporal reason for denying to things the status of cause:

> If, as we typically believe, physical individuals persist through time and through change, then it is senseless to speak of a particular *simpliciter* as a cause; for it is at one time involved in a causal interaction and at another time not involved in it. There would be no way to explain this fact if we could not refer to the differing properties had by that individual at various times during its existence. Nor could we explain why certain particulars enter into causal relations and not others.[9]

In the light of such reasoning, philosophers have turned to events, states, and processes in the hope of finding in these categories the resources for an accurate and metaphysically respectable ontology of causation. There has, of course, been disagreement about whether entities in all three categories answer to the purpose equally well and about what characterization they must be given if they are to do the job required.[10] But many philosophers have found, in one or more of these categories, suitably defined, a combination of particularity, qualitative specificity, and temporal impermanence that looks exceedingly promising as a profile for the ontological basis of a unified and systematic account of causation.[11] In this chapter, I want to begin to explore the question whether any

---

[9] Ibid. 54.

[10] Particular events of a non-tropic variety, for example, have been deemed unfit to serve as causal relata by some philosophers for much the same reason that Campbell gives for thinking that things cannot really be causes—namely that it is always in virtue only of a subset of their many properties that they can be said to cause anything, and so that we should, strictly speaking, regard the instantiations of just these causally relevant properties, rather than a whole individual event, as the cause of any given effect. Indeed, the recent controversy over whether or not Davidson's anomalous monism should be regarded as a version of epiphenomenalism is largely traceable to the conviction, on the part of many of Davidson's critics, that Davidsonian events, like substances, are *too* particular to be accounted causes—that particular events are always causes 'in virtue of' certain of their properties and not others. Just as the solidity of the stove has nothing to do with the stove's burning you, so the mental properties of mental events, on Davidson's view, it is alleged, have nothing to do with the bringing about of the actions which are caused by these events. I shall consider this line of thought in Ch. 9.

[11] Some of these desiderata are noted by Campbell, who goes on to argue that only abstract particulars, or tropes, have the requisite characteristics: 'what is required is an element that combines particularity with a very restricted qualitative character, since causes are always features (almost always a small selection from the host of features present) and every particular cause is a particular feature or constellation of features' (*Abstract Particulars*, 23).

of these categories can really fulfil this promise. It will be my eventual conclusion that there is no hope whatever of ridding ourselves of commitments to causal relationships in which one or more of the relata is a fact; and that none of the arguments proffered by Campbell, Fales, and others show, either, that continuant things cannot be causes. In short, I shall be trying to argue against the common suggestion that we ought to try to reduce the rich and varied assortment of causal idioms found in ordinary causal explanations to a single paradigmatic form, and correspondingly, to suggest that there is not really any sensible question of the form 'What are the "true" or "real" relata of the causal relation?' But first, the views of those who believe that individual events, or token states, or some unified category of entity which includes both of these and perhaps processes too, can be pressed into service to illuminate the structure of causal reality deserve closer examination. I shall begin this chapter, therefore, by looking at some different forms of causal explanation, with a view to exploring the connections and relationships between them and assessing the prospects for a simplification of the rich diversity of constructions which constitute the data of our ordinary causal-explanatory practice.

Before beginning, I want to enter one caution and one restriction. The caution concerns my use of the term 'causal explanation'. I shall be assuming that any statement (or indeed collection of statements) which might conceivably be given as a reasonable response to a question which asks for illumination of a causal sort can count as a causal explanation. Questions which ask for illumination of a causal sort are often 'why' questions, but it does not seem to me that they have to be; one can also ask, for example, *what* caused something, or *how* something came about, and the answers to such questions, on my usage, could count as causal explanations. This has the consequence that certain sorts of statement which are not accounted causal explanations by some philosophers do (or at least could, given the right context) count as such, given my terminology. In particular, singular causal claims, such as 'The flood caused the famine', can count as causal explanations, using the terminology in the way that I prefer, since it seems to me that, for example, 'What caused the famine?' is a request for enlightenment on a causal matter, to which 'The flood caused the famine' might be a perfectly adequate, explanatory response. In his paper 'Causal Relations', Davidson appears to make a distinction between singular causal claims, on the one hand, and causal explanations, on the other; those statements which he accounts causal explanations have a logical form which requires the invocation of non-truth-functional connectives, and thus stand in stark contrast to singular causal claims.[12] But I shall treat singular causal claims simply as one interesting subclass of causal explanations. I do not think anything significant turns on this difference in terminology, but to avoid confusion, it is important to be clear about it.

The restriction is one which I need to introduce for simplicity's sake. I shall, for the moment, be considering only causal explanations which can be construed as answers either to the question why something happened (e.g. 'Why did the cars collide?') or to the question why some particular event occurred (e.g. 'Why did that collision occur?') or to the question what caused some particular event (e.g. 'What caused that collision?').[13] It is not true, of course, that all causal explanations are concerned, in one or other of these ways, with the occurrence of events. One can explain causally why something is or was so, as well as why something happened or why some particular event occurred. But, for simplicity's sake, I restrict myself for now to consideration only of explanations of these kinds—for my eventual aim is to say something about those explanations which are commonly termed 'action explanations'—and I take it that these all fall squarely within one or other of the above categories.

1. FORMS OF CAUSAL EXPLANATION

Anyone attempting to draw up a neat typology of the forms of causal explanation found in the English language confronts a huge array of confusing data. The verb 'cause' can stand between

[12] D. Davidson, 'Causal Relations', *Journal of Philosophy*, 64 (1967); repr. in his *Essays on Actions and Events*.

[13] It perhaps needs to be noted here, partly because I shall concentrate in what follows on discussion of the *explanantes* of causal explanations and say rather little about the *explananda*, that the first sort of explanation seems to me vastly more common than the second, i.e. that it is rare that we take ourselves to be explaining the occurrence of *particular* events. Indeed, even when the grammatical form of a question might suggest that what is wanted is an explanation of the occurrence of a particular event (as in 'Why did that collision occur?') it seems to me that often we do not really mean our question to be distinct from the question why an event of that sort occurred (e.g. 'Why did a collision occur?'). Nevertheless, it seems *possible* to take oneself to be explaining the occurrence of some particular event—and I shall try to speak in ways which do not preclude this possibility.

singular terms for events ('The flood caused the famine'); between
singular terms for things and ones for events ('The dictator caused
the famine'); between terms for either things or events and complex
infinitive constructions ('The flood caused the land to become fertile again', 'The dictator caused me to become angry'); between
complex nominals and either singular terms or infinitive constructions ('The flood's being so sudden caused the famine', 'My being
late caused me to miss the train'); and there are numerous other
sorts of combination too. Then there is the sentence functor 'because', and the extremely common and much neglected expression
'because of', which typically stands between a whole sentence and
a singular term ('I missed the train because of you'). And as well as
these there is a huge array of specific verbs which can function in
the provision of causal explanations of different sorts ('The avalanche crushed the village', 'The stone broke the window', 'The boy
melted the chocolate'[14]) and a similarly large pool of very general
causal verbs and phrases ('make a difference', 'affect', 'matter',
'produce', 'prevent', 'bring about', 'interfere with') which can
figure in the provision of causal explanations ('What makes the
difference is the presence of a catalyst'; 'The temperature interfered
with the result'). Is there any hope of finding order amongst all this
complexity?

I shall not here attempt to investigate the so-called causal verbs
or the many varieties of phrase which can replace or provide
variations on 'caused' or 'because'. It is quite plausible that analyses
of at least some of these causal verbs and general variants in terms
of the plainer 'caused' and 'because' are available—but if any are
not reducible to these forms, it will not affect any of the arguments
to follow; it will merely mean that more work needs to be done in
order to supply a fully satisfying account of the different forms of
causal explanation. I shall focus on causal explanations which are
framed explicitly in terms either of the verb 'cause', the sentence
functor 'because', or the expression 'because of'; as we shall see,
these will provide us with complexities enough.

It is probably not a vast over-simplification to say that most

---

[14] Several philosophers have rightly stressed the centrality of these sorts of actions
and transactions in our understanding of causality: see e.g. G. E. M. Anscombe,
'Causality and Determination', in her *Collected Philosophical Papers*, ii (Oxford,
1981); P. F. Strawson, 'Causation and Explanation', in B. Vermazen and M. B.
Hintikka (eds.), *Essays on Davidson: Actions and Events* (Oxford, 1985); W. Child,
Causality, Interpretation and the Mind (Oxford, 1994), 192–204.

philosophical accounts of the semantics of causal explanations can be seen as committed to one or other of two views about the way in which such explanations should be represented. On the one hand, there are those who regard 'cause' basically as a 'more or less concealed sentential connective',[15] regarding its apparent occurrence, on occasion, as a straightforward relational predicate as a kind of encryption of the real logical form of the explanation and/or a misleading representation of the structure of causal reality (depending, I suppose, on the philosopher's view about the connections between semantics and metaphysics). A prominent recent exponent of a view of this sort is D. H. Mellor.[16] On the other hand, there are those such as Davidson who think that 'cause' *is* usually a straightforward two-place predicate whenever it appears to be one, and that it is rather the apparently sentential constructions that require special accounting for. I shall consider whether either of these two competing views can give a complete account of the logic of causal claims later in the chapter. But for now, I am simply seeking a typology of causal explanation, and the reason I want to focus on the two views is that the distinction between them suggests one. I shall distinguish, to begin with, between *singular causal claims*, where 'cause' features apparently as a relational predicate flanked by singular terms; and *sentential causal claims*, where there is either an explicit use of the sentential connective 'because' or a use of the verb 'cause' which suggests that the underlying structure of the explanation is better represented by means of a sentence functor than by a two-place predicate. I do not mean to suggest that it is always easy to decide which of these forms best represents the logical form of a particular explanation, nor, at this early stage, that neither of the two kinds of claim is reducible to the other. The distinction is merely a starting-point.

2. SINGULAR CAUSAL CLAIMS

In recent years, a good deal of attention has been directed towards the singular causal claim—a kind of explanation in which two singular terms appear to be linked by the relational predicate 'cause'. Davidson's work in general, and his paper 'Causal

---

[15] The phrase is Davidson's; see his 'Causal Relations', 153.
[16] See *The Facts of Causation*.

Relations' in particular, are undoubtedly responsible for much of the interest which explanations of this kind have generated, and for the focus on events which this attention to the singular causal claim has brought in its train; for the singular terms of Davidson's examples—'The flood caused the famine', 'The stabbing caused Caesar's death', 'The burning of the house caused the roasting of the pig'— are all singular terms for entities which appear to be best construed as individual events.[17] I shall call such explanations as these, where the cause cited is referred to by means of a singular term for an event, *event-citing* singular causal explanations. But it is worth noting that events are not the only entities reference to which can figure in singular causal claims. In particular, as noted above, ordinary usage permits terms for substances, or things, as well as events, to occur in cause-position in singular causal claims— consider 'The log caused the flood', 'Brutus caused Caesar's death', 'The match caused the burning of the house'.[18] I shall call these sorts of singular causal explanations, where it is not an event but rather a thing which is cited as the cause, *thing-citing* singular causal explanations. As I have already noted, however, few philosophers are prepared to allow that things can be causes in anything other than a loose and derivative sense, primarily, perhaps, for the temporal reasons to which Fales draws attention. The thought is that since things persist through time, normally existing at times prior to the occurrence or obtaining of the *explanandum* effect and continuing to exist long afterwards, their citation in a causal explanation cannot really be an accurate way of saying what produced or triggered the effect in question. We can normally be more specific than that. Thus, though in a sense there may be nothing wrong with saying that the log caused the flood, we pin-point more precisely the relevant causal factor by citing its falling across the river, say—an event.

I shall not say much, for the moment, about thing-citing explanations, though I think they are interesting; I shall return briefly to the role played by things in causation in the next chapter. But it is perhaps worth pointing out that we ought to be cautious about drawing over-hasty conclusions from the fact that thing-citing ex-

---

[17] 'Causal Relations', in his *Essays on Actions and Events*, 149.

[18] It is, however, most unusual to find terms for things figuring in what might be called 'effect-position'. Things are not normally said to be caused—though their creation may be.

planations can usually be supplemented by more specific and informative event-citing ones, about the status of things as elements of causal reality. For a start, it is one thing to say that things are causes only in a derivative sense, quite another to say, as Fales does at one point, that it is 'senseless' to speak of them as causes at all.[19] And secondly, we must be cautious of assuming too readily that facts which are really facts about what sorts of factors need to be cited in order to satisfy certain explanatory requirements are a guide to the structure of something which might be thought of as language-independent causal reality. It is true that an event-citing explanation which enlarges on a thing-citing one normally gives us extra information and so usually serves to provide a better explanation of why the *explanandum* event occurred. For example, to know that it was the throwing of the stone that broke the window is to know more than one knows if one knows only that the stone broke the window. But that does not show that the sentence 'The stone caused the breaking of the window' is false or misleading or inaccurate, or that real causal relations 'in the world' hold between events rather than between things. It is not simply obvious from the fact, if it is a fact, that event-citing explanations can always be offered to supplement or enlarge upon thing-citing ones that it is the former rather than the latter that reveal the ontological basis of the causal relation, if we think we understand that idea. Indeed, we have as yet been given no reason to think that, faced with two apparent sorts of singular cause, things and events, there is any pressure to make a choice between them. Just as there is no obvious reason to think that spatial or temporal relations hold only between objects or between events, or that any very clear sense can be given to the claim that spatial or temporal relations between objects are more basic than those between events, or vice versa, so it is not obvious why we need to reduce the relata of the causal relation to a single ontological category.[20] This is as much, though, as I want to say for now about thing-citing singular causal claims; I want to turn now to the event-citing variety of singular causal explanation.

[19] Fales, *Causation and Universals*, 54.

[20] This is not to say, of course, that someone could not think of reasons for saying, for example, that spatial relations between things are more basic than those between events—just that philosophers have not generally been troubled by the question 'What are the relata of spatial relations?' in quite the same way that they have worried about the question 'What are the relata of the causal relation?'

It is quite natural, though perhaps wrong, to suppose that when an event occurs, a true event-citing singular causal claim must always be available—that wherever anything happens, wherever there is an event to be explained, at least one of its causes must have been a preceding *event*, a trigger of some sort, and that we can always supply *one* sort of explanation of why the effect-event occurred by noting that this trigger-event caused it.[21] This, arguably, is the thought encapsulated by the doctrine that every event has a cause. The power to cause something in this particular way— to trigger it off—is not something that can be possessed by a state, since states are normally supposed to be persisting things, not happenings, and although a satisfactory causal explanation of why a particular event, or an event of some particular kind, occurred can be given by mentioning a state, states are not usually thought to be the sorts of things that can act as 'triggers'.

It is not true, of course, that any singular causal claim which states truly that one event caused another must provide a good explanation of why the effect-event occurred. Event-citing singular causal claims can be true (in the sense that the extensional causal relations they invoke can hold) without offering the kind of illumination that we normally expect from a good causal explanation. This kind of explanatory failure can happen for at least two reasons. First, the event which is cited in the explanation may be described in such a way that the connection between cause and effect remains opaque. For example, if the *Titanic*'s striking an iceberg happens to be the event that I thought of at 4 p.m. on 18 April 1991, then it will be true, but not normally illuminating, to say that the event that I thought of at 4 p.m. on 18 April 1991

---

[21] Though one does not need to consider the Big Bang or quantum phenomena in order to feel uneasy about the insistence that every event is 'triggered' by some preceding event. This is particularly obvious if one is inclined to want to count as events those entities which I called 'non-paradigmatic' events in Ch. 3—events like annual falls in the average number of children per household. Surely there could be an annual fall in the average number of children per household in some country without there having been any 'triggering' event which caused that fall. There *may* be some event-citing explanation available (e.g. perhaps the fall was caused by a rise in the availability of birth control), but, firstly, the relationship between a rise in the availability of birth control and a fall in the average number of children per household does not fit the ordinary, physical 'triggering' model very comfortably; and secondly, it does not seem mandatory that there should be any such explanation at hand, in any case. Many individual decisions by individual people may simply have produced the fall, without there being any true causal explanation of an event-citing kind available—particularly if the fall is not especially large or striking.

caused the sinking of the *Titanic*. The second kind of failure occurs where the causal connection between cause and effect is clear enough—but where it would not be pragmatically useful to cite the event as cause. For example, there may have been an explosion in my kitchen because I struck a match, but explosions do not normally follow when matches are struck in kitchens, and so it may not be particularly helpful to cite the striking of the match as the cause of the explosion. When we know that the kitchen was full of methane, we are in a better position to understand why the explosion occurred; and so we are more likely to be inclined to cite this as the cause.

This second kind of explanatory failure is apt to prompt the thought that event-citing singular causal explanation is necessarily *partial*, even in those cases where explanatory success is achieved. The recognition that 'standing conditions' as well as events have a part to play in causal explanation makes tempting the Millian view that there is something called the cause, 'philosophically speaking',[22] a kind of huge conjunction of events and standing conditions, any part of which might, for explanatory purposes, be singled out and cited as 'the cause', the choice in any particular case depending on pragmatic considerations. Effects are then conceived of as the resultants of a sort of 'vector addition' of these multifarious factors. In offering an event-citing singular causal explanation, then, the thought is, we are normally mentioning just one of a large number of the causal antecedents which were causally pertinent to the effect in question—and pragmatics alone excuses our referring to any such event as 'the cause' of that effect.

It seems to me that this Millian view of the metaphysics of causation is still extremely widespread. But it has been subjected to a very powerful critique—and it will be one of my main contentions in later chapters that the consequences of this critique for the Millian view of causation are much more radical than have yet been realized. The critique is supplied by Davidson in his paper 'Causal Relations', and I shall be discussing his arguments in greater detail in Chapter 7. But the full understanding of those arguments requires an appreciation of the difference between singular and sentential causal claims; and so it is to that second variety of explanation that I now turn.

---

[22] See J. S. Mill, *A System of Logic*, 8th edn. (London, 1873), 214.

3. SENTENTIAL CAUSAL EXPLANATIONS

I said earlier that sentential causal explanations involve either an explicit use of the sentence functor 'because' or a use of the verb 'cause' which suggests that the underlying structure of the explanation is better represented by means of a sentence functor than by a two-place predicate. But there are two problems with this definition of sentential causal explanations. The first is that not every explanation couched in terms of the sentence functor 'because' is a causal explanation. One might say, for example, that I broke the law because I parked on a yellow line, or that it is more likely than not that a random selection of twenty-three people will contain two with the same birthday, because the probability of their all having different birthdays is $(365 \times 364 \times \ldots 343) \div 365^{23}$, which is less than one-half[23]. But neither of these seems to be a causal explanation. We face the question, therefore, of how we are to tell the causal variety apart from the rest. The second difficulty has to do not with the sentence functor 'because', but with the verb 'cause'. I suggested above that there are some uses of the verb 'cause' which are better represented by means of a functor than by a two-place predicate. But how are we to tell which these are? When is 'cause' a relational predicate and when a functor?

I do not intend to say a great deal in this chapter about what distinguishes specifically causal uses of the connective 'because' from uses of other kinds; I shall return to the question in Chapter 6. It will suffice for present purposes if the following can be agreed:

1. There are at least some explanations of the form '*P* because *Q*' which are causal explanations.
2. There are at least some explanations of the form '*P* because not-*Q*' which are causal explanations.
3. There are at least some explanations of the form '*P* because *Q*' where '*Q*' is a stative predication (see Chapter 4) which are causal explanations.

The arguments of the present chapter can proceed independently of any decision about what distinguishes causal from non-causal explanations, provided (1)–(3) are conceded.

---

[23] These examples are owed to W. Child—see his *Causation, Interpretation and the Mind*, 91–2.

The second question, though, is more pressing. If the distinction between singular and sentential explanations is to be viable, we need a way of deciding when the verb 'cause' is to be represented as a predicate, and when a sentence functor. One test which might suggest itself at this point is the following: if an explanation containing the verb 'cause' can be accurately paraphrased by means of the sentence functor 'because', then the explanation is a sentential causal claim. Explanations involving infinitive and gerundive constructions seem to satisfy this test: for example, 'The flood caused the land to become fertile again' can be paraphrased as 'The land became fertile again because the flood occurred'; 'My being late caused me to miss the train' as 'I missed the train because I was late'. Explanations involving apparent reference to causal relations between facts also meet this criterion: 'The fact that there was so much unemployment caused the crime rate to soar' can be paraphrased 'The crime rate soared because there was so much unemployment'. But this criterion is in danger of making it look as though there is really no genuine distinction to be drawn between sentential and singular causal claims at all. For many event-citing singular causal claims seem to satisfy this criterion too. 'The flood caused the famine', for example, could surely be paraphrased as 'The famine occurred because the flood occurred'. Should we then conclude that *all* causal claims can be represented sententially? Is the singular–sentential dichotomy just a superficial grammatical phenomenon that can be made to disappear by means of paraphrase?

One reason for suspecting that this conclusion cannot be right is that the trick which seemed to work for delivering a sentential paraphrase of 'The flood caused the famine'—i.e. the introduction of the verb 'occur'—will only work for event-citing singular causal claims. Thing-citing causal claims will not succumb to any parallel treatment. If the log caused the flood, then the flood occurred because of the log—but here, 'because' is not functioning as a sentence functor. We might try: 'The flood occurred because the log existed'—but that does not seem to be true—the flood occurred not because the log existed but because it fell across the river. We could, of course, offer this as our explanation—i.e. 'The flood occurred because the log fell across the river'—but this is not a paraphrase of our original explanation; it rather builds on it by importing extra information.

And there are also other sorts of causal claim that do not really seem to be paraphrasable by means of the sentential connective 'because'. Consider, for example, the following causal explanation: 'Jones's indignation caused his outburst'. It will not do to paraphrase this using the verb 'occur', for 'indignation' is a stative noun. Thus 'Jones's outburst occurred because his indignation occurred' is not right. His indignation might have existed for years—the causal explanation which invokes it does not depend for its truth on any sudden onset of indignation. And neither is it clear that we can paraphrase by means of the adjective 'indignant'; 'Jones's outburst occurred because he was indignant' need not make quite the same claim as the original explanation. One can see this by considering that one might want to say that it was not because he was indignant but because his indignation was so fierce that the outburst occurred. If we are to take such an explanation literally, it would presumably be wrong to say in this case that Jones's outburst occurred because he was indignant—but true that his indignation (fierce as it was) caused it.[24]

What is happening in this case is an instance of a general phenomenon—a stative noun can in certain cases refer to something which can be regarded as itself a possessor of causally relevant properties and this enables it to figure in a causal explanation as a sort of singular term. Someone's belief that p, to take another example, might be either firm or tentative—and that subject-relative fact might matter in a case where the belief is cited as the cause of one of that person's actions, making it impossible simply to substitute a sentential explanation involving only the verb 'believes'. For example, suppose I pray five times a day because of my belief that God exists—which happens to be a very firm belief of mine. I concede that if my belief was less firm than in fact it is, I probably would be unable to summon up the necessary self-

---

[24] Whether one finds this example persuasive is going to depend on one's view of what it takes to make a sentence of the form 'p because q' true. If one thinks that q must be not only a necessary but also a sufficient condition for p, then one will agree that the sentential explanation is not true in the envisaged circumstances; for Jones's being indignant is not sufficient to cause his outburst—his indignation needs, in addition, to be fierce. But it does not matter to my position if someone thinks that the sentential explanation is still true under the imagined conditions—indeed, it merely dispenses rather more quickly than I have been willing to do with a kind of case that is slightly awkward from my point of view, given my claims about token states, for these usages provide a kind of evidence for the view that we are prepared, at least sometimes, to treat certain sorts of state as quasi-particulars.

discipline and would cease to pray so frequently. But then it is arguably not true that I pray five times a day because I believe that God exists.[25] A particular quality of the actual belief that I have— its firmness—matters causally; and so it might be alleged that the pure sentential explanation does not provide an adequate paraphrase.

Having said that, it seems to me that the vast majority of cases in which a stative noun is used to refer to a cause are cases in which a sentential paraphrase would capture perfectly well the intent of the explanation. Someone who cited Jones's indignation as the cause of his outburst, for example, would very likely accept the sentential paraphrase involving the adjective 'indignant'; and an explanation which cited a belief as the cause of an action would normally be regarded as nothing more than a notational variant on a sentential explanation involving the verb 'believes'. I mention the possibility that stative nouns *can* be understood as singular terms in causal explanations only for completeness' sake; it is not part of my view that it is usual or natural to read them in this way.

To return, though, to the point at issue, I think it is fairly clear that the paraphrase test does not utterly undermine the distinction between singular and sentential causal claims. But given that it looks as though we must retain the category of singular causal claim to deal with thing-citing and (perhaps) certain state-citing explanations, it seems perverse to exclude event-citing singular causal claims from the category. Surely if there is a relational predicate 'cause', it figures in sentences like 'The flood caused the famine' just as clearly as it figures in 'The log caused the flood'. What I propose, then, in order to ensure that the paraphrase test yields a coherent verdict, is that it be supplemented by a restriction on the resources which may be involved in producing the paraphrase: if the original explanation contains a singular term for an event, this must not be conjoined with the verb 'occur' (or its synonyms 'happen', 'take place', etc.) to produce the sentential paraphrase. This restriction will ensure that event-citing singular causal claims remain in the singular category.

It might seem as though this restriction is simply *ad hoc*. But it is not really so. What consideration of the above examples of those singular causal claims that will not yield to sentential paraphrase

[25] See previous note.

shows is that what distinguishes singular causal claims from others is that they are utterly non-committal about which specific features or properties of a particular thing are causally relevant to the effect it produces; all they involve is the claim that the particular thing in question—be it event, thing, or state—is somehow involved in the production of that effect. This is what makes it impossible in the case of thing-citing and certain state-citing explanations to supply a sentential paraphrase. We cannot deduce that it was because the log had this or that or the other property that it caused the flood if all we know is that it was the log that caused it; nor, arguably, that it was because Jones was indignant that his outburst occurred if all we know is that it was his indignation that caused it (for certain specific properties of his indignation, other than its being a case of indignation, e.g. its fierceness, may have been crucial). Where the singular cause is an event, though, the fact that we do not know which particular features mattered does not prevent us from supplying a sentential paraphrase—for the very existence of an event consists in its occurrence, so that when an event causes an effect, the effect can be said to occur because the cause does. But the verb 'occur' is in a sense an empty verb—it tells us nothing more about the event than what we can anyway glean from a true singular causal claim. The function of such an explanation is still to point us towards a causally efficacious singular cause, not to tell us what it was about any such singular cause that was causally relevant ('occurrence' is not a genuine feature of any event). So explanations of the form '*C* occurred because *E* occurred', where '*C*' and '*E*' are singular terms, genuinely belong with singular causal claims of other sorts—for they serve the same explanatory function.

Another problem with the introduction of the restriction on paraphrase is that it means we must reverse the sentential verdict on an explanation already considered: 'The flood caused the land to become fertile again', and those like it, which mix singular terms with infinitive or gerundive constructions. So far I have spoken as though the singular–sentential dichotomy were simply exhaustive; but if we restrict sentential paraphrase in the way suggested, certain causal explanations will fall clearly into neither category. Explanations like 'The flood caused the land to become fertile again' will be neither singular nor sentential; 'the land to become fertile again' is certainly not a singular term, but neither can we paraphrase sententially without using 'occur' or some similar verb. Similar

explanations containing singular terms for things are also possible—e.g. 'The President caused the country to fall into desperate
decline'. What are we to say about the logical form of explanations
such as these?

I think it would be wrong to try to force these explanations into
either singular or sentential moulds. The cause cited in these explanations is a singular cause, but the effect is only expressible
sententially—and there is no getting away from either of these facts.
'Because of' is the natural construction for dealing with these
hybrid cases: if the flood caused the land to become fertile again,
then the land became fertile again because of the flood; if the
President caused the country to fall into desperate decline, then the
country fell into desperate decline because of the President. I shall
not deal further with these sorts of explanations; but I note here my
view that they cannot be reduced to either of the other forms; they
are genuine hybrids which combine features of both the other
varieties of causal claim. I shall return now to sentential causal
explanations.

For someone who begins with a certain view of what causal
relations must be like, sentential causal explanations can appear to
present a prima-facie puzzle. What sentential causal explanations
appear to assert is that certain relationships hold between *facts*—
that one thing is, was, or will be the case because (causally speaking) another is, was, or will be. But many philosophers are inclined
to think that causation, conceived of as a real-worldly phenomenon, cannot require an ontology of facts—that facts are just not
the sorts of things between which 'natural' causal relations might
hold, not the sorts of things which might have 'efficacy' or causal
power. What, then, is the connection between the truth of a
sentential causal claim and real causation, the 'pushing and shov-
ing' that goes on in the language-independent world? It is tempting
to think that whatever account we give of sentential causal explanations, it must show that their causal character does not need to be
construed as resting upon the existence of causal relations which
are irreducibly sentential, that it does not imply any commitment to
ineliminable causal connections between facts.

What might such an account look like? In the next section, I shall
describe one very influential idea about the logical relations between a certain range of sentential explanations and a corresponding class of singular causal claims which has seemed to many to

provide a clear and straightforward way of understanding the relationship which is expressed by the sentential connective 'because', in its causal uses, which does not commit us to any worldly causal relations that are not relations between particulars. I do not think the account is precisely Davidson's own view of the causal 'because'—I shall consider later what I take to be the Davidsonian position—but I believe that Davidson's views, specifically those outlined in 'The Logical Form of Action Sentences' and in 'Causal Relations', have nevertheless been highly influential in encouraging its adoption. Davidson certainly suggests, at any rate, that *some* varieties of sentential connective which express causal relationships (in particular, the connective 'caused it to be the case that') might be treated in the way that this account suggests we might treat 'because'. I shall call the account I have in mind the *existential generalization account*, for reasons which will shortly become clear. I shall try to show that the existential generalization account cannot be right. My argument will have two parts. I shall begin by trying to argue that the relationship between singular and sentential claims cannot be as the existential generalization account suggests even for the central class of cases in connection with which it might be thought most attractive—namely, those cases in which both *explanans* and *explanandum* are event predications, in the sense described in Chapter 3. I shall then go on to argue that even if this first argument is not found persuasive, there is certainly no prospect of generalizing the account to many important varieties of sentential causal explanation—in particular, to explanations with negative and stative *explanantes*.[26] Given, then, that we will in any case need another way of understanding the causal 'because' in these recalcitrant cases, then, and given that there seem to be reasons also for supposing that the existential generalization account fails even for those explanations whose *explanantes* are event predications, I shall conclude that we need to abandon the account and look elsewhere for a plausible account of sentential causal explanations, one which can be unproblematically extended to explanations with negative and stative *explanantes*.

---

[26] Davidson himself expresses serious doubts about whether causal idioms might quite generally be dealt with in the extensionalist framework of events which he proposes ('Causal Relations', 161). But it seems to me that insufficient note has been taken of his cautionary remarks to this effect by many of those who have made use of his ideas about singular causal relations.

4. THE EXISTENTIAL GENERALIZATION ACCOUNT

According to Davidson, certain sorts of sentence are best regarded as involving implicit quantification over events. The paper in which the view is expounded and defended in most detail is entitled 'The Logical Form of Action Sentences', but there seems no reason why the idea need be restricted to sentences involving agents and action verbs; it can be applied just as easily to any sentence in which the main verb is an event verb. 'The bomb exploded', for example, contains no term for an agent, and no action of any kind need be involved, but Davidson's points about adverbial modification are no less telling in connection with such a sentence than they are in the cases he considers explicitly. 'The bomb exploded loudly', for example, entails 'The bomb exploded', and all of Davidson's powerful arguments for the view that action sentences involve implicit quantification over events can be adapted for these agentless events. I shall not spend time describing Davidson's view or explaining the way in which he defends it; I merely assume familiarity with his main line of argument. What I want to do here is simply to question whether a certain view of the relation between singular and sentential causal claims which is made attractive by Davidson's views about events can be correct.

Suppose I explain why some particular match lit on some particular occasion by saying that the match lit because it was struck. Here we have a sentence of the form 'S_1 because S_2'—i.e. we have a causal explanation which fits the sentential paradigm. But though we have no singular terms for events here, it is easy enough to see that in such circumstances as we would usually be inclined to use such a sentential explanation, there will also be an associated event-citing singular causal explanation available—an explanation of the form 'X caused Y' where 'X' is a singular term which refers to some individual striking event and 'Y' a singular term for an individual lighting event which was caused by 'X'. Suppose we just call the relevant striking event 'the striking of the match' and the relevant lighting event 'the lighting of the match'. Then, corresponding to the sentential explanation 'The match lit because it was struck' we have the singular causal claim 'The striking of the match caused the lighting of the match'.

What is the connection between these two causal explanations? Davidson's account of the logical form of action sentences might suggest that we should represent the logical form of the sentential causal explanation as follows:

$(\exists x)(\exists e')(\exists e'')$[Struck $(x$, the match, $e')$ & Lit(the match, $e'')$ & Caused (e', e'')].[27]

No *particular* singular causal claim is, strictly speaking, entailed by this formulation—since nothing in it logically guarantees unique referents for definite descriptions like 'the striking of the match' and 'the lighting of the match', where these are understood as referring to particular events.[28] But the existence of *some* true singular causal claim relating a striking to a lighting event is guaranteed—just as the statement 'Someone locked the back door' entails the existence of at least one true statement of the form '*A* locked the back door', where '*A*' refers to a particular individual, though it does not entail any specific statement of this form (e.g. it does not entail 'Fred locked the back door'). And in such cases as this, those like Davidson, who take singular causal claims involving events at face value may be tempted to see the truth of the sentential formulation as dependent for its ontological grounding and causal character on the truth that is expressed by the singular causal claim in question. In such a case, that is to say, it might appear that there is no difficulty about how the sentential explanation—that the match lit because it was struck—relates to real causation 'in the world'. It relates to real causation 'in the world' by entailing that there were at least one striking event and at least one lighting event which were related one to another by the causal relation. The sentential explanation can be regarded as a sort of existential generalization of the singular causal claim.

Before looking at some sentential explanations which are clearly unrelated in this way to any singular causal claims, let me note that even in cases of the favourable sort in which both *explanans* and

---

[27] Davidson explicitly offers this sort of formulation as the logical form not of any sentences of the form 'S_1 because S_2', but rather of a sentence of the form 'S_2, which caused it to be the case that S_1'. It may be that there are important differences between these forms; indeed, it strikes me that the objection I make below to the idea that singular event-citing causal claims entail certain sorts of corresponding sentential ones is somewhat less plausible in connection with the formulation Davidson actually uses. Nothing important, though, turns on this point of interpretation.

[28] The qualification is necessary because it might be possible to read these definite descriptions as referring rather to states of affairs—in which case, uniqueness is guaranteed.

explanandum sentences are straightforward event predications, there might be room for doubt about whether the relation between sentential and singular claim can be quite as straightforward as the account implies. One pertinent question is whether the singular causal claim implies the sentential one—as it ought, if the sentential one has the logical form suggested by Davidson. 'The striking of the match caused the lighting of the match' surely implies 'A striking of the match caused a lighting of the match'—and if this latter claim is to be equivalent to 'The match lit because it was struck', as the above formulation suggests, it ought to imply that claim too. But does it? Might we not be able to imagine a case in which we wanted to say that the striking of the match caused the lighting of the match—and yet not because it was a *striking*—so that it would not be correct to say that the match lit because it was struck? Suppose, for example, that the situation is as follows: Someone is attempting to invent a procedure for igniting matches by remote control, and tests of the mechanism are under way. One experimenter is holding one of the specially designed matches in his hand. At a signal from this first experimenter, a second experimenter, who is sitting beside a push-button which triggers the ignition mechanism, is supposed to press the button. The signal arranged is an up-and-down motion of the hand. The first experimenter gives the signal a number of times, but the attention of the second experimenter has temporarily wandered and he does not immediately notice that the signal has been given. The first experimenter, who is holding the box from which the match came in his other hand, while attempting to signal more vigorously, strikes the match he is holding accidentally against the box—it just so happens that the up-and-down motion of his arm is noticed this time by the second experimenter, who presses the button, and the match lights as a result. In such a situation, it seems to me correct to say that the striking of the match—which happened also to be an up-and-down motion of the hand—caused the lighting of the match (though it was not, of course, the most proximate of the causes we are able to identify in this case). But it is not true, it seems to me, that the match lit because it was struck. It is irrelevant that the match was struck— any one of the other up-and-down motions of the first experimenter's arm might have caused the lighting. The singular causal claim is true, but the sentential one, which was supposed to be a mere existential generalization of it, is not.

4.1. *Negative* Explanantes

Reflection on a number of other kinds of case confirms the suggestion that the sorts of causal relationship which the sentential connective 'because' can encode are not simply dependent on straightforward extensional relations between causally efficacious particulars, such as might be expressed in a singular causal claim. Consider, for example, what we ought to say about the sentence 'The match did not light because it was not struck'. It is vastly implausible that this sentence is well represented as

$$(\exists x)(\exists e')(\exists e'')[\text{Not Struck } (x, \text{ the match}, e') \ \& \ \text{Not Lit (the match}, e'') \ \& \ \text{Caused } (e', e'')],$$

i.e. as the claim that there was an event which was a not-striking of the match and an event which was a not-lighting of the match and that the first caused the second. It is obvious that this representation would be grotesque—like representing the claim that 'No one came to my party' as the claim that $(\exists x)(x$ came to my party $\& \ x = \text{no one})$. The sentence is a negative existential claim if anything is— what it says is that there was no lighting of the match because there was no striking of the match—i.e. its logical form ought to be:

$$\neg\exists e'[\text{Lit (the match}, e')] \text{ because } \neg\exists x \exists e'[\text{Struck } (x, \text{ the match}, e')].$$

But this formulation retains the sentential connective, which is clearly not going to be illuminated in this case by any appeal to the two-place predicate 'cause'. There are no events available to stand in this relation—that is precisely what the sentence tells us. Some other account of the causal 'because' is going to be needed for this case.[29]

I have found that it is not an uncommon reaction to this point about negated *explanantes* and *explananda* to suggest that explanations of this sort cannot be causal explanations precisely because they do not assert the existence of causal relations between events. One important lesson which needs to be drawn from this reaction, I think, is that there simply is no clear, pre-philosophical notion of a causal explanation; what a philosopher will be prepared to count as falling into the category is going to depend, at least partly, on her other philosophical opinions and commitments. But that is not to

---

[29] See Mellor, *The Facts of Causation*, 132–5, for a similar argument.

say that reasons cannot be given for thinking that it would be strange to grant causal status to 'The match lit because it was struck' while denying it to 'The match did not light because it was not struck'. It would be prima facie curious if the 'because' in these two explanations carried a causal meaning in one case and some different sort of meaning (and *what* different sort of meaning?) in the other. It would be at least superficially odd if the logical form of the first were to be represented using a two-place predicate, while the second required retention of an irreducibly sentential connective. And even if we were to accept the need for divergent accounts of the two explanations in this particular case, where the *explanandum* sentence is negated, as well as the *explanans*, there are other kinds of case where only the *explanans* is a negative sentence—e.g. 'The man died because he did not take antibiotics', 'The train crashed because it did not hoot', and so on. In such cases, the grounds for thinking that the explanations in question are causal are arguably even stronger, since they are explanations of why events of particular sorts occurred.[30] Could there be an explanation of why an event of some particular kind occurred—as opposed to an explanation of why some event, which occurred, was of a particular kind—which was not a causal explanation? I am inclined to think that there could not be. But there is no prospect of representing these explanations in the way suggested by the existential generalization account, by invoking a causal predicate, unless we are prepared to count omissions and failures as events. And this, it seems to me, would involve a distortion, in that the non-occurrence of a *type* of event (a taking of antibiotics, a hooting of a train) would be wrongly represented as the occurrence of a *particular* event (a particular failure to take antibiotics, a particular failure to hoot by a train).

4.2. *Stative* Explanantes

Another kind of causal explanation which presents difficulties for the existential generalization account is that in which the main verb in the *explanans* is a stative verb.[31] In sentences like 'The bridge

---

[30] See Child, *Causality, Interpretation and the Mind*, 92–3, for a defence of the idea that any explanation of the occurrence of an event must be causal.

[31] For these purposes, I count the occurrence of some part of the verb 'to be' together with an adjective as stative.

collapsed because it was weak', 'I missed the train because I was late', 'I turned on the TV because I wanted to watch the news', there does not seem to be a reference, or implicit existential commitment, to any *happening* which could serve as the cause-event in a singular causal claim which might ground the causal relationship which is expressed by the sentential one. It does not follow from the fact that the bridge collapsed because it was weak, for example, that there was any 'event of being weak' (whatever that would mean) which caused its collapse (though it may be tempting to postulate the occurrence of an event of *some* sort, prior to the collapse, for metaphysical reasons).[32] But it might be thought, by those who are inclined to suppose that the distinction between events and states is not particularly significant, that this presents no real obstacle to the generalization of the strategy. For it might be tempting to deny that such explanations differ in any very important way from the sentential event-citing explanations of which the account outlined above was supposed to provide the logical form, on the grounds that, though they do not entail the existence of any event-citing singular causal claims, they do entail the existence of what might be called state-citing ones. For we can always nominalize the sentence which serves as *explanans* in one of these stative sentential explanations (as I shall call them), in order to come up with some sort of stative nominal—and it might be thought that by this means we can generate an explanation which involves the two-place predicate 'caused', and which grounds the original explanation ontologically in much the same way that I suggested above event-citing singular causal claims might be thought of as grounding their sentential counterparts, by someone who accepted the existential generalization account of those sentential counterparts. For example, while it might be conceded

---

[32] Some will want to insist, indeed, that there must have been relevant precipitatory events in all the cases cited; e.g. that there must be some event related to my wanting to watch the news which makes me turn on when I do: my coming to believe or realize that the news is on now, for instance. I shall not quarrel; all I wish to point out, for now, is that the original explanations (in this case, that I turned on the TV because I wanted to watch the news) do not *entail* the existence of any such event. If there is a reason to think there must have been such an event, it is a metaphysical, not a logical one.

In case it should be thought that the suggestion that 'events of being weak' are so preposterous as not to be worth bothering with, let me point out that talk of 'events' of believing and desiring, equally preposterous by my lights, is extremely common in the philosophical literature on mental causation.

that the truth of the sentences 'The bridge collapsed because it was weak' and 'I turned on the TV because I wanted to watch the news' does not depend on the existence of *events* of being weak or wanting, respectively, it might be said that it does depend on the existence of *states*—specifically *token states*—of being weak and wanting, which are to be conceived of as the sorts of things that might have causal efficacy, which might be the 'real-worldly' entities whose interactions with other such entities grounds the original sentential explanation. So, for example, that I turned on the TV because I wanted to watch the news could be regarded as entailing that there is a sentence of the '*X* caused *Y*' form available, where what replaces '*X*' is the stative nominal 'my wanting to watch the news', or perhaps 'my desire to watch the news', and what replaces '*Y*' is a definite description supposed to refer to an action, namely 'my turning on of the news'. Both kinds of explanation, it might be thought, basically work by quantifying existentially over particular causes: in the one case, over events, in the other, over token states, the existence of which help to explain, because they help to cause, the *explanandum* events in question. Obviously, states cannot do the kind of precipitatory causing that is characteristic of events, because they are not happenings—that will generally be conceded—but token states, it may be thought, are nevertheless required in order that we can come to understand the connection between the truth of stative sentential causal explanations and real-world causal relations.

It seems to me, though, that it is absolutely clear that this strategy will not work for stative sententials. Though we can generate explanations which are superficially similar in their form to singular event-citing causal claims, by nominalizing the *explanans* and *explanandum* sentences in a stative sentential, we fool ourselves if we think that by doing so we have generated a genuine singular causal claim. Consider, for example, the stative sentential 'The bridge collapsed because it was weak'. Nominalizing, we can obtain 'The weakness of the bridge (or the bridge's being weak, or the bridge's state of weakness) caused the collapse of the bridge'. But the relation between these claims and the original stative sentential cannot be the same as the relation which was supposed by the existential generalization account to hold between an event-citing singular causal claim like 'The striking of the match caused the lighting of the match' and the sentential 'The match lit because it was struck'. On the existential generalization account, recall, the sentential explanation was supposed to be an existential generalization of the singular one—it was supposed to assert that there was a striking event and that there was a lighting event and that the one caused the other. But we cannot likewise suppose that 'The bridge collapsed because it was weak' asserts that there was a weakness or being weak of the bridge and a collapse of the bridge and that the one caused the other. For what would be meant here by 'a weakness' or 'a being weak'? As Mourelatos notes, stative nominalization transcriptions are almost always *mass-quantified*; generally speaking, they do not accept the indefinite article and do not have plural forms. Understood as they demand to be understood in this context, the plural forms 'weaknesses' and 'being weaks' make no sense whatever; and neither does the count-quantified expression 'a weakness'. It is possible, of course, to speak of weaknesses in the plural in certain contexts—one can speak, for example, of the weaknesses of a person or of a design or of a form of government. But 'The bridge collapsed because it was weak' cannot be regarded as involving implicit quantification over weaknesses in *this* sense. Understood thus, the plural form 'weaknesses' quantifies over entities which are still *types*—things like greed or instability or corruptibility, not particulars of a sort whose interactions might ground stative sentential causal explanations in the requisite manner.

It might be suggested that it is unimportant if the English language provides, in many cases, no natural means of quantifying over and referring to the token states whose interactions are supposed to ground those causal explanations whose *explanantes* are stative in form. For it might simply be said that we can, after all, use the philosophers' term of art 'token state' itself in order to designate the wanted entities—thus, we can, for example, speak of the particular, token state of weakness which caused the bridge's collapse. But it is important to see that we do not help ourselves in the slightest to understand the causal nature of the explanation we offer in saying that the bridge collapsed because it was weak by suggesting that the underlying causal relation in this case is a relation between a token state of weakness and a collapse. Even if we were to admit the existence of particular, token states of weakness, and accepted that they could stand in causal relations, an explanation of the form 'The bridge's token state of weakness caused the bridge's collapse' would fail even to entail the sentence 'The bridge collapsed because it was weak'—and so cannot be offered as an elucidation of what grounds the latter sentence. For if the token state of weakness in question really were a genuine particular, it would have other intrinsic properties, aside from being a state of weakness. Particulars are not the sorts of things that have only one intrinsic property; anything which could satisfy the secret life requirement outlined in Chapter 1 would have to be many-propertied. But once we admit that token states have more than a single property, a gap opens up between any explanation which cites such a token state as a cause of some event, and a sentential explanation which cites the property (or a fact involving the property) by means of which the token state is purportedly identified. For example, a gap opens up between 'The bridge's token state of weakness caused the collapse of the bridge' and 'The bridge collapsed because it was weak'. The first neither says the same thing as, nor entails, the second, since it is conceivable that the token state in question might have caused the collapse of the bridge in virtue of one or more of its other properties—other, that is, than its being a state of weakness—and in such a case, the bridge's being weak would have been causally irrelevant to its collapse. It would then be true that the bridge's token state of weakness caused the collapse of the bridge; but false that the bridge collapsed because it was weak. In other words, the causal efficaciousness of a token state of weakness does not secure the causal relevance of the fact that the bridge was weak, provided it is accepted that a token state of weakness is the sort of thing that might have more than one property of a kind which might figure in a causal explanation.

Someone might think that the obvious answer to this problem is to drop the suggestion that token states are many-propertied individuals of the sort which I have been supposing they must be conceived of as being. Couldn't token states be 'fine-grained' entities?—so that, for example, we could just deny that a token state of weakness of a particular bridge has any intrinsic properties other than being a token state of weakness of that very bridge? Some of those philosophers who hold that the ultimate relata of causation are property instances may, I think, have something like this idea in mind. But it seems to me that someone who was prepared to make their ontology of causation fine-grained in this way would have no coherent reason to resist what the surface form of sentential causal explanations anyway suggests—namely that there are causal relationships, of a sort, between *facts*, relationships which require sentential forms of expression for their formulation and which cannot be regarded as grounded in relations between particulars. It is true that facts are often classified as 'abstract', while the defenders of property instances are apt to insist that property instances are 'concrete', spatiotemporal entities. But it is hard to see what this labelling really amounts to. As I suggested in Chapter 1, there seems to be no reason for granting 'concrete' or spatiotemporal status to a property instance that could not also be a reason for granting it to the corresponding fact, no reason for denying it to a fact that could not also be a reason for denying it to the corresponding property instance. In addition, the defender of 'concrete' property instances will need to have something to say about those causal explanations in which the *explanantes* predicate something of a subject which cannot be easily located in space and time—e.g. 'Investors were nervous because inflation was high'; 'Crime has soared because society is no longer cohesive'; 'Ancient Egyptian art flourished because its culture was so far advanced in other respects'. Doubtless some complicated story about the supervenience of economic, social, and cultural property instances on other sorts of property instance could be told. But is it not vastly implausible that these explanations depend for their status as *causal* explanations on the availability of some such story? Is it not better to embrace the view that these explanations do exactly what they appear to do—namely relate facts one to another by means of a sentential connective? I am inclined to think, then, that the introduction of property instances offers only the illusion of a solution to the problem of the causal 'because'. Property instances are not obviously better fitted to be the relata of an unproblematically real-world causal relation than are the facts with which we began. It seems to me that there is no prospect of accounting for sentential causal explanations without taking their sentential form seriously. Our task, therefore, is to neutralize somehow what I earlier called the prima-facie puzzle about sentential causal explanations, either to diminish the appeal or dispute the relevance of the claim that facts are just not the sorts of things between which 'natural' causal relations might hold, not the sorts of things which might have 'efficacy' or causal power.

5. CAUSATION AND CAUSAL EXPLANATION

One suggestion about how we might dispute the relevance of the claim that facts are not the sorts of things between which natural causal relations might hold to an irreducibly sentential understanding of the causal 'because' is considered by Davidson himself, towards the end of 'Causal Relations'. The suggestion is that sentential forms of causal explanation should be thought of as asserting the existence not of causal but of *explanatory* relationships between facts.[33] After considering some forms of causal claim which cannot easily be made to square with the idea that the causal relation can be expressed by means of a two-place extensional relation holding between events, Davidson suggests that what is needed to deal with the phenomenon is simply the recognition that there is an ambiguity in the verb 'cause'. In the case of singular causal claims, when we say that something was the cause of some event we can be taken to mean that an extensional relation of causation holds between it and the produced event. Where an event, like the striking of the match, is cited as the cause of the lighting of the match, for example, this is what we mean. But in other cases, we cannot interpret the phrase 'was the cause' in the same way. In such cases, the assertion that something 'was the cause' of something else has to be understood rather differently. We might say, for instance, that the bridge's being weak was the cause of its collapse, but 'the bridge's being weak' is really a *fact*, not a singular cause, and so cannot stand in this same extensional causal relation to any event. Indeed, it might be said that since facts are not part of the natural world at all, they cannot, strictly speaking, be said to bear causal relations to anything at all.[34] The relation which holds between the bridge's being weak and its collapse (or perhaps we ought to say more exactly, between the bridge's being weak and the fact that it collapsed) is really the relation of *causal explanation*.[35] Explanations which point to facts rather than events

---

[33] 'Causal Relations', 161.

[34] There will be those who dispute this claim about facts; indeed, in a sense I shall be disputing it myself in the next chapter.

[35] Cf. Davidson, ibid. 161–2: 'What we must say about such cases is that in addition to, or in place of, giving what Mill calls the "producing cause", such sentences tell, or suggest a causal story. They are, in other words, rudimentary causal explanations. Explanations typically relate statements, not events. I suggest there-

in this way, even if they can be given something like the surface form of singular causal claims by nominalization (e.g. 'The bridge's being weak caused its collapse'), retain the characteristics of their un-nominalized forms ('The bridge collapsed because (of the fact that) it was weak'); and we must respect the difference between the 'caused' which occurs in explanations such as this and the 'caused' which occurs in event-citing singular causal claims.

I shall call this view of the difference between singular causal claims and sentential ones *the Davidsonian view*.[36] It attempts to respond to the differences between singular and sentential causal explanations by invoking a distinction between those uses of the word 'caused' (and variants on it) which invoke extensional causal relations holding between particular causes and effects, and those which rather have to do with relations of causal explanation holding between facts. The view, while promising, immediately raises two very significant questions. First, what is it for the relation of causal explanation to hold between facts? What is it for one fact causally to explain another? And second, how are we to understand the connection between the existence of causal-explanatory relations holding between facts and that worldly phenomenon which we are inclined to think of as real causing? What, for example, is the relation between the causal explanation which adverts to the bridge's being weak to explain why it collapsed, and real metaphysical causality in the world? I have so far used the word 'fact' in what I have hoped is a metaphysically non-tendentious way: a fact exists, in my usage, when any proposition is true—there is no more than this to the existence of facts.[37] But unless we introduce some stronger conception of a fact, we might struggle to see how expla-

fore that the "caused" of the sample sentences . . . is not the "caused" of straightforward singular causal explanation, but is best expressed by the words "causally explains".'

[36] Though the view that I am calling 'Davidsonian' is not exactly Davidson's own view; in particular, I think Davidson would be a great deal more chary than I have been of supposing that causal explanation is a relation which can hold between *facts*—his account makes *statements* the relata of the relation of causal explanation. But the suggestion on which I wish to focus, that 'cause' can in effect operate as a sentence functor, whose import is more clearly revealed by the phrase 'causally explain', is Davidson's.

[37] See Mellor, *The Facts of Causation*, 9, for what I think is a similar usage. According to Mellor, facts are just entities which correspond by definition to true statements. But Mellor is pressed by worries similar to those I have just touched upon to introduce a more substantial category of entity—which he calls 'facta'—to serve as the truth-makers for causal explanations which appear to advert to facts. I

nations which appear to advert only to facts are rooted in real causality. Put crudely, if the bridge's being weak is a fact in this thin sense, and not a thing in the world, how can it be in a position to *do* anything? Vendler, arguing for the view that causes are facts, puts the difficulty well: 'At first blush my view seems unlikely. What I describe is a metaphysical hybrid, a mésalliance between flesh-and-blood event and shadowy fact.'[38] How can there be causal relations between 'shadowy' facts or between shadowy facts and the 'flesh-and-blood' events they are supposed to explain? But if there are not, how can the explanations in question—explanations which advert to such matters as the fact that the bridge was weak—be genuinely causal?

An account of the relation between causation and causal explanation which in some ways fits well with Davidson's insistence on the distinction between singular causal claims and those sentences which, on his view, 'tell or suggest a causal story'[39] is outlined by Strawson in his paper 'Causation and Explanation'. According to Strawson, causation is a natural relation; it holds between 'things in the natural world, things to which we can assign places and times in nature'.[40] The things thus related are said by Strawson to be 'particular events and circumstances'.[41] Causal explanation, on the other hand, is said to be a relation which holds rather between facts or truths; and its holding in any particular instance depends, in Strawson's view, upon the propensity of human beings to find certain facts comprehensible in the light of others. Unlike causation, then, explanation is not a natural relation; it is an 'intellectual or rational or intensional relation',[42] though its holding in any particular case is conceded by Strawson to be a matter of 'natural facts about our human selves'.[43]

As Strawson notes, ordinary language is not always careful about the distinction. We freely mix the language of facts and reasons, which Strawson associates with the relation of causal explanation, with singular terms for events, which he regards as relata of the

---

am interested in seeing whether we can make sense of the role played by facts in causality without the need to appeal to any such entities as these.

[38] Z. Vendler, 'Causal Relations', *Journal of Philosophy*, 64 (1967), 705.
[39] Davidson, 'Causal Relations', 161.
[40] 'Causation and Explanation', 115.
[41] Ibid.
[42] Ibid.
[43] Ibid. 117.

natural relation of causation. For example, we might say that the fact that there was a short circuit caused the fire, or that the parade was the reason why the traffic was diverted. But we should realize that facts, being abstract entities, cannot enter literally into natural causal relations, on the Strawsonian view. *Short circuits* cause fires, not facts about short circuits, though the occurrence of fires—and certain of their specific features—may perfectly well be explained by citing facts about short circuits.

Strawson accepts the need for an account of the connection between the two relations: 'Surely the power of one fact to explain another must have some basis in the natural world where the events occur and the conditions obtain and the causal relations hold. We must think this on pain of holding, if we do not, that the causal relation itself has no natural existence or none outside our minds.'[44] In the next chapter, I shall say a bit more about Strawson's own suggestions as to how the connection might be forged. But for now, I just want to concur with Strawson's insistence that we need an account of the connection between causal explanation (conceived of as a relation between facts or truths) and causation itself—and to note the shape of the puzzle confronting us by making use of Strawson's example. According to Strawson, facts about short circuits do not enter into natural causal relations. But facts about short circuits not only explain the occurrence of fires and certain of their specific features—they explain them *causally*. And this cannot, on pain of the unacceptable consequences that Strawson mentions in the above quotation, be a matter merely of our finding those particular facts enlightening, of the existence of the intellectual relation that Strawson mentions. Part of what it is to find a particular fact about some situation enlightening with respect to the question why some event occurred or why some circumstances are as they are is to regard the fact as throwing light upon the causal order, conceived of as something existing quite independently of oneself and one's propensities to find certain facts helpful in the causal explanation of others. We cannot be content simply to say that, when we explain a fire by citing, say, not the short circuit which caused it but rather some fact about it—say, the fact that it occurred in the vicinity of a large mass of inflammable gas—the fact that inflammable gas is present, though it adds to our understand-

---

[44] 'Causation and Explanation', 118.

ing of why the fire occurred, has nothing whatever to do with natural causal relations 'in the world'. So even if we are inclined to accept the Strawsonian account of the difference between causation and causal explanation we cannot just stop there. We need an account of how the intellectual relation depends on how things are, an account of what makes the illuminating 'because' sentences true. In the next chapter, I shall try to say something about how we might go about answering this question

It is time to take stock. I have suggested that there is an important distinction to be made between singular causal claims and sentential causal explanations. A certain mode of analysis of a class of sentential explanations made tempting by Davidson seemed to offer the promise that their ontological grounding might be made unmysterious by reference to the singular causal claim (or claims) whose existence the sentential explanation implies. But I have suggested that there are very strong grounds for being sceptical both about whether this mode of analysis will generalize to causal explanations involving negative and stative *explanantes*, and also about whether it is right even for explanations in which the *explanans* and *explanandum* are both straightforward event predications. We must, then, look for another account of the workings of such sentential explanations. And though it may be a useful first move, it is not sufficient simply to say that sentential explanations are based not on causal but on explanatory relations between facts. For we need an account of what the connection is between the holding of these explanatory relations and the holding of other relations which are not merely intellectual ones, which have to do with the workings not only of the human intellect but also of the rest of the animate and inanimate world.

6

Efficacy, Causing, and Relevance

I ARGUED in the last chapter that a proper appreciation of the important differences between singular and sentential explanations is essential if we are to understand properly the ontological and metaphysical implications of our causal talk. Towards the end of that chapter, I outlined a view, which I called the Davidsonian view, which attempted to account for these differences by drawing on the distinction between two relations—the relation of causation and that of causal explanation. I suggested, though, that this answer seemed to leave unexplicated the connection between the relation of causal explanation—a relation whose holding, at least on one fairly plausible view, is dependent upon the tendency of human beings to find one fact, or set of facts, to be useful in achieving a certain kind of understanding of another—and what I called 'real metaphysical causality in the world'. In this chapter, I want to try to provide the outline of an account which might help us to understand this relation. An outline, I should say, really is all that I shall provide; it would take another book to deal properly with all the different sorts of complication and objection that might arise in connection with the sort of account I advocate. My aims are only (1) to insist that we must make a proper place in our account of causality for relationships which are essentially relations between facts, not relations between particulars, and (2) to try to explain how we might do this without simply consigning these relationships to the realm of the intellect, as Davidson's account appeared to do. I do not pretend that the account is complete; but I shall be content if I have said enough to deflect immediate accusations that the wanted account is (1) unnecessary, and (2) impossible.

In Section 1, I shall look at William Child's discussion of the relation between causation and causal explanation.[1] Child distin-

---

[1] *Causality, Interpretation and the Mind*, 100–10.

guishes between two different sorts of view about what makes an explanation a causal explanation. I shall try to suggest that there are strong reasons for preferring the second of these two views to the first, and that making this choice may be a first step towards the clarification of the role played by facts in causation. Then, in Section 2, I shall move on to discuss Jackson and Pettit's account of the distinction between program and process explanations. After explaining the distinction, in Section 2, I shall go on to argue, in Section 3, that Jackson and Pettit's account of the workings of program explanations sheds a lot of light on the functioning of sentential causal explanations, and can help us to see both how we should and why we have to overcome the prejudice which inclines us to suppose that no explanation of a particular effect can be genuinely causal which does not explain that effect by invoking some causally efficacious particular which participated in its production, thus enabling us to get clearer about the sorts of causal relationships which facts can bear one to another. But I do not agree with everything that Jackson and Pettit say about the program–process distinction; indeed, I do not believe that process explanations, in their sense, really exist at all. In Section 4, then, I shall explain what the differences are between my views and those of Jackson and Pettit, by challenging their suggestion that some properties, namely microphysical ones, bear on the effects to which they are causally relevant in a way quite different from that in which other properties belonging to non-physical discourses bear on theirs—by being causally efficacious rather than merely counterfactually relevant.

1. CHILD ON CAUSATION AND CAUSAL EXPLANATION

Child begins his account of the relation between causation and causal explanation by distinguishing two different kinds of answer which Strawson offers at the end of 'Causation and Explanation' to the question what makes an explanation a causal explanation:

On one view, what causal explanations have in common is this: wherever there is a true causal explanation there is, behind it, an instance of causation, a 'natural relation which holds in the natural world between particular events or circumstances, just as the relation of temporal succession does, or that of spatial proximity' . . . On another view, causal explanations are united not by their dependence on a natural relation of causality, but rather by the fact that they are all explanations of the occurrence or persistence of particular events or circumstances, or of general types of event or circumstance; 'cause' is the name of a general categorial notion which we invoke in connection with the explanation of particular circumstances and the discovery of general mechanisms of production of general types of effect.[2]

Child does not make a definite choice between the two views; though he says at one point that he 'incline(s) in the latter direction'.[3] He recognizes that there are difficulties associated with the first view, though he argues that some of the objections which have been raised in opposition to it are less troubling than they have sometimes been thought. And he is anxious that his shift away from the first position, which he regards as a 'broadly Davidsonian picture',[4] towards the second should not be considered a big departure from the Davidsonian view, many important elements of which, he claims, can be retained within the broad outlines of the second model. In short, his position seems to be that though the first position is flawed in detail, it is not hopeless in overall conception, and that many of its insights can be salvaged.

In what follows, I want to discuss these two kinds of answer to the question what makes an explanation a causal explanation. I am in agreement with Child, for reasons already adumbrated in the previous chapter, that the first model cannot be correct—at any rate, not once we accept a particularist conception of the sorts of entities that can stand in 'natural' causal relations. I shall argue, though, that Child seriously underestimates the scale and significance of its failure. Adoption of something like the second position seems to me to be essential if we are to make a place for a view of causation which permits us a non-reductive yet not exclusively human-centred understanding of the relationships between facts which the causal 'because' is used to express. In Section 1.2, therefore, I shall try to say something about the 'general categorial notion' which is our concept of cause.

---

[2] *Causality, Interpretation and the Mind,* 100.
[3] Ibid. 109. Strawson does not choose between them either.
[4] Ibid.

1.1. *Causal Explanation and Natural Relations*

One very straightforward suggestion about the connection between causal explanation and natural causal relations combines the following two theses:

(1) Any true causal explanation must depend for its truth on the holding of a natural relation of causation, and

(2) The relata of the relevant natural relation, where not explicitly mentioned by the causal explanation in question, are nevertheless implicitly revealed by it.

On the assumption, then, that 'natural' causal relations must be relations between particulars of some variety (an assumption which appears to be made both by Child and Strawson) it looks as though (1) and (2) in combination commit us to the view that sentential causal explanations, despite the fact that they do not work straightforwardly by stating that a relation of causation holds between certain particulars, nevertheless manage somehow to point towards particulars between which the natural relation of causation does hold. But it is hard to see how a sentential explanation could point towards these particulars without mentioning them, unless we adopt the view of sentential causal explanations I rejected in Chapter 5, whereby nominalization transcriptions of sentential explanations are thought of as delivering descriptions of the particular entities whose interactions constitute the causal relations which lie behind the original sentential explanation. Nominalization would seem to be the only device available for extracting reference, or apparent reference, to events and states from sentences which contain no singular terms of the appropriate sort to begin with. But I argued in Chapter 5 that this view of sentential explanations could not account either for causal explanations with negative *explanantes* or for stative sententials, and that there was also serious reason to doubt whether it gave a correct account even of causal explanations whose *explanantes* are event predications. Any version of the 'natural relations' view of causal explanation which is committed to (1) and (2), then, I suggest, has already been demonstrated to be untenable.

Another view, though, might be that while we should hang on to the connection between causation and causal explanation which is expressed by (1), there is no need to embrace (2), and in particular, no need to permit the existence of natural relations of causation between entities that are not events, in an attempt to deal with stative and negative sentential explanations. Child suggests one way of thinking about the stative cases. He suggests that reference to causally related events does not have to be 'near the surface' of a causal explanation in order for it to remain the case that the explanation depends for its truth on the presence of appropriate causal relations between events; such reference to events can be 'buried'. He gives the following example. Suppose that we are told that a train crashed because the driver was drunk. We do not need, according to Child, to suppose that this explanation rests on a causal relation between a token state—the drunkenness of the driver—and an event—the crash. Rather, the natural relation of causation on which the truth of the explanation depends is concealed:

Though it is not explicitly mentioned in the explanation, there was an event which caused the crash—the train's crossing the points. Since trains often cross points without crashing, an explanation should tell us what was special about this crossing, why it caused a crash when most crossings do not . . . in saying that the crash happened because the driver was drunk, we select one particularly salient feature of the cause. In some cases we may offer such a feature-citing explanation without even knowing what the cause was; knowing that the driver was drunk, we are sure that, whatever the exact cause, its involving a drunken driver will be a relevant feature. But, even in this case, the truth of an explanation depends ultimately on the obtaining of a causal relation between events.[5]

What are we to say about this suggestion?

The first question that seems worth raising is whether Child is really justified in his assumption that it is always possible to find an appropriate event to serve as the cause of an effect-event, whenever we are faced with a true, sentential, causal explanation of that effect. In dealing with his own example, Child simply helps himself to the assumption that the train crossed some points. But presumably, it need not have done so. Suppose, for example, that what happened before the train crash was this: the driver was supposed to radio ahead to a waiting signalman to notify him of the train's approach—but because he was drunk, he simply failed to do so.

---

[5] *Causality, Interpretation and the Mind*, 102–3.

The signalman therefore failed to notify the driver of a second train that he ought to pull into a siding and wait until the first train had passed. No crossings of points or passings of red lights or any other salient events in the journey of the train are available in this case to be lighted upon and singled out as the cause of the crash. But this does not seem to prevent the driver's drunkenness from figuring in a true causal explanation of the crash.

Child himself notes what is a rather similar difficulty for the modified 'natural relations' view which commits itself only to (1) above, in connection with those explanations which cite the continuous operation of causal *processes*.[6] Suppose, for example, that a bridge collapses because its supports have been slowly rusting for many years, and finally the corroded pillars have become too weak to support the structure. One might try citing this 'becoming' as the event which was the cause of the collapse: the bridge collapsed because one of its pillars became (at that moment, as it were) too weak to support the bridge. Or one might insist that even if we do not know what it is, there must have been some event which triggered the collapse—the final dissolving of some crucial piece of steel, say. But it does not seem to me as though we *have* to conceive of the collapse as triggered by some crucial prior event in order to be justified in regarding an explanation of it which cites the corrosion that has been going on over many years as a causal explanation. If there is any temptation to think that there must have been some such triggering event, I think it has to do with the thought that something must explain why the collapse of the bridge happened when it did, rather than at some other time, rather than being a requirement on the nature of causal explanation as such.

Another difficulty is presented by those explanations which are not themselves explanations of the occurrence of any events, but rather of the existence, or persistence, of certain states of affairs. Here are some examples: 'Why is my suitcase on the rack? That man lifted it up'; 'Why is your dress so creased? I've been sitting on the floor'; 'Why do you believe that this man can perform miracles? Because I saw him heal someone'. All these seem to me to be clear cases of causal explanations—but none is (ostensibly, anyway) the explanation of why some event occurred. It might, of course, be

[6] Ibid. 107.

said, as before, that reference to the events in question is 'buried' in these explanations. For example, the truth of the first explanation might be regarded as dependent upon a relation between the man's lifting up of the suitcase and the suitcase's *coming to be* on the rack, where this latter nominal is intended to pick out an event; the second dependent on a relation between my sitting down and my dress's *becoming creased*, or its *creasing*; the third dependent on a relation between my perception of the healing and my *coming to believe* that the man could perform miracles. But this will not work everywhere; not all causal explanations of static effects can be construed as explanations of how those effects came into existence in the first place. I could ask, for example: 'Why is the water at 78°C after all this time?' and be told 'Because the container is insulated'. This seems to me, again, to be a causal explanation—but it is not an explanation of an event, nor even an explanation which adverts implicitly to an event which caused the onset of some state. Reference to events here, if it exists, is buried deep indeed.[7]

I think, then, that the appeal to underlying events cannot really be the key to understanding why the explanatory power of certain sentential explanations should be regarded as a *causal* variety of explanatory power. We need to look elsewhere for an answer to the question what makes an explanation a causal explanation. And in particular, I think we need to beware of too heavy a reliance on an ontology of events for the explication of our conception of causality. Of course, events can precipitate or trigger other events—that is one important kind of relationship which counts for us as causal. But it is not the only sort. And it will be one of the main contentions of the arguments to follow in Part III that there are great dangers in failing to recognize that there are other sorts, specifically, that the causal relevance of certain facts to certain others is neither assimilable to nor necessarily dependent upon underlying relations between events or other alleged particulars, such as token states or property instances.

---

[7] Someone might think that we could appeal here to certain microphysical events—collisions between water molecules and the container, and so on. But as Child himself notes with reference to a different sort of example (ibid. 108), such an appeal involves a shift from the original position. The original claim was that causal explanations tell stories about causally related events. But in what sense is the explanation 'The water is still at 78°C because the container is insulated' a story about causally related molecular events? I say (and Child seems to agree) that it is not, though there is doubtless a dependence of a different kind here.

What about the second of the Strawsonian models mentioned by Child—the one towards which he inclines? This alternative suggestion is that *cause* 'is the name of a general categorial notion which we invoke in connection with the explanation of particular circumstances and the discovery of general mechanisms of production of general types of effect'.[8] To say this, it might be felt, is not, as yet, to say very much. In a sense, it just seems obvious and trivial; a natural response might be that *of course cause* is the name of a general categorial notion which we invoke in connection with the explanation of things which it seems reasonable to call 'particular circumstances' (e.g. why the water was still at 78°C, why the train crashed, etc.) and also with the discovery of general mechanisms of production of general types of effect (e.g. that smoking causes cancer, unemployment has an effect on the crime rate, etc.). But perhaps if more flesh could be put on the bones of the idea, it could be made the basis of an alternative to the 'natural relations' view. In the next section, then, I shall try to say something about some different ways in which one might attempt to fill out the account.

1.2. 'Cause' as a General Categorial Notion

It may be useful to begin this discussion of the nature of causal explanation by considering some explanations which seem clearly to be of a non-causal variety. Let us begin by considering one which is mentioned by Child—namely that I broke the law because I parked on a yellow line. What is it about this explanation which convinces us that it is not a causal explanation?

A first suggestion might be that the explanation 'I broke the law because I parked on a yellow line' is not causal because it is not an explanation of the occurrence of anything. It does not genuinely explain why a breaking-the-law type event *occurred*—only why an event which occurred anyway, my parking of my car, *counted* as a breaking of the law—what it was about that event which constituted an infringement of legal requirements. But as we have seen, there are plenty of causal explanations which are not explanations of why an event of some sort occurred. Even if it is a sufficient condition of some explanation's being a causal explanation that it

---

[8] 'Causation and Explanation', 135.

explain why an event of some sort occurred, it cannot be a necessary one. So this answer is not good enough as it stands; we need to say something more.

Nevertheless, there is something about this suggestion which seems to be on the right lines. Even if not every causal explanation is an explanation of why some type of event occurred, an explanation of *why I broke the law* that was causal would surely have to be an explanation of the occurrence of a breaking-the-law type event—as, for example, if I were to say that I broke the law because I was feeling rebellious. One hypothesis that suggests itself at this stage, then, is the following: explaining why an event of some sort occurred is one variety of causal explanation—a kind which is associated with those *explananda* which are event predications. And perhaps if we could give some parallel account of those varieties of causal explanation which are associated with kinds of *explananda* which are not event predications, we might be able to find some commonalities between the different varieties which would account for their shared causal status. It would seem sensible, then, to turn to look at some explanations in which the *explananda* are of a different sort, in the hope of discovering what these commonalities might be.

Stative predications can serve as the *explananda* in both causal and non-causal explanations. I can explain, for example, why my porridge is warm by saying that it is because I have just heated it up on the stove—and this would seem to be causal. But I could also say that it is warm because the mean kinetic energy of the particles in the porridge has a value of V—and this seems to be a rather different sort of explanation; intuitively, the relation between my porridge's being warm and the mean kinetic energy of the particles in it is constitutive, not causal. It is tempting to try to make time the crucial factor here—to say that the former explanation adverts to an event which precedes the onset of the state which is my porridge's being warm, whereas the latter adverts to a state which obtains simultaneously—and that this is what explains the difference in their status. But this cannot be right. I could explain causally why my porridge is warm just as easily by saying that it is because it is in an insulated bowl—a state of affairs which we can suppose for the sake of argument does not precede its being warm.

The first causal explanation of why my porridge is warm—the one which adverts to my previously heating it up on the stove—

explains how that state of affairs *came about*, how it was that my porridge came to be warm. The second explains why it is warm by adverting to a condition that helps to maintain it is a warm state. Both these sorts of explanation, I suggested, seem to be causal. Can we say anything about what unifies these two kinds of explanation?—what it is about them which renders both *causal*?—but which disqualifies the explanation which adverts to the mean kinetic energy of the particles in the porridge?

One common resort of philosophers considering examples of this kind is to appeal to the necessity for causes and effects to be distinct from one another. The mean kinetic energy of the particles in the porridge being of value V, for example, might be said not to be a state of affairs distinct from the porridge's being warm. This strategy promises to deal also with the law-breaking case; it might be said that the explanation of my breaking the law which adverts to my parking on a yellow line cannot count as causal because the relationship between my breaking of the law and my parking on a yellow line is constitutive—the fact that I parked on a yellow line constitutes the fact that I broke the law and so cannot cause it. Obviously, anyone employing such a strategy would need to say something more about how we are to decide when one fact constitutes another. But even if we were able to do this satisfactorily, it would seem that it helps us only to detect one variety of non-causal explanation rather than to say what positive characteristics are shared by those which are causal.

A next move might be to draw up a more generous list of the sorts of thing that can be causally explained, at the same level of abstraction and generality as the orginal proposal that a causal explanation is an explanation of why an event of some sort occurred. But any such list would, I think, have to be quite long; and it is hard to see how such a list might be made both liberal enough to include every sort of fact which might conceivably be causally explained and yet strict enough to exclude all non-causal explanations. Here are some of the sorts of thing one can explain causally (doubtless many other categories could be added):

1. Why some sort of event occurred (e.g. why did the light come on?)
2. Why some sort of event failed to occur (e.g. why didn't the light come on?)

3. Why some sort of event occurred when it did (e.g. why did the bridge collapse just then?)
4. Why some event had a certain property (e.g. why was your parking of the car so clumsy?)
5. Why some state of affairs exists (e.g. why is my suitcase on the rack?)
6. Why some state of affairs doesn't exist (e.g. why isn't my suitcase on the rack?)
7. Why some state of affairs still exists (e.g. why is the water still at 78°C?)

But both (4) and (5) look to be in danger of admitting the explanation of why I broke the law that adverts to my having parked on a yellow line. It is not obvious why this explanation should not count as an explanation of why my parking had the property of 'being an infringement of the law', thus falling under (4); or alternatively it might be argued that it is an explanation of why the state of affairs which is my having broken the law exists, thus coming under (5). It seems to me, then, as though this strategy will not work. There is nothing useful to be said at this kind of level of generality about the kinds of questions which are answered by causal explanations. We need to focus instead on what it is about specifically causal explanations of why certain states of affairs exist, or of why events have certain properties, which both distinguishes them from non-causal explanations which also fall into these categories, and unites them with causal explanations of other sorts (e.g. with explanations, both singular and sentential, of why certain events or kinds of event occurred).

Another kind of suggestion might be to look to the counterfactual claims which are associated with explanations and to the generalizations which support these counterfactuals, in an attempt to show that the relevant generalizations in the case of causal explanations are of a special sort. I am not at all inclined to be sympathetic to what is perhaps the most common suggestion of this kind—namely that causal counterfactuals are distinctive in being supported by strict laws. There are too many explanations which seem to me to be clearly causal which are associated at best with loose generalizations to make this an attractive strategy. But there are more appealing ways of linking the concept of causal explanation to the sorts of generalization which support associated counterfactuals. David Owens, for example, has put forward a more moderate account of this sort in his book *Causes and Coincidences*.[9] Owens's suggestion is that only causal counterfactuals are supported by generalizations which have what he calls 'empirical content'. The subjunctive conditional 'If I had not parked on a yellow line, I would not have broken the law', for example, is supported, as Owens puts it, 'by a law of the state rather than a law of nature'.[10] That anyone parking on a yellow line thereby breaks the law is a general truth which it would make no sense to attempt to verify empirically, case by case.[11] It would, I think, be too stringent to insist that all causal explanations must be associated with counterfactuals which are supported by laws of nature, as Owens seems to imply in some places, unless the concept of a law of nature is to be made extremely weak—weak enough to include, for example, all the loose social, economic, and psychological generalizations on which the intelligibility of a given causal explanation might depend. But the idea that the sorts of generalization which might be associated with causal explanations are of a special sort—a sort which have 'empirical content'—is quite attractive, and promises to deal with a range of non-causal explanations quite successfully. All of Child's other examples of non-causal explanations, for instance, succumb without difficulty to the Owens criterion.[12] That the delivery was a no-ball because the bowler overstepped the crease, for example, is associated with the counterfactual: 'If the bowler hadn't overstepped the crease, the delivery wouldn't have been a no-ball'—and this is supported by a rule of cricket, not an empirical generalization about what tends to give rise to no-balls. That Xanthippe became a widow because she was married to Socrates and Socrates died is associated with a generalization that is a priori, not empirical; as Owens remarks in connection with a similar example, it would be silly to say: 'Are you sure that's why she became a widow? Let's not commit ourselves until we've investigated a bit further'. And

[9] D. Owens, *Causes and Coincidences* (Cambridge, 1992).
[10] Ibid. 72.
[11] One could verify empirically, of course, that many or most people parking on yellow lines receive parking-tickets or end up with demands for fines. But the corresponding explanations in these cases, namely 'He received a parking-ticket because he parked on a yellow line' and 'He received a demand for a fine because he parked on a yellow line', arguably *are* causal explanations.
[12] *Causality, Interpretation and the Mind*, 91–2.

Child's final example—that it is more likely than not that a random selection of twenty-three people will contain two with the same birthday because the probability of their all having different birthdays is $(365 \times 364 \times \ldots 343) \div 365^{23}$, which is less than half—can also be accommodated by Owens's criterion; the generalization which supports it is a priori, not an empirical, but a mathematical, truth.

There are, however, examples which might seem to be more troubling for Owens. That my porridge is warm because the particles in it have a mean kinetic energy of value V, for instance, seems to be associated with a generalization which has empirical content, even though, as I remarked earlier, it is tempting to deny that the explanation is causal. And I have three further, more general concerns about Owens's account—two of which amount really to nothing more than vague feelings of unease about its shape, but the third of which seems to present a real difficulty about accepting it as the right way of distinguishing causal from non-causal explanations in the context of the rest of my views. The first worry, one which is bound to assail almost any philosopher, and which Owens does a good job of trying to allay, is just about whether the notion of a generalization's having empirical content can be made clear and determinate enough to do the work required of it by Owens. The second is that Owens's account of what it is for an explanation to be a causal explanation seems, in a sense, to be *too complicated*. One might put the point by saying that even if it were true that the application of Owens's criterion served perfectly well (and for non-accidental reasons) to divide causal from non-causal explanations in a way that squared perfectly with ordinary intuitions, it does not really explain what, at root, it is that *makes* these explanations causal. It seems to me that we ought to be able to say something more basic about the general categorial notion of *cause*, without having immediately to invoke the sort of complex theoretical machinery that Owens relies upon. It might be, of course, that anything available to be said without the help of this kind of philosophical machinery would fail necessarily to explicate the concept of causal explanation in terms analytically independent of the concept of causality itself—but the concept of causality being as basic as it is, it might be foolish to think we can really say what a causal explanation is while remaining outside the circle of a certain small family of related concepts.

My third worry is that Owens's account leaves unanswered the question what relates those sentential explanations which pass his test, and therefore count as causal explanations, to singular causal claims, like 'The dictator caused the war' or 'The famine caused the flood'. These explanations might be thought to support counterfactuals of a kind—e.g. 'If it hadn't been for the dictator, the war wouldn't have happened'.[13] But there don't seem to be any obvious empirical generalizations to be made about dictators and wars—or even if there are, they are not necessary to the causal status of the singular causal claim, as one can see by reflecting that other uniquely identifying descriptions of the dictator could perfectly well be substituted for 'the dictator'—e.g. 'the man with the largest model-train collection in the Western hemisphere'—without damaging the causal status of the explanation. Owens leaves this question unanswered because he assumes that it is possible to treat singular causal claims as sentential ones—he suggests, for example, that 'the match's striking caused the match's lighting' should be construed as equivalent to 'the match lit because it was struck'.[14] I argued, however, in Chapter 5 that the former is neither equivalent to, nor even implies, the latter—so this strategy is untenable. How, then, are we to fit singular causal claims into Owens's account of what makes for a causal explanation?

One possibility at this point would be to try to bind singular causal explanations together with their sentential counterparts by means of something like the following hypothesis: to say that X caused Y, where X and Y are particulars, is simply to say that there is some description $D(X)$ of X and some description $D(Y)$ of Y such that a sentence of the form '... $D(X)$ ... because ... $D(Y)$ ...' is true, where the 'because' can be read as a causal 'because', according to the Owens criterion. For example, to say that the dictator caused the famine, on this hypothesis, would be to say that there is some description of the dictator and some description of the famine which would enable us to bring the singular causal relation between them within the scope of some generalization with empirical

[13] Though there is room for debate, I suppose, about whether they actually imply such counterfactuals. Arguably, it is possible to think that the war might have occurred anyway, even without the dictator, compatibly with its being true that he did in fact cause it. What one thinks about this issue is going to depend on complicated questions to do with transworld identity for events which I do not want to get involved in here.

[14] *Causes and Coincidences*, 60.

content. Perhaps we could find such descriptions (perhaps, for example, the dictator could be brought under the description 'powerful ruler with territorial ambitions who began a war against a neighbouring country, thereby ensuring that insufficient people remain in agricultural production') and the relevant empirical generalization might connect the existence of such rulers with the occurrence of famines during their rule. But once again, this seems to me much too complex an account of what it is for a dictator to cause a famine. Do we really commit ourselves necessarily to all this theoretical baggage about empirical generalizations, the moment we make a singular causal claim? And can we be confident in any case that we will always be able to find such generalizations?[15] There are doubtless important things to be said about the relationship between causes and empirical generalizations, but it seems wrong to me to suppose that the latter can be used to give any kind of reductive explication of the former.

It may be that the best hope of explicating the 'general categorial notion' which is our concept of *cause* may lie with the possibility of resigning ourselves to acceptance of the point I made earlier—namely that we will be unable to say much at all about it in terms which are genuinely independent of the concept of causation itself—it is too basic to admit of analysis in the strict sense. What we must do, if we are to understand what it is that binds together all those explanations which we are disposed to think of as offering a *causal* rather than some other kind of understanding of a phenomenon, is to say something about our purpose in providing specifically causal explanations of events and circumstances, and of producing generalizations on the basis of the specific instances of causality which we encounter.[16] Perhaps, for example, we might say

---

[15] Cf. Anscombe, 'Causality and Determination', ii. 147: 'Meanwhile . . . it is clear enough what are the dogmatic slumbers of the day. It is over and over again assumed that any singular causal proposition implies a universal statement running 'Always when this, then that'; often assumed that true singular causal statements are derived from such 'inductively believed' universalities. Examples indeed are recalcitrant but that does not seem to disturb . . . Such a thesis needs some reason for believing it!'

[16] This is, of course, a rather tendentious description. It is a very widespread view that, as Strawson puts it, 'causal generalisations are not generalisations of particular instances of causality; rather, particular instances of causality are established as such only by the particularising of causal generalisations' ('Causation and Explanation', 119). But I have hoped to distance myself somewhat from this widespread view.

that a causal understanding of something or other is an understanding of why the world is as it is in a certain respect—either why it is or why it is not a certain way—which appeals either to how it came about that it is as it is in the first place or to what maintains it as it is. It is a feature of our world that we can bring things about by bringing other things about, or maintain things in a certain way by ensuring that conditions remain a certain way, or prevent things from happening by preventing certain other things from happening. We have an enormous interest in this feature of our world; it is tremendously important to our survival and to the success of all our projects. And reference both to particulars and to facts may figure in the provision of the wanted sorts of understanding—which is what explains why there are both singular and sentential forms of causal explanation. I might, for example, want to find out what specifically is causing the rattle in the back of my car in order to be able to intervene and fix it—and this search will be the search for a particular cause, for the thing which is making the noise. But there are also kinds of causal enquiry where the search is not for a particular, but rather for a fact about the way things are, which contributed to an effect, and which, if it could be manipulated, might enable us to control similar sorts of effect in the future. I might, for example, be interested in finding out what conditions are favourable to dust-mites in order to discourage them from living in my carpets—if I discover that humidity is helpful to them, I might consider installing a dehumidifier. But to discover that humidity is helpful to dust-mites is not to discover anything about the role played by a particular in the production of some effect; it is to discover that a kind of fact (a fact about the number of dust-mites living in my carpet) depends on a certain other sort of fact (a fact about the amount of humidity in the room)—a dependence which counts as causal because it is associated with the possibility of effecting a change in the one fact by changing the other.

A question, though, seems to arise at this point about the structure of the dialectic so far. I began by accepting for the purposes of discussion the contrast drawn by Strawson and endorsed, in some measure, by Child, between those accounts of causal explanation according to which every causal explanation is underpinned somehow by a 'natural' relation of causation, and those which suggest rather that cause is a 'general categorial notion which we invoke in connection with the explanation of particular circumstances and the discovery of general mechanisms of production of general types of effect'. I have suggested that the second of these kinds of account is to be preferred to the first, and I have tried to say something about what sorts of explanations of 'particular circumstances' might count as the causal ones. But it may seem that in the process of doing so, the distinction between the two sorts of account has been made unclear. Surely, it might be said, the possibility of reaching a causal understanding of any phenomenon has to depend somehow on the existence of causal relations in nature. That we are able to cause or prevent one thing by bringing about or preventing another, or maintain some state of affairs by maintaining some other, or make one thing the case by making something else the case—all these sorts of fact surely depend on the existence of causal relations in nature. It might be doubted, therefore, whether we are at liberty simply to consider the 'general categorial' view as an *alternative* to the 'natural relations' view; it might be said that its very intelligibility depends on the possibility of regarding causal explanations as dependent upon underlying 'natural' relations.

It needs to be recalled, though, that what I rejected was not the view that causal explanations depend somehow on causal relations which exist in nature, but only the very specific doctrine that each causal explanation depends upon a natural relation of causation, where 'natural' relations are permitted to hold only between *particulars*. What I argued specifically was that there were many varieties of causal explanation which could not be regarded in any straightforward way as dependent for their causal status on any underlying causal relationships between events. But perhaps we ought not to be so quick to make the assumption that 'natural' relations have to be relations between particulars. Strawson says two things about natural relations. The first characteristic of natural relations is that they are supposed to hold as a matter of objective, human-independent fact; they are contrasted with those relations (like explanatory relations) which are, in Strawson's words, 'intellectual or rational or intensional', which depend for their existence on 'natural facts about our human selves'.[17] And if we are realists about causation, then causal relations 'in the world', those which underwrite the possibility of our reaching a causal

---

[17] 'Causation and Explanation', 117.

understanding of the way things are, and of our changing and manipulating the way things are in various respects, ought not to fall on the non-natural side of *this* divide. But Strawson also suggests that natural relations 'hold between things in the natural world, things to which we can assign places and times in nature'.[18] And perhaps there is some room for manœuvre in the recognition that there may be a need to separate these two senses of 'natural'. If we could do this, we might be able to make room for the idea that there could be causal relations which were natural in the first sense, but not natural in the second; whose holding was not essentially dependent on human enlightenment or understanding, but which could nevertheless not be fully understood or expressed without invoking resources which outrun those which are provided by a simple two-place predicate and a domain of spatiotemporal particulars. For it seems clear that we use the language of causation not only to record causal relations between particular events, but also to express our commitment to broad, counterfactually supported dependencies of phenomena of different sorts on *facts* of various kinds. And there seems to be no reason to suppose that when we speak in this way, the dependencies to which we thereby draw attention are relations which hold only in virtue of the propensities of human beings to find the mention of these facts explanatorily compelling. Just because facts are not things 'in the world', at least not in the same sense as particulars are things 'in the world', it does not follow that we cannot use the language of facts to record dependencies which *are* objective, rooted in reality. There may simply be no need to retreat from the perception that the relata of some relation are not 'natural' entities in Strawson's second sense to the assumption that any sentence which affirms that the relation holds between two such entities asserts that some explanatory, or otherwise human-dependent relation obtains.

In the next section, I want to attempt to say something more about how this idea might be developed. What we need to achieve is an understanding of the causal relationships between facts which are 'natural' in Strawson's first, but not in his second sense; and in order to achieve this, it seems to me, we need to loosen the grip of the idea that since facts cannot literally *do* anything, since (quite plausibly) they cannot literally be the bearers of causal power or

[18] Ibid. 115.

causal efficacy, they cannot stand in relations to one another that deserve to be called causal. The concept which I shall place at the heart of my account is the concept of *causal relevance*. Facts, I shall suggest, though evidently they cannot be causes of the same sort as either events or particular things, can be causally relevant to various effects—and it is essential for the proper understanding of a very large category of causal explanations that we understand properly the distinction between causal relevance, in this sense, on the one hand, what I shall call *causing*, the extensional relation which is expressed by the two-place predicate 'cause', and *causal efficacy*, a property which I shall suggest is best conceived of as belonging only to particulars, on the other. But I shall introduce this distinction in something of a roundabout way. I want to begin by looking first at Jackson and Pettit's account of the distinction between two sorts of explanation which they call, respectively, *program* and *process* explanations.[19] According to Jackson and Pettit, program explanations succeed in throwing a kind of light on the effects which they explain which justifies their classification as causal, even though they do not work by directly invoking any causally efficacious entities; and since this is the very possibility that we are interested in understanding, it seems reasonable to suppose that Jackson and Pettit's distinction might be worth consideration. I disagree significantly with many aspects of Jackson and Pettit's account; but I do think that their account of the workings of program explanations is enormously helpful as a means of understanding the role played by facts in causality. Without more ado, then, I shall turn to their explication of the distinction between program and process explanations.

2. PROGRAM AND PROCESS EXPLANATIONS

Jackson and Pettit's account of the program–process distinction starts from a consideration of a class of explanations which they take to express commitment to the causal relevance, in respect of certain sorts of effect, of the dispositional properties of objects.

[19] The most important papers are 'Functionalism and Broad Content', 'Program Explanation: A General Perspective', 'Causation in the Philosophy of Mind', and 'Structural Explanation in Social Theory'.

They take it to be natural to make the assumption that dispositional properties are sometimes causally relevant to particular effects, and offer various examples in support of this assumption: a glass can break because it is fragile, Fred's life can be saved because his seatbelt is elastic, and so on. It needs to be noted immediately, though, that the explanations which Jackson and Pettit take to be revelatory of the causal relevance of certain *properties* are sentential explanations. Jackson and Pettit construe these sentential explanations as evidence of the causal relevance of properties, rather than taking them, as I have done, to express causal relationships, of a sort, between facts. But for the moment, I shall speak as they do, and talk of the causal relevance of properties. As a matter of fact, I do not think there is any real distinction between the two ways of putting things—any sentence necessarily contains a predicate, and any sentential *explanans* which occurs in a causal explanation will therefore necessarily contain some expression which can be readily converted into the name of a property—a property which can then be said to have causal relevance to the effect in question. I am not really averse, then, to speaking of the causal relevance of properties. But it will become clear later that Jackson and Pettit's preference for properties over facts is associated with an understanding of the role which can be played by properties in causal explanations which I do not share—and for this reason, I shall ultimately return to an ontology of facts in order to explicate the concept of causal relevance.

Jackson and Pettit point out that given certain widely held assumptions the attribution of causal relevance to dispositional properties can come to seem puzzling. For how are we to understand the role played in causality by properties such as fragility and elasticity, given that (in their view) a fully satisfying account of why the glass broke, why Fred's life was saved, and so on can be given in terms of the dispositions' categorical bases? Doesn't this make it seem as though the dispositional properties, at least once we admit them to be distinct from the categorical properties which may ground them in a particular case, must have been causally impotent, and therefore causally irrelevant?

Jackson and Pettit insist that we should not draw this conclusion. The causal relevance of a dispositional property, they allege, is a matter of the existence of a phenomenon which they label 'invariance of effect under variation of realization'.[20] Here is the non-dispositional example which they use to elucidate the idea. Suppose that Smith takes ten grains of arsenic which causes him to die about ten minutes later. Jones also takes ten grains of arsenic—and he also dies ten minutes later. Jackson and Pettit ask when it would be right to say that the fact that they both died in about the same time is explained by the fact that they both took the same amount of arsenic. Clearly, not if the time taken to die after taking a given dose is given by a complex formula involving body weight, which gives in the case of Smith and Jones very different times to die for all possible doses, with the sole exception of the case in which the dose happens to be ten grains. In that case, the explanation of their taking the same time to die would have to be that they both took ten grains, not that they took identical doses. Jackson and Pettit suggest that this example shows something rather important about causal relevance—namely that we are often interested, when looking for causally relevant factors, not merely in the details of what actually happened, but in what would have happened in a range of other cases. There are many different particular ways in which Smith and Jones might have taken the same dose—rather than taking ten grains, both could have taken nine grains or eleven grains, and so on—or, to put it as Jackson and Pettit prefer, there are many ways in which Smith and Jones's taking the same dose might have been 'realized'. If in a large range of these cases, Smith and Jones would have died in the same time after taking the same dose, then it is right to say that the doses' being the same was causally relevant to the fact that they died after the same amount of time. If, on the other hand, taking eleven or nine grains each would have resulted in Smith and Jones taking different lengths of time to die, then the doses' being equal is not causally relevant—it is their both having taken ten grains that matters.

How is this supposed to help us see how dispositional properties can have causal relevance? The idea is that dispositional properties secure their claim to causal relevance in the same sort of way as did Smith and Jones's both taking the same dose, in a case in which the time taken to die by someone who has just taken arsenic is a simple function of the dose taken. There are many ways in which a property like fragility or elasticity might be realized by a categorical base, just as there are many ways in which Smith and Jones might have taken the same dose of arsenic. But it may not matter for the production of a particular sort of effect which of these realizations is actually present in the case in question. Provided some categorical basis or other for a certain level of fragility is present in the glass, for example, the glass will break; provided some categorical basis or other for a certain degree of elasticity is present in the seatbelt, Fred's life will be saved. And this, Jackson and Pettit allege, enables us to see how dispositional properties can have causal relevance, despite the fact that the 'causal work' in any particular case is all done, in their view, by instances of categorical properties. The relevance of the disposition to any given effect is a matter of the fact that, provided the appropriate dispositional property is present, some categorical basis or other capable of producing the same sort of effect must also be present—or, in Jackson and Pettit's terminology, the dispositional property 'programs for' the categorical ones on which it depends.

Jackson and Pettit argue that it is not merely causal explanations which invoke dispositional properties which can be illuminated by recourse to this idea of one property's 'programming for' others. Rather, they suggest, a very broad range of explanations indeed ought to be regarded as working in much the same sort of way. They call the relevant explanations 'program' explanations. It is distinctive of a program explanation that the explanatory property to which it directs us is not itself a causally efficacious property; rather, it is a property of a kind such that its instantiation in the case in question ensures that some property or other which *is* of the causally efficacious sort, appropriate for bringing about the sort of effect which is explained by the explanation, is also instantiated. Such explanations are widely used, according to Jackson and Pettit, in the social sciences and in the higher reaches of natural science, as well as in folk psychology and a wide variety of other everyday contexts. Indeed, given the view, which Jackson and Pettit appear inclined to embrace, that only microphysical properties can be causally efficacious, it looks as though almost all sentential causal explanations must be program explanations. Process explanations, those which do advert to causally efficacious properties, would seem to be confined to utterly basic physics.

Jackson and Pettit are at pains to stress that a causal explanation is not necessarily any less useful for failing to identify a causally efficacious property. In many kinds of case, indeed, as Jackson and Pettit point out, a program explanation is *preferable* to a process explanation, even when both are on offer. For we are often interested not just in what actually happened in a particular case but in what *would* have happened had certain things been slightly different. To take one of their examples, consider a situation in which Mary dies because she allows her aluminium ladder to touch some power-lines. We could say of her death that it occurred because the ladder was a good conductor of electricity. But electrical conductivity depends on the existence of a cloud of free electrons permeating the metal—so we might also say that Mary's death occurred because of the instantiation of this lower-level property by the metal. But the cloud of free electrons is the categorical basis of a large number of the properties of the aluminium ladder—its thermal conductivity, its lustre, and its ductility, for example. Yet it was not because the ladder was lustrous, or because it was a good conductor of heat, that Mary died. Why not?—given that the cloud of free electrons which 'does the causal work' is the categorical basis of all these different properties? The answer is simply that *other* possible cases matter to us in settling on the right causal explanation— would Mary have died, for example, if her ladder had been made of wood or if she had been wearing rubber shoes? To answer such questions as these we need the program explanation of her death— not the one which gives the categorical basis. If lustre is important, for example, then shiny wooden ladders might be as dangerous as metallic ones. But if electrical conductivity is what matters, we know what sorts of materials would have saved Mary's life—and we know what sorts of ladders to use in future. In a perfectly good sense, then, the electrical conductivity of the ladder is *causally relevant* to Mary's death, in a way that its thermal conductivity is not, even if we decide that it was the cloud of free electrons, the basis of both these higher-level properties, that 'did the causal work'. The causal relevance of the properties cited by program explanations is a matter of what changes would have made a difference, of which counterfactuals are true. A property thus does not need to be efficacious in order to be causally relevant to some given effect.

It is not true, then, conclude Jackson and Pettit, that causal explanations of events which cite lower-level factors always render higher-level explanations of those same events redundant; nor that the properties cited by those higher-level explanations are causally irrelevant to the effect-event. For questions about causal relevance are often questions not only about the actual scenario, but also about counterfactual ones. In asking whether or not some property is relevant to the production of some effect, that is, we need not be asking whether it (or some instance of it) was efficacious in that particular case; we may rather be asking what difference it would have made had that property not been instantiated. And the program explanations tell us this: the glass would not have broken, or would have been less likely to break, had it not been fragile; Mary would not have died, or would have been less likely to die, if her ladder had not been a good conductor of electricity.[21] It is these counterfactual conditionals which secure the right of the higher-level features in question to be accounted causally relevant, and it does not matter, according to Jackson and Pettit, if we can find other, lower-level properties which have a clear title to be regarded as the causally efficacious ones. For the fact is, the two sets of properties are simply not in competition with one another. The causal relevance of one feature is quite compatible with the causal efficaciousness of the other. Being efficacious is only one way of being causally relevant.

Should we accept the program–process distinction? In the next section, I shall try to argue that Jackson and Pettit's account of the workings of program explanations, with its insistence on the importance of counterfactual considerations, questions about what would and would not, in other circumstances, have averted the effect, etc., is a basically correct account of the workings of the huge class of causal explanations which I have classified as sentential. But at the same time, I shall try to show that the program–process distinction *as Jackson and Pettit characterize it* is confused. For they set the distinction up as though it were a distinction between those explanations which do and those which do not make reference to causally efficacious *properties* (though, as I have already mentioned, their examples indicate that, actually, the range of explanations they have in mind are of sentential form).

[21] It is not important for my purposes in this book to decide whether '*P* because *Q*' implies that *Q* be a condition causally necessary, in the circumstances, for *P*, or merely one which makes it more likely to be the case that *P*, given the other circumstances. I shall therefore normally continue to use this sort of disjunctive formulation.

The distinction is then introduced as a distinction *within* a class of explanations, all of which are understood to share this basic logical character, and roughly speaking, what it then seems to be is a distinction which has to do entirely with *levels* of explanation—a distinction between those lower-level, microphysical explanations which do, and those higher-level explanations which do not, make reference to causally efficacious properties. But in my view we need to abandon the idea that there are any explanations at all of the sort which Jackson and Pettit call process explanations, explanations which involve properties which bear on an effect in a way different from that in which the properties invoked by program explanations bear on their effects, by being efficacious rather than by merely being relevant in a non-efficacy-involving way.[22] The distinction between efficacy and relevance ought to be deployed not as a distinction between the way in which the properties of physics and properties of higher levels have their causal influence, but as a distinction between the role played by particulars in causation, on the one hand, and the role played by facts on the other.

3. SENTENTIAL EXPLANATIONS AS PROGRAM EXPLANATIONS

How does Jackson and Pettit's account of the workings of program explanations help us to deal with our original worry about making facts the relata of the causal relation? The original fear, recall, was that facts in the 'thin' sense in which I have used the term were unsuited to be the bearers of causal efficacy. But if Jackson and Pettit's account of the workings of the large number of sentential causal explanations which fall into their 'program' category is correct, there is no need to find facts to be causally efficacious in order to grant them causal relevance. Translating from Jackson and Pettit's property vocabulary to my own preferred ontology of facts, for example, we can say that Smith and Jones's taking the same dose of arsenic is a fact causally relevant to the fact that they took

---

[22] This rather clumsy way of putting things is necessitated by the fact that Jackson and Pettit regard efficacy as a *form* of relevance. From now on, though, for convenience, I shall use the term 'relevance' exclusively to mean 'non-efficacy-involving' relevance. Efficaciousness, on my usage, therefore, is not a kind of causal relevance—it is something else entirely.

the same amount of time to die—despite the fact that it is not the sort of thing that could have efficacy. The same is true of the fact that Mary's ladder was a good conductor of electricity—though it was not efficacious, that is no reason to deny that it was causally relevant. And so on. Distinguishing relevance from efficacy enables us to avoid the worry about how entities whose mode of being is quasi-linguistic can enter into causal transactions, about Vendler's 'mésalliance' between 'flesh-and-blood' events and 'shadowy' facts.[23] For what Jackson and Pettit's account of program explanations suggests is that causal relevance ought really to be understood as a *modal* notion, not a transactional one. The causal relevance of a fact is not just a matter of how something in fact came about but also of how and whether it would have come about had things been different. Since this is a matter of how things are in other possible worlds, we need modal resources to explicate the idea. For example, that the glass was fragile was causally relevant to the fact that it broke because it wouldn't have broken, or would have been less likely to break, if it had not been fragile. That Smith and Jones took the same dose of arsenic was causally relevant to the fact that they died in the same amount of time because if they had not taken the same dose, they would not have died, or would have been less likely to die, in the same amount of time. The causal relevance of a fact is a matter of what would have happened had the fact not been a fact, had the sentence which expresses the fact been false instead of true. It is a matter, that is, of which counterfactuals hold in the relevant circumstances, of what changes would have made a difference, not of what 'causing' the fact itself—or any 'token states' or 'property instances', terms for which are derived by nominalization from the sentence which expresses the fact—got up to.

It might be said that this is just a counterfactual analysis of causation and that all the usual attendant difficulties and counterexamples are waiting in the wings. I do not want here to get embroiled too deeply in the pros and cons of counterfactual analyses of causation. But I need to fend off at least a few likely objections and to explain how my account can avoid them.

The first point to make is that I am not offering a counterfactual analysis of causation. To start with, what I say here is intended only to apply to sentential causal claims, not to singular ones, so it is not

---

[23] See Ch. 5, Sect. 5.

supposed to be a general account of causation at all. But secondly, I am not interested in endorsing any straightforward equivalence of the form 'The fact that p is causally relevant to the fact that q if and only if, had p not been the case, q would not have been the case (or would have been less likely to be the case) either'. In particular, I do not want to insist on the first half of this biconditional—the half which makes the existence of a true counterfactual of the appropriate sort *sufficient* for the existence of a relation of causal relevance between p and q. It seems obvious that counterfactual claims can be true for many reasons and that the causal relevance of p for q is only one kind of relationship between p and q which supports counterfactuals. p and q might, for example, be the same fact—in which case, it seems true that had p not been the case, q would not have been the case either—but p was not causally relevant to q. Or p might be the fact that some penny fell heads up and q the fact that it fell tails down; it is then true that had the penny not fallen heads up, it would not have fallen tails down, but not true that the fact that the penny fell heads up was causally relevant to the fact that it fell tails down.[24] Neither do I want to make good this deficiency in the counterfactual analysis, as is often done, by supplementing it with the condition that p and q must be 'distinct existences'—for p and q are *facts*, not particulars, and I do not think the concept of a 'distinct existence' applies at all naturally to facts. Rather, I think it best just to accept that we will not succeed in *analysing* the concept of causal relevance—in explicating all that is meant by it—by appealing to counterfactuals. For we will need to explain what makes the difference between those counterfactuals which are associated with relations of causal relevance and those which are sustained by some other relation between facts, and to explain this, we will need to look beyond the counterfactual analysis, to the 'general categorial notion' of *cause* which I have already spent some time trying to explicate. Thus, for example, we might say that the reason why the fact that the penny fell heads up is not causally relevant to the fact that it fell tails down, despite the truth of the appropriate counterfactual, is that it does not offer an explanation which tells us how the penny *came to be* tails down. But this poses no problems, for the point of counterfactuals in my account is not to provide a reductive analysis of causality, but rather to show how a

[24] This example is due to J. L. Mackie; see *The Cement of the Universe* (Oxford, 1980), 32.

causal explanation can be true without invoking any actual causal relations between particulars.

It might seem, though, that I do need at least to accept that the truth of an appropriate counterfactual is a *necessary* condition of the existence of a relation of causal relevance between facts, or between facts and events. For if relations of causal relevance can exist between facts though no appropriate counterfactuals are true, it will need to be explained what makes for the truth of the relevant causal explanations in these cases—and we would then have another puzzle of the same shape as before. So it would be problematic if it were to turn out that relations of causal relevance between facts can exist though the corresponding counterfactuals could not be endorsed. But there seem to be such cases. For example, suppose that Mary's death by electrocution is not, after all, an accident, and that she is sent out to fix a cable with the aluminium ladder by someone who wishes to see her dead. Worried whether his plot will succeed, this person waits below in the bushes with a gun, just in case Mary manages to carry out her task without electrocuting herself; he will shoot her if she comes down alive. In such a case, assuming that the person in question has a loaded gun, is a good shot, etc., it seems false that Mary would not have died if her ladder had not been a good conductor of electricity; the circumstances being as they were, she would have died in any case. But surely, the ladder's being a good conductor of electricity was causally relevant to her death.

The key to examples like this, I think, is to distinguish between particular and sentential *effects*.[25] It is true that the fact that Mary's ladder was a good conductor of electricity was causally relevant to her *death*, to the fact that that particular death occurred. But we need not say that it was causally relevant to the fact that she died, in a case where we know she would have died anyway. Surely it would be quite natural to say that the conductivity of the ladder was irrelevant, in such circumstances. But now the relevant counterfactuals agree in their truth values with our judgements of causal relevance. We can say (1) that the fact that Mary's ladder was a good conductor of electricity was causally relevant to her death, (2) that Mary's death would not have occurred if her ladder had not been a good conductor of electricity, (3) that the fact that Mary's

---

[25] This is the basis of David Lewis's solution to similar supposed counterexamples—see 'Causation', in Lewis, *Philosophical Papers*, ii (Oxford, 1986).

ladder was a good conductor of electricity was causally irrelevant to the fact that she died, and (4) that it is not true that Mary would not have died had her ladder not been a good conductor of electricity.

Someone might, I suppose, agree with all this, but insist that it is very strange to deny that Mary died because her ladder was a good conductor of electricity. I agree that this does seem strange. But I think it would be a mistake to conclude from this that we need to abandon the counterfactual account. I think what explains our reluctance to accede to the verdict delivered by the counterfactual in this case is the fact that, as Strawson notes, ordinary language is not always careful about the distinction between sentential and particular effects, and so it is perfectly possible to understand or intend an explanation which is formally of the sentential sort as an explanation of an event.[26] Sometimes this is signalled; in the case at issue, for example, we might indicate that we mean to focus on the particular event, Mary's death, by saying something like 'Yes, but whether or not this assassin was waiting in the bushes, surely Mary *in fact* died because her ladder was a good conductor of electricity'. But what can we mean by saying that she in fact died because of this property of her ladder if not that this was relevant to her actual death? It is thus the thought that Mary's actual death would not have occurred were it not for her ladder's being a good conductor of electricity that makes us reluctant to deny that she died because of that fact.

I have still not addressed what I think many will regard as the main objection to the invocation of counterfactuals to help with the explanation of causal relevance. I think the main objection would run something like this: what we really need is an understanding of what *grounds* sentential causal explanations, what makes them true, when they are true. What we have been told so far is that they are associated with counterfactuals. But this is not satisfactory. For counterfactuals are not the sort of propositions whose truth can ground the truth of another sort of proposition; they are not the sorts of propositions which can be regarded as simply true. In particular, we cannot say that the truth of sentences of the form '*p* because *q*' is to be explicated by reference to the fact that if *q* had

---

[26] '... it simply need not be true of the ordinary language speaker either that he means to speak consistently at one level or the other or that he mixes levels. It is often simply that he does not distinguish the levels because he has no need to' ('Causation and Explanation', 116).

not been true, *p* would not have been true either. For what sustains this counterfactual, if not real causal relations in the world?

I think the answer to this question is simply that the sort of dependencies amongst facts which causal counterfactuals encode just *are* real causal relations in the world. We have to accept that it really can be objectively and straightforwardly true that something can be a fact because (causally) something else is, that one truth can depend causally on another. This is precisely to insist on separating the two senses in which a relation can be a 'natural' relation which I mentioned at the end of Section 1.2 above. Evidently, relations between facts are not relations between ordinary spatiotemporal particulars, and so they are not 'natural' relations in Strawson's second sense. But this does not make them into intellectual or rational relations, relations which are in any way whatever dependent on 'natural facts about our human selves'.[27] Even if there were not and never had been any human beings, it would still be true that the earth revolves around the sun because it is a massive body, that particular pieces of metal expand because they get hot, that explosions occur because methane is present, and so on. Facts would still be causally relevant to other facts, even if there was no one around to say so. For of course we do not create facts by using sentences, any more than we create objects by using singular terms; and neither do we create the causal dependencies amongst them merely by linking them by means of the sentence functor 'because'. It is just a mistake to suppose that we could express all the causal truths there are with a two-place predicate and a domain of spatiotemporal particulars; for the domain of causality is simply not exhausted by the singular relationships we can express with these meagre resources. As well as 'what caused . . . ?' we ask 'what mattered?', 'what was relevant?'—and these questions demand consideration not just of the productive relationships which actually existed in the case in question, but also of how things are in possible worlds other than our own.

4. WHY THERE ARE NO CAUSALLY EFFICACIOUS PROPERTIES

It remains to explain what I believe is wrong with Jackson and Pettit's account of the program–process distinction. The main

[27] Ibid. 117.

difficulty, in my view, is their assumption that a certain small number of properties—namely those which belong to microphysical discourse—owe what causal relevance they have, not merely to the counterfactually characterizable relationships which constitute the causal relevance of other sorts of properties, but rather to their possession of something which Jackson and Pettit call 'causal efficacy'.

But what exactly is causal efficacy? And why should we believe that microphysical properties have any? Why, for example, should we think that properties to do with possession of a certain mass or charge (if these are indeed basic enough to count as microphysical) owe their relevance in respect of the effects which they can be invoked to explain to relationships which are any different in kind from those which properties belonging to non-physical discourse bear to the effects to which they are relevant? Why should we believe that any properties are efficacious, rather than simply relevant in the counterfactually based, non-efficacy-involving way which Jackson and Pettit have helped us understand?

Jackson and Pettit's reason for wanting to postulate the existence of at least some properties with causal efficacy appears to be the not unnatural thought that *something* must have efficacy; something must be 'doing the causal work' which, ultimately, brings about change in our universe. Their considered view, indeed, actually seems to be that it is not properties, but rather property *instances*, which ultimately do this causal work—presumably on the grounds that properties, being universals, do not really have the right kind of presence in the spatiotemporal framework to do the pushing and pulling which is involved in 'doing causal work'. In 'Program Explanation: A General Perspective', for example, Jackson and Pettit write that a causally efficacious property is 'a property in virtue of whose instantiation the effect occurs; the instance of the property helps to produce the effect and does so because it is an instance of that property'.[28] Here, it is an *instance* of the property, not the property itself, which 'helps to produce' the effect—and which thus, presumably, 'does the causal work'. But if we are looking for entities which have the right kind of spatiotemporal presence to make it conceivable that they might help to produce effects, why turn immediately to the rather abstruse

---

[28] 'Program Explanation: A General Perspective', 108.

and philosophical category of property instance? Why not look to the more straightforward categories of *thing* and *event*, if we are looking for entities which might have efficacy? For what it is worth, it seems to me that the ordinary concept of efficacy applies far more naturally to particulars than it does to properties; a knife may be efficacious in cutting through butter, for example, or a kick may be efficacious in breaking down a door, but it seems very strange to say either that the sharpness of the knife or the force of the kick was efficacious. Doubtless, this appeal to ordinary usage does not settle anything; but it may provide at least a prima-facie reason for being cautious about the attribution of efficacy to properties or their instances.

As I pointed out at the beginning of Chapter 5, philosophers are often tempted by the thought that things and events cannot genuinely be causally efficacious, that property instances just must be the ultimate bearers of efficacy. But I think we are now in a position to see that the reasons they usually offer for thinking so are really quite spurious, that they are based on a confusion of causal relevance with the sorts of causal relationship in which spatiotemporal particulars can stand, one to another. Recall Keith Campbell's argument, for example, that a stove cannot literally burn anyone, since its solidity, iron structure, enamel surface, and smoothness have nothing to do with the burn, that it is the stove's temperature—a property instance—which 'does the damage'.[29] But in so far as we are inclined to accede to this judgement, what we are acceding to is just that the temperature is what is causally *relevant*; that if the stove had not been as hot as it was, the burn would not have occurred. We do not need, in accepting this, to concede that the stove's temperature is some sort of particular entity which 'helps to produce' the burn (unless this just *means* 'is causally relevant to'). Nor do we need to deny, as Campbell seems inclined to do, that the stove really caused the burn. It *did* cause the burn; and in so doing was efficacious. It is just that not all of its properties were causally relevant to the fact that it did so—by which is meant simply that only an alteration in its temperature (and not in any of its other properties) would have made any difference to the effect.

The reason, then, why I say that there are no such things as

[29] *Abstract Particulars*, 22–3.

process explanations in Jackson and Pettit's sense is that I do not think we should speak of causally efficacious properties. But this is not mere linguistic legislation on my part. The point is that the concept of efficacy, where it is clearly differentiated from the concept of relevance, belongs in a group of concepts (along with a number of others, including 'power', 'production', 'generation', etc.) that is tied up with a bunch of models and metaphors that encourage us to misrepresent the role played by properties in causality as a 'push–pull' role—to think of them, or their instances, anyway, as little particular bits and pieces of Universe, strung together in an almighty web of actual, precipitatory relationships. But there is no such web as this. The point of mentioning a property in a causal explanation—even a property of basic physics, like 'having mass M', or 'being positively charged'—is to assert its counterfactual relevance, not to say that the property, or an instance of it, acted, exerted force, produced anything or 'did' anything. If there is a useful role for the concept of a 'process' explanation, I think it would have to be one under which we could bring those statements of causal action on which Strawson and Anscombe focus: 'The stone broke the window', 'The boy kicked the ball', 'The atom emitted radiation'. Only here are our metaphors of production and activity unlikely to lead us astray; indeed, it is in such cases as these that they have what can be regarded as their literal application.

I shall conclude this chapter by summing up its main points. We began with the puzzle: How can sentential explanations, which appear to link facts, not things, give causal explanations if we are reluctant to allow facts to be relata of the natural relation of causation? I have argued that the key to this puzzle is to understand the workings of what Jackson and Pettit call program explanations, and to distinguish the relation of causal *relevance*, which facts bear one to another and to particular events, from the sorts of singular causal relations in which things and events can stand. Relations of causal relevance support counterfactuals; but it is not true that counterfactually relevant facts necessarily owe their relevance to the fact that the facts themselves—or the properties invoked by those facts—'do causal work'.

I said earlier that philosophers have often felt a pressure to rewrite those causal explanations which do not involve explicit reference to any causally efficacious individuals, so as to demonstrate that even these explanations depend somehow for their truth on truths of the 'X caused Y' form. But the arguments of this chapter and the previous one suggest that it is wrong to succumb to this pressure. It is not that there are kinds of causal explanation which cannot meet the demand—the grammar of our language means that we will always be able to come up with something that will permit our explanations to be forced into the canonical form 'X caused Y'. It is rather that the motivation for the insistence is ill founded and the formulations to which it gives rise misleading. The motivation for the insistence is ill founded because it does not follow from the fact that an explanation incorporates no explicit reference to a singular cause that it cannot be expressive *as it is* of the holding of a genuinely objective causal truth. Not all genuinely objective causal truths are truths about relations between bona-fide spatiotemporal particulars; it is not as though a sentence which expresses commitment to a causal relation needs to be a 'picture' of a straightforward, two-place extensional relation. We use the language of causation not only to record causal relations between particulars in singular causal claims but also to express our commitment to broad, counterfactually supported dependencies between facts or between facts and events. And the formulations to which the insistence gives rise are misleading because they invite the assumption that sentential causal explanations ultimately work in pretty much the same way as event-citing explanations—by appeal to the existence, prior to the event to be explained, of a particular cause. But this, I have argued, is a mistake. It invites the application of models and metaphors to the understanding of sentential explanations which seriously misrepresent their functioning and conceals from view the enormously important differences between sentential and singular causal claims.

In the remainder of this book, I want to argue that these misleading models of causation have had important effects on the philosophy of mind. I shall try to suggest that they have made certain general philosophical accounts of the mind seem natural which are in fact deeply problematic (in particular, the token identity theory and certain varieties of functionalism) and have, in addition, created problems (e.g. the problem how content can be causally efficacious) that would not have arisen had we properly understood how different sorts of causal explanation work. We have become committed to the existence of token states of belief and desire, for instance, not seeing how else we are to explain the 'causal efficacy' of our intentional states—and are then challenged by eliminativists to say how we can know that any states bearing the requisite causal relations to others exist. We have made intentional states material, not seeing how else they could have causal powers, and are then puzzled because our strategy seems to have rendered content causally irrelevant. I want to argue that we would be in a much better position to see our way clear of these difficulties if we paid more attention to the differences between sentential causal explanations and singular causal claims. To support this claim will be the task of Part III.

III

States and Causality in
Philosophy of Mind

7

The Network Model of Causation in Philosophy of Mind

IN this chapter, I want to describe and attempt to undermine a model or picture of causation which I believe dominates contemporary philosophy of mind (as well as many accounts of the nature of causation in general) and shapes prevailing ideas about the form of some of its most important questions. I call it the *network model of causation*, for reasons which will presently become apparent.[1] The network model informs much contemporary discussion of such matters as the status of folk psychology, the commitments of physicalism, and the efficacy of mental content. It is found lurking amongst the assumptions of philosophers whose positive theories have otherwise little in common; evidence of some commitment to it can be found in the writings of philosophers as diverse in their views on the nature of mind as Fodor and Stich, Davidson and Lewis. But the network model of causation, I believe, is badly mistaken. It ignores the important differences upon which I have been trying to insist: that between singular and sentential causal claims, for instance, and relatedly, the differences between particulars and facts, and between causing and causal relevance. I shall try to argue that once these distinctions are properly appreciated, the network model of causation cannot any longer be sustained. But without its help, it seems to me, some of the problems dogging contemporary philosophy of mind cannot so much as be raised, at any rate in their present form. In particular, I shall try to argue in Chapters 8 and 9 (1) that theories according to which token intentional states like token beliefs and desires are supposed identical, or

---

[1] Simon Blackburn also uses the phrase 'network model' in his paper 'Losing Your Mind: Physics, Identity and Folk Burglar Prevention', in J. D. Greenwood (ed.), *The Future of Folk Psychology* (Cambridge, 1991), 198. His usage, however, is not the same as mine. Blackburn employs the phrase to refer to the view that psychological terms are introduced by implicit functional definition; whereas in my usage it denotes a certain picture of the metaphysics of causality.

at any rate somehow 'congruent', with token states of the brain cannot be so much as properly understood without the help of the network model,[2] (2) that one familiar way of pressing the supposed eliminativist challenge to folk psychology is rendered null and void if the network model is mistaken, and (3) that the demise of the network model can help us see our way clear to an answer to the question how mental content can be causally relevant, compatibly with the existence of a physiological explanation for every action. But first, it needs to be explained both what the network model is, and why, in my view, it offers a deceptive means of representing the reality in which our true, causal explanations are grounded.

I shall begin, in Section 1, simply by characterizing the network model. I hope and expect that this characterization will be readily recognized as an expression of an idea whose influence can be discerned in a number of different philosophical debates: in discussions of free will, moral psychology and akrasia, as well as in the philosophical discussion of the mind–body problem. In Section 2, I shall try to explain what I think is wrong with the model, basing my explanation on Davidson's argument against Mill in 'Causal Relations', an argument the full repercussions of which, I think, have yet to be properly comprehended. Then in Section 3, I shall consider the influence that the network model has had on philosophy of mind, moving on in Section 4 to argue in particular that the use to which the idea of isomorphic causal structures has sometimes been put in philosophy of mind cannot be justified, once the limitations of the network metaphor have been understood.

1. THE NETWORK MODEL OF CAUSATION

It is, I think, more or less uncontroversial that the causal history of any particular event or circumstance is always an immensely complex affair. For one thing, there seems no reason to suppose that the causal history of any temporally located event or particular circumstance could not be traced back, in principle, to the beginning of time itself, although it is rare that we ever reach back so far for our causal explanations. But even if we disregard this aspect of causal-

---

[2] For the suggestion that congruence, rather than identity, is the best relation in terms of which to formulate token physicalism, see Papineau, *Philosophical Naturalism*, 11–12.

ity and restrict ourselves only to causal factors which are relatively close, temporally speaking, to the event or circumstance we wish to explain, it is still usually possible to think of a very large range of considerations which might figure in the aetiology of the effect in question. Sometimes, philosophers draw a distinction between conditions and causes, but mostly it seems to be agreed that if there is a distinction to be drawn here, it is really a pragmatic one; we are more inclined to regard as causes those factors which are unusual, unexpected, or particularly pertinent to practical questions such as 'How do we avoid effects like this in the future?' or 'Whom should we punish for this?', and more likely to relegate to the status of 'condition' anything which was only to be expected or which, for some reason, is of little interest or relevance to our practical concerns. Metaphysically speaking, though, it is mostly thought that causes and conditions are really on a par. Orthodoxy has it that they act jointly to produce or trigger resultant effects and if we are inclined to single out only one of these causal factors as 'the cause' we have merely made a context-sensitive selection from a range of possibilities.[3]

Our recognition that causal stories are complex matters has us reaching for models and metaphors by means of which to represent to ourselves the ontological reality in which those of our causal explanations which we are inclined to regard as true are grounded. The concept of a causal network is an almost irresistible resource in the attempt to visualize and make manageable our understanding of the highly complicated causal relationships which seem to be revealed by the wealth of alternative, equally true causal explanations we can offer of any event or circumstance. It is an obvious refinement of another exceptionally compelling image by means of which we often encode our understanding of the temporal relations which causally related events bear to one another: the image of a causal chain. But while chains are linear, each link being related only to (at most) two others—its two neighbours in the chain— networks are branching, and so they have a kind of complexity which chains lack, complexity which makes them seem well suited to the representation of the intricate systems of causal relations to

---

[3] For views of causation along these lines, see Mill, *A System of Logic*, 214–5; Mackie, *The Cement of the Universe*, 34–6; Lewis, 'Causal Explanation', 214–5; F. Dretske, 'Mental Events as Structuring Causes of Behavior', in Heil and Mele (eds.), *Mental Causation*, 121.

which our multifarious causal explanations seem to point. In a network, two or more different chains can come together and, in doing so, they can create new effects, effects which would not have resulted from any single chain alone. I have already used the metaphor of vector addition to describe the way in which spatiotemporally coinciding portions of a multiplicity of separate chains are conceived of as combining to give rise to resultant effects. At the nodes of causal networks, different causes 'add' together, the effect which results being conceived of as part-caused by each separate causal factor.

I want to concede at once that there need not necessarily be anything wrong with the use of the network metaphor in connection with causality. For the use of the metaphor might be intended to reflect nothing more than the fact that we are able to represent complex causal stories concerning the production of particular effects diagrammatically, as it were, with effects ranged lower down the diagram than their causes, and lines to indicate causal relationships. I might, for example, draw something similar to Figure 7.1 in an attempt to explain why my tyre punctured on the way to work. We could call this a causal network, if we liked, and there would be nothing wrong with the suggestion that it could be a useful way of representing some of the causal factors which I take to have been somehow involved in the puncture of my tyre. But one can find the network metaphor taken much further than this in the philosophical discussion of many topics in which causality plays a role. Implicit in some of those discussions is the idea that such a representation could, in principle, offer something more than a rough-and-ready illustrative aid to thought about causation; that a diagram of this sort, representing the causal factors which we take to have been implicated in the generation of some particular effect—if we were careful and accurate enough about it—might be capable of revealing a structure which we could reasonably think of as isomorphic with a set of natural, interactive, and productive relations between particular entities of certain sorts. The suggestion is that a causal network might be not merely a more or less detailed diagrammatic representation of a causal story, but a structure consisting of real entities, causally interconnected one with another. Figure 7.1 would be obviously unsatisfactory conceived of as a shot at the depiction of some definite, objective, actually existing causal structure—it contains indefinite phrases instead of singular terms

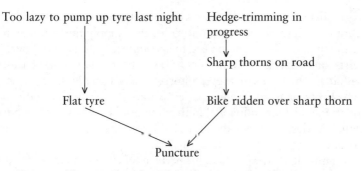

FIG. 7.1. The causal explanation of a puncture: a diagrammatic
representation

and expressions which seem unsuited to the representation of human-independent reality because of indexicality and other sorts of relativity to context (e.g. 'too lazy to pump up tyre last night'). But it is quite natural to think that perhaps we could eradicate these defects—and produce something which could be conceived of as something more than a heuristic, quasi-pictorial device for the representation of causal relations, something which accurately reflected the ontology and relationships to be found in nature wherever one set of circumstances and/or events gives rise to an effect. The picture of causal reality which is generated by this idea is what I call the network model of causation.

The ambition to model causality in this accurate way by means of a network raises two important questions. First, what should be the ontology of the network—the entities which are linked by the various interconnected chains? As we have already seen, we are content, in our everyday causal explanations, to offer as causes things in a wide variety of categories: physical objects, events, processes, conditions, facts, omissions and lacks, absences and presences, properties, dispositions, and states of affairs. But it would doubtless be attractive to a proponent of the network model, for reasons of theoretical economy, to suppose that much of this variety must be a feature merely of the linguistic expression of causal truths rather than a reflection of similar diversity at the level of the network. The question then would be: which of the ontological categories into which the things we call 'causes' fall should be retained to provide the ontology of the networks we have ambitions to model? And second, what kind of relations exist between the entities, whatever they turn out to be, that supply the ontology for the networks? We seem to need to account for at least two different sorts of connection in the networks—the relation I have called 'adding' which is, as it were, a horizontal link between the entities which combine to produce effects; and the vertical, productive relation which an individual in the network bears to what might be called its descendants—the things which are its effects. How are we to understand these two relations?

I think if it were made properly explicit, as often it is not, something like the following answer to the first of these questions would have to be proposed by those who discuss or implicitly invoke network imagery in connection with the understanding of causality. First, events must be included in causal networks. For events are needed to bring about other events—states alone cannot cause change. For example, the dryness of the ground, the density of the foliage, and the wind's being strong may all be causally relevant to the explanation of a forest fire—but these conditions might persist for ever and the forest fire never occur without an event to trigger it off—someone's lighting a match, say, or dropping a lighted cigarette into the bushes. But second, it is imperative that states be included alongside events. The cigarette's being dropped into the bushes would never have caused the forest fire had the ground not been so dry, the wind so strong, the foliage so dense— and so these factors must also be included in the causal network that describes the causal provenance of the effect-event. Events occur against the background of standing conditions, combining with those conditions to produce effects in such a way that each relevant event and state can be considered a part of the cause of the effect-event. The network ontology is thus a twofold ontology of events and states.

In philosophy of mind, where the network model of causation is often implicitly invoked, one often finds expressions which suggest, contrary to what I have proposed, that a uniform ontology either of events or of states would suffice for a causal network. One finds, for instance, talk of 'systems of states' combining to produce behaviour; or of 'networks of events'[4] constituting causal reality. But I take this simply to be a consequence of the fact that it is not

---

[4] For this phrase see e.g. L. R. Baker, 'Metaphysics and Mental Causation', in Heil and Mele (eds.), *Mental Causation*, 75.

generally thought important to distinguish between the two categories of entity; thus, philosophers come to use either the term 'state' or the term 'event' to refer indifferently to entities in either category. This usually becomes obvious when more is said about the sorts of entities that are supposed to make up these 'systems' or 'networks'—one usually finds, for example, when psychological causation is at issue, that a mixture of beliefs and perceivings, desires and decisions, intentions and rememberings, are intended to be included in the relevant networks.[5] I shall not, therefore, take seriously the suggestion that we might do without one or other of the two categories of entity in constituting the network—for besides the fact that I do not think that it is really what is envisaged by those who speak as though a single category of entity were involved, I cannot see how the model could be made into a plausible way of thinking about causal reality unless both events and standing conditions were incorporated.

The network model, then, embraces the idea that entities which are non-universal yet also stative in their nature must be amongst the causally productive items which combine in the generation of effects. Presumably, this must be because it is thought that, otherwise, it would not be possible to understand what grounds those of our causal explanations which advert to properties or features of things or situations, rather than to individual events. The role played by the wetness of the road in a car accident, for example, or the presence of oxygen in the lighting of a match need to be accommodated by the network model—and a natural solution is to include token states or 'standing conditions' of wetness or oxygen's being present in the network itself. A certain conception of the relationship between true, sentential explanations with stative *explanantes* and the network is thus part of the model; such sentential explanations are regarded as potentially revelatory of entities which require to be found a place in the causal network[6]

---

[5] Ned Block, for example, claims that his 'metaphysical stance' is 'one in which mental events are the causes of behaviour, and their contents are properties of those events that may or may not be causally relevant to the events' effects' ('Can the Mind Change the World?', in G. Boolos (ed.), *Meaning and Method: Essays in Honor of Hilary Putnam* (Cambridge, 1990), 140. But his examples of mental events are 'beliefs, thoughts, desires, and the like'.

[6] Only 'potentially' revelatory, because many philosophers think that only certain sorts of features could genuinely play a causal role (perhaps only features that have some special sort of intrinsicness, or which are physical).

and are thought of as grounded in the interactions which the model postulates. Token states thus come to be conceived of as an important species of causally efficacious particular with the capacity for interaction with other states and also with particular events.

What about the second question I raised earlier—the question of the nature of the links between the different elements in the network? It is tempting to think that the horizontal 'addition' relation might simply be a matter of spatiotemporal coincidence—though this raises questions about networks which represent causal relations between entities which have no very definite location. But I shall not pursue this issue here. Instead, I want to focus on the vertical relations between entities in the network and their effects. What relation is represented by these vertical linkages?

It is natural to think that the answer to this question is straightforward; that the relation in question is just the causal relation. Each entity is a cause (though the network model demands the concession that it is not proper to say that it is *the* cause) of its descendants in the network. But as I argued in Chapter 5, we run into ambiguity when we label some things causes of others. The things we call causes need not stand to their effects in the causal relation which is represented by the two-place predicate 'cause', the relation I earlier labelled 'causing'; they may rather be causally relevant to that effect. And the arguments of the previous chapters have shown that causing and causal relevance are significantly different. So the network model faces the question: which of these relations is represented by its vertical links?

The idea of a network could in principle, I think, be made compatible with different answers to this question. One might, for example, think of causal networks as networks of facts or states of affairs, in which case the arguments of previous chapters suggest that the vertical relation ought to be relevance. Or one might think that there is nothing in the idea of a network as such that prevents it from having room for both sorts of relationship. Later, I shall consider the suggestion that at least some of the network's vertical links might represent relevance relations. But mostly, I think, the usages of the network model in philosophy of mind with which I wish to take issue effectively suggest that each part-cause of an effect bears the same sort of relation to that effect as any other part-cause, and that this relation is a relation between particulars, and so cannot be—or include—the relation I have been calling causal relevance. I shall call this relation part-causing. For the time being, I shall simply stipulate that it is part of what I am calling the network model of causation that the vertical links in the network represent part-causing, which is to be conceived of as an extensional relation which one particular event or token state can bear to another. In Section 4, I shall consider the question whether the network model might conceivably be freed from this assumption.

What exactly is wrong with the network model of causation? I want to argue that the network model badly misrepresents the function of sentential causal explanations, and particularly of those sentential explanations whose *explanantes* are stative predications. It suggests that these stative sentential explanations are grounded ontologically in the causal activity of something which is conceived of as a kind of particular—the token state—when the truth, as I have already tried to show, is that such explanations advert not to the causal action of particulars, but to the causal relevance of facts. And though the network metaphor itself might perhaps be able to withstand the recognition that its vertical links must often be understood as relevance links, the uses to which the network model has been put—the talk, for example, of isomorphisms between mental and physical causal structures, which one finds in philosophy of mind, or of states with mental and states with physical descriptions having the same 'causal role'—cannot. I shall argue that these ideas make no sense once we have conceded that talk of the 'causal efficacy' of 'token states' is to be cashed out in terms of relevance relations involving facts, rather than productive or generative relations between particulars.

2. WHAT'S WRONG WITH THE NETWORK MODEL OF CAUSATION?

The resources by means of which to rebut the network model of the metaphysics of causation have already, in my view, been made available by Davidson in an argument which he deploys against Mill's conception of the cause 'philosophically speaking' in his paper 'Causal Relations'. This argument seems to me to suggest very strongly that events and token states ought not to be regarded as particular, causally efficacious entities which combine, one with another, to produce effects. What is surprising, I think, is that this consequence of Davidson's argument has not really been fully appreciated—perhaps not even by Davidson himself, who seems occasionally inclined to speak as though he regarded it as at least possible that events and states should interact in this sort of way.[7] My first task, then, will be to try to explain what I take to be the ramifications of the argument in 'Causal Relations' for the view that events and states are particulars which combine in the way suggested by the network model.

In his discussion of causation in *A System of Logic*, Mill speaks of the 'invariable sequence' that we find in nature between antecedents and consequents of certain sorts.[8] He appears to have in mind the thought that certain kinds of circumstances or events are always followed by an effect of a certain type—that is to say, that they are sufficient for the occurrence of an effect of that kind. But Mill goes on to note that it is seldom, if ever, that this 'invariable sequence' subsists between a consequent and a single antecedent:

It is usually between a consequent and the sum of several antecedents; the concurrence of them all being requisite to produce, that is, to be certain of being followed by the consequent. In such cases it is very common to single out only one of the antecedents under the denomination of Cause, calling the others merely Conditions.... The real Cause is the whole of these antecedents; and we have, philosophically speaking, no right to give the name of cause to one of them exclusively of the others.[9]

The antecedents which may 'concur' in the production of particular effects, according to Mill, may include both events and states. Mill is utterly explicit about this. One of his examples concerns a man who dies through eating a particular dish; Mill asks whether it would be correct to say that his eating of the dish was the cause of his death, even though there is no invariable connection between eating of the dish and death. He concludes that it would not be correct, and writes that:

What in the case we have supposed disguises the incorrectness of the expression is this: that the various conditions, except the single one of

---

[7] See below, Sect. 3, for discussion of an example.

[8] *A System of Logic*, 214.

[9] Ibid. Cp. T. Honderich: 'Causal connection of the fundamental kind, as it seems to me, typically holds between what we can carelessly call a set of events or conditions or a circumstance CC, and another event E. The first is a complete explanation of the second . . .' ('The Union Theory and Anti-individualism', in Heil and Mele (eds.), *Mental Causation*, 139).

eating the food, were not *events* (that is, instantaneous changes or successions of instantaneous changes) but *states* possessing more or less of permanency; and might therefore have preceded the effect by an indefinite length of duration, for want of the event which was requisite to complete the required concurrence of conditions ...[10]

Here we have as clear an example as could be wished for of the idea that events and states combine to produce effects. It is usually more natural, according to Mill, to single out an event than a state as a cause, but it is illusory to suppose that the connection between the event and the effect is any closer than that between any of the individually necessary standing conditions and that same effect. In Mill's words, 'All the conditions were equally indispensable to the production of the consequent; and the statement of the cause is incomplete unless in some shape or other we introduce them all.'[11]

Davidson disputes Mill's verdict about the dish-eating case, and diagnoses Mill's mistake as due to a confusion of particular causes with necessary and sufficient conditions; for the reason we are urged by Mill to deny the status of whole cause to the man's eating of a particular dish is that eating that dish would not, in general, be a sufficient condition of death amongst consumers of it—perhaps only the weak and frail would succumb to the poison contained in it, for example. But this, according to Davidson, cannot be a reason for refusing to allow that the man's eating of the dish was, in this particular case, the cause of his death. The man *did* die—he was frail—which means that this particular dish-eating can be described as a dish-eating by a man who was frail. The fact that we do not mention the frailty of the man in saying that his eating of the dish was the cause of his death does not imply, according to Davidson, that the dish-eating was not its whole cause: 'Mill ... was wrong in thinking we have not specified the whole cause of an event when we have not wholly specified it. And there is not ... anything elliptical in the claim that a certain man's death was caused by his eating a particular dish, even though death resulted only because the man had a particular bodily constitution, a particular state of present health, and so on.'[12]

Davidson's conclusion here should seem bewildering to a proponent of the network model. How can the dish-eating be the *whole*

---

[10] *A System of Logic*, 214.   [11] Ibid.   [12] 'Causal Relations', 156.

cause of the man's death, when on the network model it is only in combination with a number of other part-causes that it suffices to bring about death? It might perhaps be granted that Mill's own argument for the conclusion that the dish-eating is but part of the cause of the man's death is invalid; for it is based on the observation that there need not be any invariable connection between events of general kinds—between eatings from a certain dish of salmonella-infested macaroni cheese, on the one hand, say, and deaths, on the other. And one cannot move from the conclusion that eatings from this dish of salmonella-infested macaroni cheese do not invariably cause death to the conclusion that *this* eating of it did not (alone) do so; though certainly it will follow both that eating the dish is not *in general* sufficient for death and also that the fact that this man ate the dish may not be sufficient to *explain* why he died. But neither of these conclusions can be assumed without further argument to have anything to do with the question whether the particular eating of the dish which led to death may or may not be regarded as its whole cause. It might be conceded, then, that Davidson has pointed out a genuine flaw in Mill's reasoning. But still, it might be said, Mill's conclusion that the dish-eating event is but part of the cause of the death is unavoidable. Here is an attempt at a better argument for it.

Suppose we have a causal explanation of some event which combines reference to a particular cause-event with mention also of something which we might think of as a standing condition. Then as long as the standing condition in question is not something whose mention ought to figure in a description of the *essence* of the cause-event, we should be able to imagine a possible world in which that particular cause-event occurs—the very same one—though the standing condition does not obtain, and where the effect fails to occur as a result of the absence of the standing condition. For example, suppose we decide that our subject's being frail is no part of the essence of the event which was his eating of the salmonella-infested macaroni cheese—that that very particular event might have occurred though he was perfectly strong and healthy. Then reflection on such a case might make it seem obvious that we need the idea that what happened in the actual case was that this particular event combined with a state of frailty (of which it is, in principle, quite independent) to produce the death of the person. The additive model of combination endorsed by the network model might seem unavoidable—if the salmonella-eating could have occurred and not brought about death, did in fact bring about death, and would not have brought about death were it not for the man's frailty, how can we escape the conclusion that the salmonella-eating must have combined with the man's state of frailty to produce his death, each being therefore part, and not the whole, of the cause?

In response to this line of thought, I want to make two points. First, I think it probably ought to be conceded that, in a case like this, there is a perfectly harmless sense in which it is true and perfectly all right to say that the man's eating of the dish combined with his state of ill health to cause his death. There is not necessarily anything wrong with the mere idea that different causal factors 'combine' to give rise to effects when they are independent of one another in the way they seem to be in this particular case. It is not the idea of combination as such, but only the network model of what is involved in this so-called 'combination' of causal factors that is to be regarded as problematic—in particular, the two features of the model which I highlighted above: the idea that both the events and states involved are particular causes, and the suggestion that there is nothing very significant to be said about the differences between the relations which events and states respectively bear to the effects which they allegedly combine, one with another, to produce. It is these assumptions, as I shall shortly try to show, which make the network model dangerous, and which suggest uses of it which cannot be justified.

But second, the argument offered above which was supposed to show that we are forced to regard events and states as factors which combine with one another to produce effects is not valid in any case; and I think it is illuminating to see why it fails. It may be helpful to begin by considering a line of reasoning that is parallel in some respects to that argument, but where the parallel conclusion is more clearly out of place. To return to an example we have used before, suppose I strike a match and it lights. There was an event: the lighting of the match. What caused it? One answer I might give is that the lighting of the match was caused by the striking of the match. It might then be said that since there are possible worlds in which the striking of the match—that very striking event—occurs, but does not cause the lighting, that our original answer must have missed something out. For one thing, say, the striking had to have a particular degree of force in order for the lighting event to occur.

Let us suppose that had the match been struck ever so slightly less forcefully, the match would not have lit. And let us suppose also— though perhaps this is controversial—that this very slight reduction in the forcefulness of the strike does no damage to the identity of the striking event—that we could still regard the possible world in which the match is struck ever so slightly less forcefully as a possible world in which the very same striking event occurs as occurs in the actual world.[13] Then we would have to concede that the mere occurrence of this very striking event does not suffice for the match-lighting event—in addition, the match has to be struck with a particular degree of force. But surely this would not make us want to say that the particular striking *combines* with a property of itself—the force of the striking—that there is some second particular cause involved in the case which adds together with the striking at the nodes of a causal network to produce an effect. We are not forced to this conclusion by the mere existence of possible worlds in which the match-striking occurs and yet the match-lighting does not. Rather, those possible worlds simply reflect the fact that the match-striking had to have a certain property in order for the match to light—one which it in fact had, but which it is conceivable that it might not have had—not that it had to 'add' to anything else. The match-striking had to be a certain way—something had to be true of it—but it is surely a distortion of this fact to represent it as the need for the match-striking to combine with another causally efficacious particular. What is absent in the possible world described, where the striking occurs but the match does not light, is not a particular but a *necessary condition*—and a condition is the sort of thing that ought to be represented by a sentence, not by any kind of singular term.[14] It is a kind of fact, not a kind of particular entity.

---

[13] It is not easy to decide what should be accounted the essential properties of events. It seems to me that it makes sense to say, for example, of some individual striking that it might have been slightly less forceful than it was—but I do not think it matters much to my main line of argument if someone disagrees with me about this particular case. Other examples could readily be found. All that is needed to sustain my argument is a property of some cause-event that has the following three characteristics: (1) it is causally relevant to the effect produced; (2) it is intuitively an intrinsic, rather than a relational property of that event, and; (3) it is a non-essential property of the event. I can see no a priori reason for thinking that examples of this kind are *in general* impossible to produce.

[14] Obviously, the concept of a condition which is in use here is to be distinguished from that which I used earlier to refer to those 'states' like anger and sorrow which are not also properties.

I am not suggesting, of course, that exactly parallel reasoning might now simply be applied to the dish-eating case. For there are obviously differences between the two examples, differences which, I think, demand the concession which I have already made, that there is certainly a sense in which, in some cases, it is all right to speak of events and standing conditions as causal factors which combine. The point of introducing the case just discussed is simply to show that the mere fact that one can conceive of a possible world in which some particular event does not have the effect which it has in the actual world does not show that it combines causally with some other particular to achieve that effect in the actual world. The truth may rather be that what is lacking in the possible world where the effect does not occur is just a necessary condition, not any sort of particular, causally efficacious entity.

It might now be said, though, that even if this is conceded, it will not help us avoid the model of event–state interaction in the case with which we were dealing earlier—the dish-eating case. For it is quite plausible to suppose the reason the combinatorial idea makes no sense in the case of the match-striking is that the causally relevant property I singled out in that case—the striking's having a certain degree of force—is a property of the striking itself; whereas in the dish-eating case, things are different. Though we are enabled to assign a causally relevant property to the dish-eating in virtue of the fact that the man eating the dish was frail—the property of its being a dish-eating by a frail man—this is not an intrinsic but a relational property which the event has only in virtue of its standing in a certain relation to something else—something that it is plausible to think of as existing before the event even occurred—the standing condition which is the man's being frail. The idea that in this case an event and a state combine to give rise to an effect is therefore justified in a way that it is not in the case of the striking.

But I would continue to maintain that it is certainly wrong to imagine that this combination is a matter of two or more particular causes coming together to produce an effect. For once again, the man's so-called state of being frail is not any kind of particular cause—the man's being frail is rather a *condition* which is causally relevant to his death. The conclusions of previous chapters bear this out; the so-called 'state' is really a fact, not a particular, and so bears a quite different relation to the man's death from his eating of the dish—the relation of causal relevance, not the relation of part-causing. Indeed, once we recognize that our so-called 'state' ought to be conceived of as a fact rather than a particular cause, the idea that there is some total combination of events and states, in principle capable of complete enumeration, which together constitutes the whole cause of the man's death starts to look as though it might be senseless. For conditions can be negative as well as positive—and it is not clear to me that there is any reason why there should be a definite limit to the number of negative conditions which might have been relevant to the occurrence of some particular event. In the case of Mill's dish-eating man, for example, we might regard it as causally crucial that no ambulance was called, that no antibiotics were available, that no stomach pump was applied—and so all these factors might conceivably be regarded as necessary conditions of (or conditions which made more probable) the final death. But I see no obvious reason to think that there is any clear end to the number of alternative scenarios which might conceivably have resulted in survival rather than death, and so no clear end to the causally relevant conditions which might be generated by consideration of such scenarios.

What Davidson's argument in 'Causal Relations' suggests, then, I think, is this. Although particular events may only succeed in producing the effects which they do in fact produce because of certain 'states' or 'standing conditions', these standing conditions bear a quite different relation to those effects than do the particular events. They are conditions which are necessary in the circumstances (or conditions which make the effect more likely in the circumstances), not particular causes; and the relation they bear to their effects is causal relevance. The suggestion that each event and standing condition can be regarded as a part-cause of the effect in question therefore needs to be treated with extreme caution. It should not be taken to imply, in particular, that it makes any sense simply to sum all the relevant necessary conditions and particular causes to obtain something which might be thought of as 'the whole cause'. Davidson's own conclusion, indeed, appears to be that in so far as this expression has sense, it ought to be regarded as applying simply to the particular cause-event in any case. This is emphatically not to imply that nothing else mattered or was relevant or had anything to do with the effect in question; only that mattering and causing are not the same thing.

It might be objected, though, that whatever might be said about

Mill, I have not yet shown that it is fair to charge all those who utilize the idea of a causal network with the rather specific dogmas about the particularity of stative causes, the relationships between causal factors of different sorts and their effects, etc. to which I have been objecting above. For it might be said that there is nothing in the idea of a network as such which requires that the entities which it links together should all be particulars rather than conditions. There seems no reason in principle why a network should not be a network which links together both conditions and particulars. This may well be right. But once it is clear that the network is intended to contain both these sorts of entity, and to represent the sorts of relations which both bear to their effects, certain tempting ways of utilizing the network model, I should maintain, no longer make any sense. In the final two sections of this chapter, I want to focus on two related ideas which permeate much current thinking in philosophy of mind which I believe cannot survive the recognition that causal networks must contain conditions as well as particular causes: the idea of a state's having a determinate causal role and the associated suggestion that causal networks generated by different levels of explanation (e.g. by the folk-psychological and the cognitive-scientific or neurophysiological or physical levels) might in principle be found to be isomorphs, thus generating the possibility of mapping the individual states and events to which talk at one level appears to commit us (e.g. beliefs and desires) onto individual states and events, or complex constructions out of individual states and events, at the other level. I shall begin in Section 3 by simply trying to describe and illustrate some of the uses to which these problematic ideas have been put in philosophy of mind, before going on in the final section of this chapter to try to justify the claim that these uses require an understanding of the network model which cannot withstand the recognition that conditions as well as particulars would have to be included in any causal 'web'.

3. THE NETWORK MODEL IN PHILOSOPHY OF MIND

The causation of action or behaviour by psychological events and states is the starting-point of much current writing on the mind–body problem. The fact that these psychological entities have, or appear to have, a causal influence on the movements of human and perhaps also animal bodies is the basis of all the most widely discussed arguments for the view that we are obliged to find them a niche in the law-governed physical world. But of course, psychological causal stories can be just as complicated as any other sort— and this is where the network metaphor gets a hold. Suppose, for example, that feeling somewhat depressed one evening, I am scanning the 'What's On' column in the local paper and see that there is a good comedy on at the local cinema. I decide to go, thinking that it may cheer me up. A good explanation of why I went might advert to any of the following factors: my state of depression; my noticing a good comedy in the 'What's On' column on as I flicked through the local paper; the belief that I come to have as a result of this noticing (together, perhaps, with my belief that the 'What's On' column is generally reliable) that there is a good comedy on at the local cinema; my desire to cheer myself up; my belief that a good comedy will cheer me up; my decision to go. Evidently there are also relationships amongst some of these factors; my noticing an entry in the 'What's On' column, together with my belief that the 'What's On' column is generally reliable, for instance, might together be regarded as having given rise to the belief that there is indeed a good comedy on at the local cinema. And the representation of these relationships amongst mental events and states, and between all of these and the resultant action or behaviour, seems to cry out for the invocation of the idea of a causal network. How else but by means of the sort of complex, interrelated, causal structure that the network model depicts could the numerous different causal factors exert their influence?

It is this thought, at least in part, no doubt, which has given rise to the talk of systems or structures or patterns of causally interrelated psychological states and events which is now so commonplace in the literature on philosophy of mind. The prevalence of the idea is perhaps most obvious in discussions of functionalism, which seems to require the network model for its very characterization. Functionalists are committed to the view that between perceptual input and behavioural output is a huge network of causally efficacious entities—events, states, whatever—whose place in the causal web (their 'causal role') is the feature which determines their mental or psychological type. Fodor, for example, charting the recent history of philosophy of mind, says that functionalism offered 'a new account of the type/token relation for psychological states: psychological-state tokens were to be assigned to psychological-state types *solely* by reference to their causal relations to proximal stimuli ('inputs'), to proximal responses ('outputs') and to one another'.[15] According to the view that Fodor calls 'functionalism', then, we have 'state-tokens'—things like a subject's belief that p or desire that q—bearing causal relations to other events and states, causal relations whose instantiations of general patterns permits the psychological typing of the entities amongst which the causal relations hold—an obvious manifestation of the network model. But it is not only functionalists who speak of mental events and states in ways which reveal commitment to the network model. One need not think that psychological typing is functional typing to find the network model compelling. Here, for example, is Davidson in 'The Material Mind', giving expression to a very common view about what vindication of an identity between a rational action and physical event would require:

in identifying . . . [an action] with a physical event, we must at the same time be sure that the causal history of the physical event includes events or states identical with the desires and cognitive states that yield a psychological explanation of the action.

This is only the beginning of the complications, however, for most emotional states, wants, perceivings, and so on, have causal connections with further psychological states and events . . . And so, in saying an agent performed a single intentional action we attribute *a very complex system of states and events to him*; all this must be captured in giving the corresponding physical states and events.[16]

Davidson, though no functionalist, draws here on the idea that the individual causal links amongst token psychological events and states form a kind of causal web, the threads of which are the causal links to which folk psychology supposedly commits us. And if the token identity theory is true, the thought goes, this web must be reflected by a corresponding physical web whose threads represent causal links between physically characterizable events and states.

---

[15] J. A. Fodor, 'Fodor's Guide to Mental Representation', in Greenwood (ed.), *The Future of Folk Psychology*, 28.
[16] D. Davidson, 'The Material Mind', in P. Suppes, L. Henkin, A. Joja, and G. C. Moisil (eds.), *Proceedings of the Fourth International Congress for Logic, Methodology and Science* (Amsterdam, 1973); repr. in Davidson, *Essays on Actions and Events*, 254–5 (my italics).

Only if this kind of isomorphism exists, Davidson seems to be alleging, can mental and physical events be identified one with another—for only then would it be possible for mental events and physical ones to have the same causal role.

Once the network model of causation is in place, indeed, the concept of isomorphism is an obvious resource on which to draw to state the requirements of token physicalism. Horgan and Tye, for example, use the concept in their argument against the token identity theory, making the idea more precise with their concept of a *physical-causal isomorph*, or PCI. Using the term 'event' in a broad sense, so as to encompass states and processes, they define what it is for a set of physical events to be a PCI of a set of mental events as follows:

For any creature C with a non-empty mentality set $M(C)$, we shall say that a set of events $P(C)_i$ is a *physical-causal isomorph* of $M(C)$ . . . iff (1) every member of $P(C)_i$ is a physico-chemical event of which C is the subject, and (2) there is a 1–1 relation R between the events in $P(C)_i$ and the events in $M(C)$, such that (a) each event in $P(C)_i$ is simultaneous with its R-correlate and (b) the events in $P(C)_i$ collectively conform to all the causal principles of common-sense psychology and theoretical psychology which govern their respective R-correlates in $M(C)$.[17]

The general idea, as for Davidson, is that the shape of the causal structure which describes the psychology of an individual, as determined by the principles of folk psychology, will need to be mappable onto some physical causal structure of internal events and states, if the token identity theory, or something like it, is to have any chance of being true. For if this turns out not to be possible, some of the events and states which are being alleged identical with one another by the theory will fail to share all their causes and effects—and Leibniz's Law will therefore have been violated. One form of argument for eliminative materialism, indeed, depends on exactly this thought about what token identities require, together with an empirically grounded scepticism about whether any webs of neural events and states do correspond sufficiently closely to those which folk-psychological principles suggest exist amongst psychological events and states, for these identifications to be made.[18]

---

[17] T. Horgan and M. Tye, 'Against the Token Identity Theory', in LePore and McLaughlin (eds.), *Actions and Events*, 428.

[18] I shall consider this form of argument in Ch. 9, where I shall argue that it depends for whatever plausibility it might be thought to possess on mistakes that are embodied in the network model of causation.

What exactly is wrong with the way that the idea of isomorphism has been used in philosophy of mind? In particular, why should it carry any necessary commitment to the sorts of understandings of the ontology and relationships of the network to which I have been objecting? For it might be said that there is nothing in the idea of isomorphism itself which dictates any assumptions about the nature of the entities or the relations out of which the isomorphic webs are constructed. Provided events are mapped onto events and facts onto facts, causings onto causings and relevance relations onto relevance relations, there can surely be no objection to the invocation of the idea of isomorphism in itself. At the end of Section 2 above, I said that there need not necessarily be anything wrong with the mere idea that different causal factors 'combine' to give rise to effects, that danger only lurks when a certain conception of what the entities combined are like, and of what is involved in their combination, infects what is potentially a perfectly innocent mode of expression. Why, then, should the mere idea of isomorphic causal webs necessarily involve these mistaken conceptions? In the final section of this chapter, I shall try to show that once we suggest that causal webs are to accommodate conditional as well as particular causes, facts as well as things, the idea behind isomorphism simply becomes a nonsense.

4. CAUSAL RELEVANCE AND ISOMORPHISM

Let us suppose that we have a causal explanation of some particular event which is sentential in its form—and so which adverts to the causal relevance of a fact, according to the account of causal explanation laid out in the previous chapters. Let us suppose that the event is an action and that the fact is a folk-psychological fact, which we can call F_1 (it might, for example, be the fact that S believes that p). If we think that different levels of explanation might in principle be found to generate isomorphic causal structures, even given the suggestion that facts are parts of these structures, we must presumably be contemplating the idea that a fact like F_1 might somehow be found to map onto some other lower-level fact, P_1, possibly a rather complex conjunctive fact, in such a way that F_1 and P_1 stand in all the same causal relations as one another to other facts and events—in other words, that F_1 and P_1

have what we can call the same 'causal role'. What exactly is wrong with this suggestion?

A first difficulty is the application of the very idea of levels of explanation to causes which are conditions and not particulars. For there is a sense in which the thinking behind the causal network model implies the need to mix 'levels' from the start. I do not mean to suggest that we simply could not assign different conditions to different levels of explanation—clearly we could do this. Some causally relevant conditions will be social, some biological, some physiological, some chemical, some physical, etc. But we cannot avail ourselves of the thought that in any given case where explanations at a number of different levels are possible, each level generates a web which is, as it were, causally complete in the terms of that level, which does not require the co-operation of factors which belong, strictly speaking, to other levels. Suppose, for example, that someone leaps into a river to rescue someone. He would not have done so, let us say, if he had not wanted to rescue the person in question. That he wanted to rescue the person is then part of the psychological explanation of why he leaps into the river. But he also would not have done so—even given his desire to rescue the drowning person and various other relevant psychological facts—if some peculiar paralysis had affected his muscles or if someone had prevented him physically from taking the leap or if his motor neurons had not been working. Surely, then, on the combinatorial understanding of causal factors from which the network model starts out, all these factors, psychological and non-psychological alike, should belong to the *same* network—each is required for the leap. If we were to separate the factors into various 'levels', we would, at any rate, have to reject the idea that any web which contained factors only from a single level depicted a complete sufficient condition of any event—the psychology of the man, for example, could be as favourable as you please, yet if the man's motor neurons are not working, the leap will not take place.

Someone might object that this argument depends on an incorrect understanding of where psychology ends and 'output' begins. If motor neuron activity, rather than bodily movement, is considered to be the output, it might be said, we can hang on to the thought that folk psychology and neurophysiology each reveals a separate causal web which accurately charts the mix of events and conditions at each level which resulted in a particular pattern of motor neuron activity. But the idea that the psychological web was to be generable entirely from the resources of folk psychology is now endangered. For folk psychology invokes beliefs, desires, etc. in connection with the causal explanation of *actions*, not of the firing of motor neurons. Folk psychology does not contain any explanations which make beliefs and desires the causes of motor neuronal output.

I can myself see no reason to think that this consideration alone is not decisive. But even if it is not, there are other ways of showing that the idea that explanations at different levels might generate isomorphic causal webs is doomed to failure, once facts are part of the ontology of the web. To see this, let us ask what it would be for two facts—one at a higher and one at some lower level—to have the same 'causal role'. To demonstrate that this idea is fraught with difficulty, I propose to consider an example first discussed by David Lewis in his paper 'An Argument for the Identity Theory', which seems to me to be as good a case as any that is likely to be found for the view that different facts, associated with different levels, or types, of explanation might nevertheless have the same causal role. Lewis's example concerns cylindrical combination locks for bicycle-chains. The locks he describes contain rows of slotted discs, such that setting the combination typically causes the slots in the discs to become aligned—which frees the lock and enables it to be opened when gently pulled. Lewis's own proposal, on which he models his version of physicalistic functionalism, is that the (type) state of being unlocked for locks such as this ought to be identified with the (type) state of alignment of slots, on the grounds that the two types of state have the same causal role. I want to consider the closely related proposal, more relevant than Lewis's own for my purposes here, that the fact that a particular cylindrical lock L is unlocked at some particular time t has the same causal role as the fact that the slots S_1–S_4, which are cut into the discs in L, are aligned at t.

What would it be for L's being unlocked at t to have the same causal role as S_1–S_4's being aligned at t? Presumably, the two facts would have to have all the same causes and, in combination with all the same additional causal factors, all the same effects. For simplicity, let us just consider the second half of this condition and ask the question whether L's being unlocked at t does indeed combine with all the same factors to produce all the same effects as does S_1–S_4's being aligned at t. I want to suggest (1) that the answer to this question is 'no'; (2) that the reasons why the answer is 'no' make it obvious that no alternative candidate for identity of causal role with L's being unlocked at t is available at the lower, mechanical level; and (3) that similar difficulties are bound to dog all attempts to find facts at lower levels which share causal roles with facts at higher ones.

To begin with, then, does L's being unlocked at t have the same causal role as S_1–S_4's being aligned at t? Here is a difficulty for the unrefined suggestion that these two facts share a causal role in the sense outlined above. With a little imagination, it is undoubtedly possible to conceive of circumstances in which S_1–S_4 are aligned at t and yet where L is not unlocked at t. Suppose, for example, that a metal catch were to be attached to one of the discs in such a way that when S_1–S_4 are aligned, it springs into place to prevent the lock from opening. There is, in the actual world, no such catch, but if there had been, L would not have been unlocked at t even if its slots had been aligned at t. The absence of such a catch might therefore plausibly be accounted an aspect of the actual case which is causally relevant to the fact that L opens when gently pulled—a condition which, therefore, on the combinatorial model, ought to be thought of as combining with S_1–S_4's being aligned to ensure that the lock opens when gently pulled. But L's being unlocked obviously does not combine with any such condition—if the lock really is unlocked, the catch must be absent anyway—there is no need for L's being unlocked to combine with this condition. The two facts do not therefore have the same causal role—they do not occupy precisely the same position in the causal web.

It is likely to be objected to this line of reasoning that facts concerning absences and similar negatively characterized conditions ought simply not to be included in causal networks at all. But it is hard to provide a suitably independent rationale for this suggestion, once we have made the concession that the network is to represent causal relationships involving facts. For it is undeniable that facts which concern absences and lacks can be counterfactually relevant to certain effects. Once it is clear that the causal relation with which we are concerned when speaking of facts is relevance, and not efficacy, there seems to be no good reason whatever for making distinctions between positive and negative facts. All the intuitions which support the idea that there is something odd about absences, lacks, and other negative states of affairs participating in causal relations seem to me to stem from ideas—no doubt quite plausible ones—about the sorts of things which can and cannot have efficacy, or which can and cannot stand in the two-place extensional relation which I have called 'causing'. But if I am right, and relevance is simply a different sort of relation altogether, these intuitions cannot be used in support of the claim that negative facts can never be causally relevant to anything.

If it is once conceded that negative facts as well as positive ones can be causally relevant to particular effects and therefore require incorporation into causal networks, then, I think it will have to be conceded that L's being unlocked and S_1–S_4's being aligned do not share a causal role. But, it might be said, this does not mean that there is no lower-level fact at all which occupies the same causal role as L's being unlocked. We are simply going to need to specify a more complex lower-level condition, some kind of conjunctive fact, S_1–S_4's being aligned and modifications to the cylindrical lock being absent, for example. What is essential is merely that our characterization of the lower-level fact should be sufficiently rich to prevent the possibility of there being possible worlds in which the lower-level fact obtains, though the higher-level fact does not. But there is no reason to think that it is impossible to characterize such a condition, and therefore no reason to think that there is no lower-level fact whatever which shares a causal role with L's being unlocked.

In effect, what this proposal amounts to is that the best candidate for the lower-level fact which shares the causal role of L's being unlocked is a sufficient condition for L's being unlocked, specified in the terms of that lower level. I think there are strong reasons for being sceptical about the possibility of producing such a sufficient condition, partly because I see no reason to suppose that there is any clear limit to the number of negative conditions which might need to be included, partly because of the worry about whether it would be possible to supply a genuinely sufficient condition without straying beyond the bounds of any single 'level' of explanation, which I noted above. But even supposing it were possible to characterize such a thing, what reason is there to think that this proposal would produce a fact which stood in all the same causal relations to other facts and events as L's being unlocked? It might, for example, be causally relevant to L's being unlocked at t_2 that I forgot to lock L at t_1. But is the fact that I forgot to lock L at t_1 also going to be causally relevant to the complex conjunctive sufficient condition which is the proposed candidate for occupant of the relevant causal role? Perhaps it will be relevant to some of the conjuncts (e.g. perhaps it will be relevant to the fact that L's slots are aligned at t_2) but it would seem to be utterly irrelevant to others (e.g. to the fact that there are no modifications to the lock of the sort described above). We could perhaps try to preserve the causal relevance of my forgetting to lock L at t_1 to the whole conjunctive sufficient condition by suggesting that a fact can be causally relevant to a conjunctive fact provided it is relevant to at least one of the conjuncts. But this condition is just too weak to underwrite the judgements about identity of causal role for which we were originally hoping. There would seem, were we to adopt this suggestion, to be nothing to prevent us from simply adding arbitrary conjuncts to the fact which is our candidate for identity of causal role with L's being unlocked—their irrelevance being no bar to their inclusion, once we have adopted the principle above.

In short, it seems to me that relevance relations are simply not the sorts of relations in terms of which a causal role of the sort demanded by the idea of isomorphic causal webs might be specified. One way of putting the point would be to say that causal roles for *facts*, given that they will necessarily involve relevance relations, are bound to be the sorts of things that are unique to relatively 'fine-grained' entities. There is a traditional view that facts which are expressed by means of terms and predicates drawn from very different vocabularies might nevertheless be identified one with another on the basis of the a posteriori finding that they shared a causal role. But on the current view, this is to invoke a conception of causal role which is based on a misunderstanding of the way facts function in causal explanations. Facts expressed by means of widely differing terms and predicates, on this view, cannot share causal roles, for there will simply be too many ways of finding facts which are causally relevant to the one but not to the other, or facts to which one is causally relevant and the other is not, or facts with which one has to be thought of as 'combining', on the network model, to produce an effect, but with which the other cannot be thought of as thus combining. The idea that there is a sensible general project of mapping facts whose constituents and structural properties look prima facie to be very different one onto another on the basis of their sharing causal roles is, I suggest, an illusion born of a conception of causal role which makes sense, if at all, only in connection with particular causes and extensional causal relations.

In connection with what has gone before it, this chapter has aimed to support the two conclusions (1) that the role of 'standing conditions' in the causal explanation of a given effect is a matter of certain facts being relevant to that outcome, not of particular token states part-causing the outcome; and (2) that the causal relevance of facts cannot be comfortably accommodated by the network model of causation, at any rate in such a way that the model retains those features which support the conception of causal role and of isomorphic causal webs which have been so important in the formulation and discussion of many positions and issues in philosophy of mind. I believe that these two conclusions ought to have consequences for some current mind–body debates. In the final two chapters, I want to go on to try to explain in more detail what some of those consequences might be.

8

Token Identity Theories

THE views about causation and causal explanation which I have been expounding throughout the previous chapters have, I believe, important repercussions for philosophy of mind. In the next two chapters, I want to explain what I take some of these repercussions to be. I shall be looking at three areas of philosophical debate, all within the general area of the mind–body problem, which seem to me to have been distorted in various ways by untenable versions of the network model of causation and unacceptable, particularist views of the nature of states. My three targets will be the token identity theory, conceived of as a general theory of the nature of mind; a certain kind of argument for eliminative materialism; and a popular way of making the case for the view that intentional content is doomed to be an epiphenomenon, incapable of having any genuine causal relevance to action. Eliminativism and epiphenomenalism I take to be linked in an interesting way; the two positions can be regarded as the alternative, unattractive horns of a dilemma with which one fairly quickly finds oneself faced if one fails to come to a proper understanding of the distinctions between different sorts of causal explanation, upon which I have been insisting. I shall therefore treat eliminativism and the problem of epiphenomenalism together in Chapter 9. In this chapter, though, I begin with the token identity theory—which can, I think, also be seen to be connected with the other two areas which I shall be discussing, though in a way different from that by which they are connected to one another. The connection is constituted, as I see it, by the fact that the token identity theory often serves as a kind of starting-point from which arguments either for eliminativism or for the epiphenomenality of mental properties are able to take off. If we are to rescue both the reality and the causal relevance of mentality, it seems to me, we will have to be clear about the mistakes which are embodied in the position from which they both take their departure.

Before proceeding, a word may be in order about the term 'token identity theory'. Not many philosophers these days, I suspect, would use the term 'token identity theory' to describe either their own views or those of other philosophers. Partly, this has to do with a (perfectly justifiable) fear, which besets many physicalistically inclined philosophers, of burdening themselves with absurdly strong commitments by making use of the identity relation in order to state their claims; partly, it is doubtless just a matter of changing philosophical fashions. But in case it should be thought that an attack on the token identity theory is an attack on a straw man, it may need to be said that the absence of the terminology from much recent literature does not reflect the absence of belief in the theory. There are plenty of token identity theorists around; it is simply that new ways of dividing up the philosophical territory upon which today's mind–body battles are fought have obscured the common ontological presuppositions which many of the main antagonists share. 'Intentional realism', 'functional specification theory', 'anomalous monism', and so on, all sound very different—and no doubt, in many respects *are* very different—from one another, but there are exceedingly influential versions of each in the literature which are quite evidently committed to the idea that mental events and states are to be identified with events and states which can be described in terms which involve no essential reference to persons or to intentional contents—most usually, events and states which are conceived of as occurring or persisting in the brain. I have no particular liking for the old terminology of 'token identity' myself; indeed, I argued in Chapter 4 that we ought to eschew the use of the type–token distinction in connection with the attempt to make the sorts of distinctions which the phrase 'token identity theory' was originally introduced to clarify. But I am concerned that new, less ontologically rooted classification schemes have obscured once dominant ontological issues; and in insisting on this somewhat outmoded term of classification, I hope to be able to argue simultaneously against quite a large number of contemporary views by presenting a general argument against the ontological presuppositions which I believe they have in common.

The theory which is usually called the token identity theory by philosophers is normally stated and argued for as a theory about mental events; it is often said, for example, to be the view that all mental events are physical events.[1] But it is sometimes thought that when the theory is stated in this way, the term 'event' ought to be construed rather broadly. In particular, it seems frequently to be taken for granted that the theory can be readily extended to cover items which it is more natural to regard as mental states. Indeed, the literature in this area of philosophy of mind is littered with catch-all references to 'events, states and processes', it being simply assumed, seemingly, that for the most part, what goes for one of these categories goes for all.[2] Beliefs, desires, and other propositional attitude states have thus come to figure amongst the entities which the token identity theory is thought of as covering— and on many interpretations, that theory therefore implies the view that these psychological states are identical with states of the brain.

In the rest of this chapter, I want to argue that the mistakes embodied in the view of causation which I have been calling the network model—the view according to which states are to be thought of as separate, causally efficacious particulars, each of which acts in concert with other events and states in a causal network—have lent illusory support to the token identity theory, and to other particularist theories of mind.[3] I shall argue for the strong claim that the token identity theory is not only untrue of beliefs, desires, and the like, but that without the support provided by the imagery associated with the mistaken causal picture, it is probably unintelligible, conceived of as a theory which encompasses these states. In previous chapters, I have suggested that token states cannot be regarded, as they are so often regarded, as particulars of the same calibre as such bona-fide individuals as physical objects and events. In this chapter, I want to make out a case for the correlative thesis that certain conditions on the intelligibility of identity statements which are automatically satisfied where the terms of the identity are genuine particulars go unfulfilled in the case of the token state identities which are of interest to the philosopher of mind—identities between 'token states' like beliefs and desires and so-called 'token states of the brain' (or of its parts).

---

[1] Davidson's argument for anomalous monism in 'Mental Events' is certainly the best-known example. But others have also argued for and against the token identity theory using an ontology of events; see e.g. Christopher Peacocke's argument for the token identity theory in *Holistic Explanation* (Oxford, 1979), 134–43.

[2] See above, Intro., n. 5, for some examples.

[3] See my Intro. for this notion.

1. UNDERSTANDING IDENTITY STATEMENTS

It is usually conceded by the token identity theorist that we do not know the precise content of any of the mental–physical state identity statements in which she believes, because of neurophysiological ignorance; her commitment to their existence is independent of the knowledge of any particular identities of this kind. Let us imagine, though, that we have one such statement at hand. Let us suppose that the token identity theorist is proposing to identify the belief of some subject *S* that his friend Jones owns a Ford Fiesta with some state of his brain (possibly a very complex state which might require a highly detailed neurophysiological description). We can call this description *D*. The identity can now be expressed by means of the following identity statement:

(I) *S*'s belief that Jones owns a Ford Fiesta = the brain state described by *D*.

What I want to ask is whether we could really understand the content of this identity statement, and others like it, even if we knew the precise description for which *D* stands. What does it mean? Do we really understand the idea of a single thing which could be identified both as a belief with a particular content, and also by a neurophysiological description? What kind of fact does *I* express?

It might be thought initially that this is a strange question. For it is natural to think that the understanding required in order to make sense of an identity statement of any kind is really fairly rudimentary; in short, that to understand any identity of the form '*a* = *b*', one needs only to know what '*a*' refers to, to know what '*b*' refers to, and to understand the identity relation. Propositions concerning identity, one might think, are primitive propositions which make claims about simple one-and-the-sameness which cannot be expressed in other terms. One might answer the question above, then, simply by saying that the kind of proposition which *I* expresses is just an identity proposition, perhaps true, perhaps false, and that there is nothing more to be said.

It is probably not unreasonable to think that the identity statements with which we are most familiar are those whose relata are ordinary physical objects of various kinds—and perhaps it is true that there is no very elaborate story to be told about the content of such identity statements as these. It is true, of course, that identity statements have been associated with various kinds of philosophical puzzlement—but it is nevertheless easy to understand why informative identities involving physical objects arise, and it is easy also for an ordinary speaker to understand the information conveyed by them. In learning, for example, that Hesperus was Phosphorus, the ancient Babylonians learned a fact whose content is quite plain to us once we understand the context—once we know, for example, that 'Hesperus' and 'Phosphorus' are names of a planet, and once we understand how the two names came to be associated with different modes of presentation of that planet.[4] Even if background stories are sometimes needed (sometimes ordinary stories which explain how it is that we have come to possess two names for a single item in the first place; sometimes philosophical stories which adjust our preconceptions about language in order to deal with certain problems thought to be raised by identity statements), we do not need to supply any philosophical account of *what it would be* for Hesperus to be identical with Phosphorus. As ordinary language-users, we know already what it would be. The content of the identity stands in no need of further explication.

It seems to me, though, that token state identities lack this simple intelligibility. Let us return to *I*. I believe that we have no comparably clear and straightforward grasp of the claim *I* makes—that no 'primitive' understanding of this identity claim is available to us. It is an identity claim that needs a mooring; we need to be provided with a special sort of background before we can make the claim properly intelligible to ourselves. It does not suffice for understanding *I* merely to know which belief is involved in the identity, and which state of the brain, and to understand the meaning of the identity relation. In this case we need something further—we need an account of *what it would be* for a belief to be identical with a state of the brain. Until we have that, we are floundering, being asked to countenance an identity between two things which belong to entirely different realms of experience between which we do not understand how there *could* be an identity without further help. We do not know what *I* means—what would make it true—until we have such an account.

---

[4] The example, of course, is Frege's; see his 'On Sense and Meaning'.

Why do we need this extra resource in order to understand state identities—and why is there no need for any similar account in the physical-object case? The answer, I think, is that it is a condition of understanding the sense of names like 'Hesperus' and 'Phosphorus', a condition of knowing what Hesperus and Phosphorus *are*, that one know enough about them to render it already comprehensible that they should be one and the same thing. It is tempting to use the idea of a sortal concept to make the point (though, as we shall see in a moment, this cannot be the whole story). Sortal concepts often aid our comprehension of identities involving physical objects (and events) in a manner to which nothing corresponds in the case of token state identities—which puts a great, and ultimately insupportable, burden on the general concept of a token state itself. Hesperus and Phosphorus, for example, are the same *planet*. If one understands the names 'Hesperus' and 'Phosphorus', one already knows that both are planets (or thinks that both are stars, depending on the state of one's astronomical knowledge) and so the identity statement which relates them imparts what is, as it were, an already metaphysically comprehensible fact to anyone who knows what the names refer to (though it may not be an empirically comprehensible fact until one has some background story about the movements of the planets). If Hesperus and Phosphorus are both planets, they are, at any rate, the same *sort of thing*—which is, after all, a condition of the possibility of their being one and the same thing. In this case, the sortal concept 'planet' (or 'star'—or even 'heavenly body') mediates our understanding of the relevant identity statement; understanding the relevant sortal is at once part of understanding the sense of the terms which flank the identity sign and also a key to the metaphysical comprehensibility of the identity statement.

But in the case of the states which the token identity theorist wishes to see identified, there is no sortal concept which could play this mediating role. No level of description more specific than the categorial concept 'state' (or 'token state') is available. If we ask the question: '*S*'s belief and the brain state described by *D* are the same . . . what?', there is no way of responding more determinately than with the answer that they are the same state.[5] And so the

---

[5] If the identity is true, of course, *S*'s belief will be a brain state and the brain state described by *D* will be a belief—and so it will be true both that *S*'s belief and the brain state described by *D* are the same belief and that they are the same brain state.

attempt to make sense of identities like *I* is considerably more difficult than in the 'Hesperus = Phosphorus' type case. We do not have an automatic understanding of how the identity *could* be true, simply in virtue of knowing what the terms of the identity statement refer to.

It might be asked, though, whether this lack of a sortal mediator is really enough, in itself, to render mental–physical state identities unintelligible. For it might be pointed out, with justice, that it is not only stative identities which require to be understood without help from mediating sortal concepts. The event identities between mental events and events in the brain to which token identity theorists are committed, for example, seem to be like stative identities in this respect—there is no level more specific than the categorial level 'event' in terms of which they can be understood. If '*M*' is a mental event, and '*P*' some physical event, that is, there is no answer to the question '*M* and *P* are the same . . . what?' more specific than that they are the same event. But though token mental–physical event identities may be problematic for all sorts of reasons, unintelligibility is not any longer a common charge, and it is doubtful whether it is really a sustainable one. It is surely not *unintelligible* that someone's sudden feeling of a pain, say, should be identical with a neural event. The challenge, then, is to say whether, and how, such event identities differ from state identities of the kind expressed by *I*.

In my opinion, it must be accepted that there *is* an important difference here. The claim that a pain event, for example, might be identical with an event in the brain—that one and the same event might be both felt as pain and witnessed as an occurrence in the brain by a third person suitably equipped to observe it—seems to me to be a suggestion which we have no real difficulty in understanding, of a kind comparable to that which attends the attempt to make sense of an identity statement like *I*. But if there is a difference here, what is its source? Why should mind–brain event identities be easier to understand than identities involving states?

It seems to me that there are several related reasons for the contrast. To begin with, unlike the concept of event, the concept of

But what is needed is a sortal under which both terms of the identity can be unhesitatingly brought, quite independently of the question whether or not the identity is true, and neither 'belief' nor 'brain state', nor any more-detailed variants on either, will serve this purpose.

a token state is strictly a philosophers' concept. This is not merely a matter of the fact that the *name* of the category would be unfamiliar to a person without any philosophical background. Rather, I should like to suggest, there is really *nothing* one could point to, no fact about grammar or linguistics, no idiomatic modes of expression, no practice of any kind, outside technical philosophy that could be used to argue that we have an everyday understanding of token states comparable to the grasp of the concept of an event which every ordinary speaker possesses, an understanding that might throw some light on the question what makes one token state distinct from, or identical to, another. States in general, it is true, make plenty of appearances in ordinary language, but firstly, the uses to which the concept is put are too diverse to yield anything which could be called a folk conception of a metaphysical category; and secondly, in so far as we bring the linguistic apparatus of identity and individuation to bear directly on states in our ordinary practices, it is in connection with questions of diachronic, not synchronic, identity. Sometimes, for example, a state has been in existence continuously for a length of time and we wish to draw attention to the fact (e.g. 'I'm still in the same state of depression as I was when you last saw me'), but even if it can be argued that we can make sense of the idea of identity over time for states, it is not identity over time which is at issue for the token identity theorist. What she needs to render intelligible is identity of individual states, not over time, but over radically differing modes of presentation; the controversial relations of identity to which she is committed are synchronic, not diachronic. The question is whether we can really understand what it is for an individual state to be describable from two entirely different points of view—describable in the terms of two entirely different vocabularies—the folk-psychological and the neurophysiological. And it is certainly arguable that no practice, linguistic or otherwise, with which we are familiar from everyday contexts gives us any pre-philosophical understanding of the conditions under which states may be identified synchronically, one with another. This is one reason why we need a philosophical account of what it would be for a belief to be identical with a token brain state—ordinary practice leaves us in the dark.

A second point is that even though sortal event concepts may be unavailable to perform a mediating role in the case of certain individual identity claims, there at least exists a huge and varied assortment of such concepts to underpin and enrich our general understanding of the category: explosion, eruption, run, sneeze, wedding, picnic, demonstration, movement, etc. Any of these could be used to answer the question 'What kind of event was x?' But there is nothing comparable to underwrite our hazy understanding of the category of state. The question 'What kind of state was x?' is more comfortably answered with an adjective than with any kind of individuative sortal (e.g. 'x was an untidy/depressed/excited state'); or else with a phrase incorporating the 'state of . . .' idiom (e.g. x was a state of untidiness/depression/excitement). But neither of these gives us any independent help with understanding the identity conditions of individual states—both depend already on the concept of a state for any individuative power they might be thought to possess. Other possibilities for answering the question, perhaps significantly, fail to be count-quantifiable (e.g. 'x was anger', 'x was hatred', 'x was indigestion'). There are exceptions, of course: 'belief' and 'pain', philosophy of mind's two favourite examples, are two count-quantifiable nouns which have been thought to denote kinds of state. But it is arguable that in so far as pains are count-quantifiable, it is not pain *states* that are the objects of the individuation thereby effected, but rather locatable feelings which ought rather to be regarded either as pain events, or as items in the category of phenomenal object, along with, for example, mental images, hallucinations, and ringings in the ear. 'Being in pain' is the stative idiom. And nothing which is afforded us by the capacity to individuate beliefs according to their content gives us any idea of how to understand the suggestion that these very same beliefs might be identical with brain states.

A third point is that we are given a certain kind of grip on the content of many identity statements concerning genuine spatiotemporal particulars by our understanding of the ideas of occupancy and location which go with our conception of the spatiotemporal framework itself. Space provides us with the clearest imaginative model we have of the possibility that a single thing might be approached epistemologically in two ways—it is the source, indeed, of the 'two-route' metaphor which I invoked in Chapter 1. A thing in space, whether it is a physical object or an event, can be seen, literally, from two sides, without one necessarily realizing that it is the same thing which has been seen in each case. Frege's Afla–Ateb example can serve as a kind of paradigm case here.[6] In Frege's example, it is the fact that a spatially located object presents two different faces to the world that generates the informative identity statement 'Afla = Ateb'. It is, of course, manifestly false that a story of this particular, spatially orientated variety must underlie *every* identity statement concerning spatial particulars (consider, for instance, 'Tully = Cicero', 'the heaviest thing in the room = the largest thing in the room', 'the sinking of the *Titanic* = the event mentioned on page 5 of *The Times*', none of which depends on differences in modes of presentation which are essentially spatial). However, it is arguable that the particular event identities to which the token identity theorist is committed *do* rely for their intelligibility on the fact that the idea that an event might quite literally be seen from more than one side already makes sense to us.

The governing idea in the case of these mental–physical event identities is normally that of a single event which could in principle give rise to two different kinds of experience—the first-personal experience of feeling a pain, having a mental image, making a decision, or whatever, and the third-personal experience of observing an event in the brain. The idea of two epistemological routes to the same entity is involved, just as in the Afla–Ateb case, and it is not implausible that this idea is easy for us to understand because we are able to model it on such cases. We can imagine what it would be for a single event to present us with two aspects, without there being any question of a threat to its unity as a spatiotemporal particular—a single happening in a single place at a single time. But it is not possible to conceive so readily of a single token state presenting both a mental and a physical aspect, because we are not already equipped with any basic spatial understanding of how a token state might appear to us in more than one way. The spatiotemporal particularity which would guarantee the intelligibility of this 'two-route' picture is absent. Being neither occupants nor occurrents, states do not have a presence in the spatiotemporal framework of the kind which might enable us to make sense of informative identities involving them in this simple way; we need ways of conceiving of their one-and-the-sameness which are not dependent primarily on the idea of spatiotemporal coincidence.

---

[6] See Ch. 1 n. 44 for this example.

None of this is to say, of course, that we can make no sense at all of token state identities. I have merely attempted to show that we cannot simply assume that the ready understanding we have of identities between particulars is available in the token state case. There can be no 'primitive' understanding of the content of token state identities—a philosophical account is needed to give sense to the question when one token state can be regarded as identical with another, to give sense, indeed, to the concept of a token state. Nothing I have said so far in this chapter has proved that such an account would be impossible. However, I think it can be shown that the only account which could conceivably give intelligible content to the identity statements between mental and physical states which the token identity theorist endorses would need to depend crucially on the mistaken picture of stative causation against which I have been arguing.

2. TOKEN STATE IDENTITIES AND THE NETWORK MODEL OF CAUSATION

According to many philosophers, our commitment to the existence of beliefs and other propositional attitude states is a quasi-theoretical commitment.[7] Our reason for believing in them, roughly, is this: we use them in order to explain our own rational behaviour and that of others, and in doing so, we invoke generalizations which belong to a theory called 'folk psychology' which tells us roughly how mental states and events interact with one another, so as to give rise to behaviour (such pearls of wisdom as that if someone desires x and believes that he can get x by y-ing, then, other things being equal, he will y). Our commitment to their existence in the first place, then, is based on our commitment to their existence as *causal* entities—they are supposed to be needed in

---

[7] Unfortunately, there is not space here to enter into the debate about the extent to which folk psychology shares the characteristics of a scientific theory. My own feeling is that the 'theory-theory', as Stephen Stich calls it (see his *From Folk Psychology to Cognitive Science*, ch. 2—he attributes the original use of the term to Adam Morton, *Frames of Mind* (Oxford, 1980)), usually brings in its tow the undesirable picture of stative causation against which I have been inveighing. In my view, the 'ontological commitments' of folk psychology are usually best understood as commitments to abstract entities, not unobservable concrete ones, as the 'theory-theory' is apt to imply.

order to explain causally why we do what we do. But this in turn suggests a means of getting a grip on the identity statements of which I alleged in the previous section it was not possible to have what I called a 'primitive' understanding. Might not the idea of a causal network of interacting mental states and events, such as is alleged to be involved in folk psychology, supply what the spatiotemporal framework supplied in the case of more straightforward particulars?—namely a way of understanding *what it would be* for a mental state like a belief to be identical with a state of the brain? Once the idea of a causal network relating psychological individuals to one another and to resultant actions is in place, we can give sense to the claim that these individuals are identical with states and events in the brain. What it would be for some individual belief to be identical with a state of the brain would be for there to be a neurophysiological reflection of the folk-psychological causal story in which that belief figures—in other words, the idea of isomorphic causal networks is essentially involved in giving sense to the identity.

It is common to find the claim made that the token identity theory cannot be true unless there is isomorphism between the causal structures generated by folk psychology and those which neurophysiology delivers.[8] But if I am right, we can make a stronger claim. For in my view, the idea that psychological events and states are linked to one another in a causal web whose shape is dictated by folk psychology and which might or might not prove to be isomorphic with some similar causal web which specifies the interconnections between neural events and states is the only resource we have to draw on in the attempt to make the relevant token state identities comprehensible to ourselves. It is the idea of a state as a causally efficacious individual occupying a definite position in some causal structure that helps us to form a conception of what it would be for such a state to be identical with a physical state. Without this picture, there is nothing in our understanding of the nature of states which could render the token identity theory metaphysically comprehensible. It is not just a necessary condition of the token identity theory's being true that such an isomorphism should exist; the possibility of such an isomorphism is a necessary condition of its making any sense at all.

[8] See e.g. Davidson, 'The Material Mind', 254–5, and Horgan and Tye, 'Against the Token Identity Theory', 428, for claims to this effect.

Why should the causal network picture be so helpful in this regard? One reason is that the network picture provides us with a concept other than 'state', under which both mental and physical states can be brought—not a sortal, exactly, but something which will serve at least as well as 'event' to underwrite the mental–physical identities to which the token identity theorist is committed. With the network picture in place, we can say that an individual mental state is the same *causally efficacious entity* as some individual physical state, and then we can appeal to the concept of isomorphic causal webs to elucidate what it is for one causally efficacious entity to be identical with another, using something like Horgan and Tye's concept of an R-correlate.[9] In this way, the possibility of isomorphism grounds the identity—it gives us some conception of what would have to be the case in order for the identity to be true—which can make up for the absence of any more primitive understanding of the relevant identity statement. And secondly, the idea of a causal network can be thought of as a kind of analogue of the spatiotemporal framework. I argued above that the idea of spatiotemporal coincidence helps us understand many two-route identity claims, where genuine particulars like physical objects and events are concerned, but that this idea cannot help out with two-route identities for token states. The idea of a causal network, however, gives us a conception of a different kind of coincidence—a different way in which a framework might define a space in which there is room for only a single individual—and hence a need to make identifications. Where a plurality of isomorphic causal webs exists, each of which purports to represent the causal antecedents of some action, identifications seem to be demanded if causal overdetermination of the action is to be avoided. The analogy between the spatial and the causal frameworks here is doubtless loose in many ways—but it seems clear, nevertheless, that they perform a roughly similar function in providing a background against which we can make sense of certain kinds of identity statement.

It looks, then, as though the network model of causation is essential if we are to be able to regard the token identity theory as a meaningful hypothesis, as far as states are concerned. I have already argued in previous chapters, though, that in treating states

---

[9] See Chapter 7, Sect. 3, for an elucidation of this idea.

as individual, causally efficacious entities of much the same kind as events, the network picture overlooks the crucial differences between singular and sentential explanations. Of course, the idea that we might try to represent the aetiology of some particular action by means of a diagram detailing the beliefs, desires, thoughts, intentions, emotions, whatever, that are thought to be involved in its provenance is not in itself objectionable; what is mistaken is the thought that such a diagram represents the causal interactions of a set of separate, particular entities. What it actually represents is a collection of the nominalized *explanantes* of the various sentential explanations which we deem appropriate in the particular case—a picture of the relevant facts, not the structure of a physically realized web of causal interactions amongst particulars. The causal character of belief–desire explanation need not be threatened by this realization, provided we recognize the causal relevance relation—one need not find beliefs to be causally efficacious particulars in order to think that one does things, in part, because of what one believes. But the intelligibility of the token identity theory *is* threatened. If the only representation we can manage of the role of mental states in the causation of an individual action is a diagram detailing the causally relevant *facts*, we cannot draw on the idea of a causal network, isomorphic with some network of neural events and states, to license identifications between mental and physical states.

In case it should be tempting to think that the production of a network which either consisted of or included facts would be no less useful for the generation of token identities than the production of a network of individual, causally efficacious particulars, let me point out that I have already given an argument in Chapter 7 to explain why we cannot countenance the identification of facts, one with another, on the basis of their having 'the same causal role'. I argued there that once causal roles are conceived of as things whose specifications need to include relevance links, it becomes clear that they are bound to be unique to fine-grained entities—since facts stated by means of different terms and predicates will not be able to preserve all the same counterfactual relationships to all the same elements of the web. The fact that token states are not proper particulars really *is* crucial. Of course, I am not attempting to deny that there must be important connections and dependencies between psychological states of affairs and physical ones—or even that we might be able to state some important dependencies of this kind with a high degree of accuracy. All I wish to maintain is that relations like identity and composition are out of place in the statement of the relationships between the two domains—at any rate, as far as states like beliefs are concerned. We should cease to formulate physicalism primarily as a doctrine about the nature of a class of particulars; what it needs to be, if it is to have any chance of being true, is a statement about the relationships between the different truths which specify the way things are with a person and with her body, or parts of her body—a statement about relationships between different sorts of fact.

It seems to me, then, that we cannot make sense of the stative identity statements to which the token identity theorist is committed without relying on the conception of stative causation against which I argued in Chapters 5–7. It is not just that the token identity theory is false of beliefs and desires—it is incomprehensible, once it is appreciated that the picture of states as causally efficacious particulars cannot be sustained. We do not have any conception of what identity amounts to for states, of the rich kind which a proper understanding of the token identity theory demands—and the role played by states in causal explanations cannot meet the deficiency.

9

Eliminativism and the Problem of Epiphenomenalism

In the previous chapter, I argued that the token identity theory is not only false, but proves ultimately to be unintelligible, when it is conceived of as a general theory of the nature of mind, i.e. as a theory which is intended to encompass such psychological 'states' as beliefs, desires, intentions, and so on. In this chapter, I want to trace two lines of thought which can be seen to be rooted in the token identity theory, in the sense that both, in their different ways, arose out of the perception that that theory was not satisfactory, despite its attractive simplicity, as an attempt to provide a physicalistically respectable understanding of the nature of psychological states. The first line of thought led to a radical conclusion and to what might justly be called a new position in the philosophy of mind—eliminativism; the second has not really resulted in the emergence of a new philosophical position, as such, since its end-point—the conclusion that mental properties have no causal relevance to anything (a conclusion which I shall henceforth refer to as 'epiphenomenalism')—has (rightly) normally been regarded as a *reductio ad absurdum* of its presuppositions. But this difference between the two lines of thought, it seems to me, is really no more than a historical accident; eliminativism ought also to have been regarded, not as a possible resting-place, but as a sign that something had gone badly wrong with philosophy of mind. In this final chapter, I want to try to show how both eliminativism and epiphenomenalism can be regarded as the upshot of the ontological mistakes and the misunderstandings of the workings of causal explanations which I have tried to highlight in earlier chapters; and how both can be safely and easily avoided once these errors are expunged from our ways of thinking about the mind.

1. TWO CHARACTERIZATIONS OF ELIMINATIVISM

Eliminativism can be characterized as a thesis either about the non-existence of certain sorts of mental *entity*, or about the lack of applicability of certain mental *predicates*. When characterized in the first way, the eliminativist's conclusion is that there are no such things as beliefs, desires, intentions, and so on—that no genuinely existent entities fall under the categories with which we are provided by what is tendentiously called 'folk' psychology. Beliefs and desires are like witches and demons and caloric fluid, on this view— they are entities which we invoked, before we knew any better, in an attempt to explain why people did and said the sorts of things they did and said, just as we once invoked witches and demons to explain certain sorts of illness and madness, and just as we once invoked caloric fluid to explain the transfer of heat from one body to another. Now, though, we know there are no such things as witches, demons, and caloric fluid; we have theories which provide us with much better explanations of the phenomena in question. And similarly, according to the eliminativist, cognitive science and the neurosciences will soon have provided us with much better explanations of why we do and say what we do and say than folk psychology ever did, or could. The 'entities' which folk psychology invokes, therefore, will come to be regarded as fictional creations, products of the outmoded categories of a falsified theory of rational behaviour.

When characterized in the second way, the eliminativist conclusion is that mental predicates, predicates like '. . . believes that Beijing is the capital of China' or '. . . hopes that Dave will mow the lawn on Saturday', are not genuinely true of anything. Nobody *really* believes or wants anything; nobody *really* hopes for anything or intends to do anything. Predicates like '. . . believes that Beijing is the capital of China', on this view, are like predicates such as '. . . contains such-and-such an amount of caloric fluid' or '. . . is possessed by demons'; they are predicates which will be revealed, as scientific theories progress to encompass the realm of human psychology, to be true of nothing.

I have distinguished these two ways of characterizing eliminativism because it seems to me that it is not an utterly straightforward matter to see them as equivalent (though they are often regarded as such). The first characterization is less clear, because it is not obvious quite what is meant by saying that there are 'no such things' as beliefs, desires, intentions, and so on; one difficulty with this formulation is that there are (admittedly not very natural) ways of construing this claim on which I should say it is most definitely *true*; though I am no eliminativist. For one might perhaps take the claim that there are 'no such things' as beliefs, desires, and so on, to mean that there are no such entities as I have been calling 'token states' of belief, desire, etc.—no stative entities which are particulars in the sense I have tried to characterize, which have impersonal, neurological descriptions as well as person-involving, content-involving ones. It is only when one characterizes eliminativism in the second way, it seems to me, that the conclusion appears in unambiguously eliminativist guise, only when one characterizes it in the second way that one sees the conclusion for the truly incredible position it is. But the preparedness of eliminativists to embrace the second conclusion as well as the first disambiguates the first for us. There are no such things as beliefs and desires, for a genuine eliminativist, in the strong sense that there are no believers and desirers—nobody who truly satisfies predicates of the form 'believes that φ' or 'desires that ψ'. And this conclusion is in no danger of being confused with the claims about the non-existence of token states of belief and desire which I have attempted to make; it is evidently a far more radical and far-reaching doctrine. It is also quite obviously false.

It seems to me that the staying-power of such an absurd doctrine as eliminativism needs explaining. The explanation, I believe, is that although arguments against the eliminativist *conclusion* are not wanting in the literature, it has not yet really been clearly, straightforwardly, and correctly pointed out what is wrong with certain eliminativist *arguments*—so that these arguments continue to persuade, despite the evident preposterousness of the conclusion to which they lead. I believe that the key to understanding where at least some eliminativist arguments go wrong lies with the distinction between causing and causal relevance which I have offered in Chapter 6 and with the associated denial, on which I have tried to insist, that beliefs and desires are particular states, in the sense of 'particular' characterized in Chapter 1. In order to make good this claim, I want to discuss one very influential kind of argument for eliminativism, whose conclusion fits the first of the characterizations above—the conclusion is formulated as the claim that there are no such things as beliefs. I shall try to show (1) that one of the premisses of the argument is simply false, and (2) that whatever prima-facie plausibility it might at first be thought to have is based on precisely the sorts of confusion about states and their role in causation that I have attempted to undermine.

2. AN ARGUMENT FOR ELIMINATIVISM

There is a kind of argument which is sometimes supposed to justify the conclusion that there are, strictly speaking, no such things as the states to which folk psychology appears to commit us—beliefs, desires, and the like. The resulting position can be conceived of, when argued for in this way, as derived from two premisses, one of which sets out a necessary condition for the existence of propositional attitudes, the other of which expresses scepticism about whether this condition is likely to be met, given the current state and likely development of cognitive science and neurophysiology. Stephen Stich is the best-known proponent of this form of argument, and I shall therefore concentrate here on the case against belief which is presented in his book *From Folk Psychology to Cognitive Science*. My suggestion will be that the first premiss of Stich's argument commits him to an untenable version of the network model of causation.

The following quotation from Stich's book contains the gist of the case against belief in which I am interested:

For folk psychology, a belief is a state which can interact in many ways with many other states and which can be implicated in the etiology of many different sorts of behaviour. A pattern of interaction which looms large in our commonsense scheme of things is the one linking beliefs to their normal, sincere, linguistic expression . . . But of course, the belief that p does much more than merely contribute to the causation of its own linguistic expression. It may interact with desires in many ways, some of which will ultimately issue in nonverbal behaviour. It is a fundamental tenet of folk psychology that *the very same* state which underlies the sincere assertion of 'p' also may lead to a variety of nonverbal behaviours . . . What is striking about the results I shall sketch is that they strongly suggest that . . . states similar to the one underlying our own ordinary utterance of 'p' do *not* also participate in the production of our nonverbal behaviour . . . And under those circumstances, I am strongly inclined to think that the right thing to say is that *there are no such things as beliefs.*[1]

As suggested above, this line of reasoning can be represented as a two-premiss argument, as follows:

(1) It is a necessary condition for the existence of beliefs that there should exist states characterizable in the vocabulary of some respectable science that have the causal roles which folk psychology ascribes to beliefs.

(2) Various experimental results show (or at least strongly suggest) that no states characterizable in the vocabulary of any respectable science have the causal roles which folk psychology ascribes to beliefs.

So (3) There are (or at least, it is very likely that there are) no such things as beliefs.

What I want to ask is why we have to accept (1).

It is striking that (1) has been quite widely accepted, even by the opponents of eliminativism. Many of those who have been concerned to defend folk psychology—intentional realists like Fodor, for example,[2] and functionalists like Jackson and Pettit[3]—have largely accepted that the vindication of folk psychology requires that scientifically respectable states having the causal roles which it ascribes to propositional attitudes exist. It is just that they suppose what Stich denies in premiss (2), that such states *do* exist. But fortunately, the defence of folk psychology need not turn on any such estimation of the likelihood of science turning up particular sorts of empirical results. The case against Stich's argument for eliminativism can, in my view, proceed entirely on the grounds that premiss (1) invokes a conception of beliefs which wrongly represents their role in causal explanation and requires an understanding of states according to which they are particular entities which combine additively with events and other states in just the way in which I have argued they should not be supposed to do.

Why should it be a necessary condition for the existence of beliefs that there exist states characterizable in the vocabulary of some

---

[1] *From Folk Psychology to Cognitive Science*, 230–1.
[2] See J. A. Fodor, *Psychosemantics* (Cambridge, Mass., 1987).
[3] See e.g. F. Jackson and P. Pettit, 'In Defence of Folk Psychology', *Philosophical Studies*, 59 (1990).

respectable science which have the causal role which folk psychology attributes to beliefs? Stich's idea (which is widely shared) is that folk psychology is a folk theory of the causation of behaviour, and that entities such as beliefs therefore have a status similar to that of many other theoretical entities; they are invoked in order causally to explain certain effects. In principle, then, as with all folk theories, it is possible that science should turn up findings which suggest that the sorts of causal processes which in fact underlie behaviour are very different from those hypothesized by the folk theory, or as Stich puts it, that 'the functional economy of the mind postulated by folk theory is quite radically mistaken'.[4] According to Stich, this 'functional economy' is subserved by beliefs which are 'states' and which 'interact' with other states. But given the radical conclusion which this premiss so readily generates, ought we not to question whether folk psychology does indeed make any such assumptions?

What is the 'raw data' which permits Stich the assumption that folk psychology postulates causally interacting states in order to explain behaviour? Presumably, it is our ordinary, everyday use of folk-psychological explanation. But which particular sorts of explanations are supposed to demonstrate our folk commitment to interacting propositional attitude states? It is in philosophical, not in everyday discourse that one finds talk of interacting token states of belief and desire combining to produce actions. No straightforward commitment to causal relations between such things as individual beliefs or desires (or 'token states' of belief and desire) and individual actions can be extracted from ordinary discourse. We do not, for example, say such things as 'My belief that it was about to rain caused my taking of an umbrella to work', or 'My desire to see the Crown Jewels caused my visiting of the Tower of London'. What we do say is rather such things as 'I took an umbrella because I believed (thought) it was going to rain', and 'I visited the Tower of London because I wanted (desired) to see the Crown Jewels'. But in these sentences, 'because' appears as a sentential connective. These sentences fit the sentential paradigm outlined in the previous chapters—they are not singular causal claims. Of course, we can rephrase these explanations in such a way as to yield explicit reference to individual actions and beliefs and

---

[4] *From Folk Psychology to Cognitive Science*, 231.

desires. If I did something intentionally, then some action of mine occurred. And if I did it in part because I believed that p, then it is all right to say that my belief that p 'was the cause of' my action, particularly if other causally relevant factors (e.g. desires) are already known, or can be taken for granted—just as one might say that the bridge's being weak was the cause of its collapse. But as I argued in Chapter 5, we must interpret the 'was the cause of' differently in these sentences from the way in which we interpret it in a sentence like 'The flood was the cause of the famine'. For the predicate 'cause' does not occur in these sentences; rather, the word 'cause' operates here as a disguised sentence functor. My belief is therefore not 'the cause' of my action in the same sense as the flood was 'the cause' of the famine. It is not even one of several causes of this straightforward kind which act jointly to bring about the action. As I have already argued, a cause of this kind cannot be a particular cause *at all*. The relation here is causal relevance, not causing. The often made claim that beliefs and desires (or 'reasons') are causes can obscure this; it makes it sound as though beliefs and desires stand to individual actions in the relation which is expressed by the two-place predicate 'cause'. But there need be no commitment to that thesis in the mere claim that rationalization is a species of causal explanation.

I suggest, then, that folk psychology contains no commitment whatever to token propositional attitude states, understood as particular entities which combine to produce actions. What it contains are predicates of a special kind—'believes that p', 'desires that q', and so on—whose nominalized forms, 'believing that p', 'desiring that q', etc., refer to properties, a person's possession of which can be causally relevant to what she does and says. But the fact that someone can do something because they believe that p and desire that q does not imply that anything which is characterizable in other terms must share the 'causal role' of the fact that the person believes that p or desires that q. As I argued in Chapter 7, once relevance relations are incorporated into the concept of causal role (as they must be) there is no reason to expect (and indeed, every reason not to expect) that causal roles will be shared by facts expressed by means of very different terms and predicates. Again, it needs to be emphasized that this is not to deny that which propositional attitudes a person has might depend (at least in part) on facts about her brain. It is to deny only that there is nothing

problematic about converting physicalistic commitments to de-
pendency or supervenience relations into commitments to particular identities or constitution claims.

The 'existence' of beliefs, then, I suggest, has nothing whatever to
do with the existence of any individual, causally efficacious entities.
The claim that someone's belief that p 'exists' can mean nothing
sensible unless it just means that the person in question believes that
p—that the property of believing that p is one that he or she
possesses. It is doubtless a necessary condition of this that certain
other things also be true of the person—and facts about her brain
may be amongst these. But it is a gross misrepresentation of
this simple truth to represent it as the requirement that physical
states must share the causal roles of beliefs. That way, indeed,
eliminativism lies, but it may be safely and easily avoided by refusing the eliminativist's first step: the introduction of 'token states'
into the characterization of folk-psychological commitment.

3. THE PROBLEM OF EPIPHENOMENALISM

Eliminativism presented what its proponents conceived of as an
empirically based challenge to the token identity theory by suggesting that no states characterizable in the vocabulary of any respectable science were likely to be found which shared the 'causal roles'
of beliefs and other 'folk-psychological' states. But the prospects for
finding an acceptable, non-reductive variety of physicalism have
been made to seem rather less bright over the last fifteen years for
reasons other than those mooted by eliminativists. A number of
issues have shaken the confidence of philosophers in theories of this
sort—one of the most prominent being the suggestion that non-
reductive renderings of physicalism do not after all secure the
reconciliation between mental and physical causation of human
action that was one of their original claims to distinction. Versions
of this worry vary, but roughly, the suggestion is that if we are
looking for a variant of physicalism which genuinely saves the
phenomenon of mental causation, it will not be sufficient merely to
identify mental particulars with physical ones. It will have in addition to be true that the mental properties of those particulars—an
event's being a thinking of the thought that p, or a state's being the
belief that q, for example—matter causally. It is not enough to

assure oneself that mental events and token mental states are physical entities. It must also be true—if mental causation is to be a reality—that what is caused to happen by those mental events and states happens 'in virtue of' their mental properties.[5] But this, it is alleged, is something which most versions of non-reductive physicalism end up having to deny. It is argued that claims made in order to defend the non-reductive aspects of such physicalisms—such as, for example, the claim that mental properties do not figure in any strict laws—effectively imply that the mental properties of mental events and states are causally irrelevant to the effects which those events and states combine to produce. Such theories, it is therefore concluded, do not, after all, save the phenomenon of mental causation.

To indicate just what the problem is supposed to be, it may be helpful to look briefly at an analogy. Suppose a person throws a stone which breaks a window. Using an ontology of particular events and a two-place causal relation, we can say that the person's throwing of the stone caused the breaking of the window. But we might also note that only certain properties of the event which was the person's throwing of the stone were causally relevant to its having had the effect it did. Perhaps its being a throwing of a stone such that the stone left the thrower's hand at a certain speed and in a certain direction mattered, for example, or its being a throwing of a particularly heavy stone, etc. But many of the properties of the throwing event will have been causally irrelevant to its having caused the breaking of the window—e.g. its taking place at 3.05 p.m. on a Tuesday, or its being a throwing of a *brown* stone.

Applied to the psychological case, now, the idea is this. Suppose we accept the token identity theory—namely that the mental states and events which bring about our actions are states and events which have physical descriptions. We might have thought initially that this was enough to secure the causal relevance of mentality. But the question seems to remain open, once we have said that our actions are caused by mental events and states, whether it was

---

[5] For views of this general kind, see T. Honderich, 'The Argument for Anomalous Monism', *Analysis*, 42 (1982); F. Stoutland, 'Davidson on Intentional Behaviour', and M. Johnston, 'Why Having a Mind Matters', both in LePore and McLaughlin (eds.), *Actions and Events: Perspectives on the Philosophy of Donald Davidson*.

really the mental *properties* of those mental events and states—properties like 'being a belief that *p*' or 'being a desire that *q*'—that mattered causally. If it were to turn out, the argument goes, that it was only really the physical properties of these events that mattered causally, we would not really have saved mental causation, for all the 'causal work' would be being done, in this case, by the physical properties of the mental events. It is not enough, therefore, to assure oneself that mental events and token mental states are physical entities. It must also be true—if mental causation is to be a reality—that what is caused to happen by those mental events and states happens 'in virtue of' their mental properties—otherwise, the truly mental aspects of mental events and states will not have mattered in the slightest.

One possible reaction to this argument would simply be to accept the claim that mental properties are not causally relevant to anything; that they really are epiphenomenal. As I remarked earlier, though, this has not, in general, been a popular response—unsurprisingly, for it is indeed a view that we can barely take seriously. We surely cannot embrace a doctrine which says that what we think and want is utterly irrelevant (causally speaking) to anything we do or say. To accept that we have beliefs, desires, thoughts, intentions, etc., but that their content is utterly irrelevant to anything we do, is, if anything, even more peculiar than accepting that there are no such things as beliefs, desires, thoughts, intentions, etc. at all; indeed, one can see how epiphenomenalist worries might lead one quite quickly to embrace eliminativism, for it is hard to see what content there would be in the insistence that we are indeed the subjects of propositional attitudes once the causal relevance of those attitudes to our actions has been severed.

A more frequently made suggestion is that the problem of epiphenomenalism shows that contemporary non-reductive physicalism has gone soft, so to speak, and that we need to move some way back towards the stronger physicalisms of days gone by, insisting on bridge laws, mental–physical property identities, and the like. It is often argued that the problem indicates that it was not enough, after all, to secure the physical status of our tokens—a workable physicalism will also have to find psychological types to be in some sense physical. But I shall try to suggest that this response is a move in the wrong direction. To solve the problem of epiphenomenalism, we do not need to gird up physicalism with extra reductionist claims, but rather to understand that the token identity theory burdened us with the wrong kinds of commitment in the first place.

4. THE SOLUTION TO THE PROBLEM OF EPIPHENOMENALISM

The first thing I should like to note about the way in which the problem of epiphenomenalism is normally stated is that it involves a kind of unnecessary detour through just the kinds of particularizing manœuvres to which I have been objecting throughout the last few chapters. The usual formulation of the difficulty poses a question about the causal relevance of the mental properties of events and states. Philosophers have offered different reasons for supposing that the mental properties of mental events and states can have no causal relevance to the effects they cause—the most prominent, perhaps, being the idea that mental properties do not figure in laws, together with the premiss that a property can only be causally relevant to an effect if it figures in some law or other, relating possession of that property by an individual to the production of effects of that sort. In a moment, I shall say something about this line of reasoning. But for now, I just want to ask what events and states are doing in the statement of the problem at all. Events and states, after all, are not the most obvious bearers of mental properties; the most obvious bearers of mental properties are *subjects*—human beings, and perhaps other sorts of creatures too. If there is a problem about the causal relevance of mental properties, then, why should it not be stated simply as a problem about how the mental properties of subjects—believing that *p*, desiring that *q*, and so on—can be causally relevant to what those subjects do and say? The usual reasons for being worried about the causal relevance of properties such as 'being a belief that *p*' or 'being a desire that *q*' seem to carry over perfectly well to the (surely more straightforward) properties 'believing that *p*' and 'desiring that *q*'—e.g. these properties do not seem to figure in strict causal laws.[6] Why, then, should we not just take a simple ontology of subjects and their

---

[6] This may not be true of all arguments for the epiphenomenalism of mental properties—I am not sure, for example, that the argument used by Ned Block in 'Can the Mind Change the World?' could be easily transposed into an argument for

properties in order to formulate the difficulty—why introduce events and states and their properties at all?

I am not suggesting, of course, that it is hard to understand why the problem of epiphenomenalism has been stated using an ontology of events and token states. The reason is writ large in the history of physicalism over the past forty years or so; it is that the ontology of events and states was originally supposed to help us *answer* the first-level problem of how someone's believing or wanting something can matter causally to what they do, given the existence of neurophysiological explanations for the bodily movements with which their actions were usually supposed identical. Individual states of belief and desire were introduced into the ontology of philosophy of mind precisely as a way of explaining how beliefs and desires could be causally relevant to individual actions, compatibly with the truths of neurophysiology. But the problem of epiphenomenalism (as usually formulated) is a symptom of the failure of this answer—and indeed, of the necessary failure of any attempt to answer the question how a certain sort of property (or fact) can be causally relevant to an effect by invoking particular causes. The difficulty is a straightforward structural one; with respect to any particular cause, the question can always be raised which of *its* properties were causally relevant to the effect in question? One cannot ever, therefore, ensure the causal relevance of a certain property (e.g. someone's believing that *p*) to an effect by postulating the existence of a particular (e.g. the 'token state' of believing that *p*) whose machinations are intended somehow to ground all the relevance relations in which the original property stood. For we will always need to be assured, if mental causation is to be saved, that it is only 'in virtue of' this token state's being the belief that *p* that it causes the effects it does; and we are back facing a problem of just the same shape as the one with which we started—a problem about how certain intuitively rather high-level properties of a particular thing can be causally relevant to the effects that particular is able to produce.

What I would like to suggest, then, is that the ontological framework in terms of which the problem of epiphenomenalism is usu-

the causal irrelevance of the mental properties of subjects. His argument uses as a premiss the claim that 'internal processors are sensitive to the "syntactic forms" of internal representations, not their meanings' (138), and this evidently takes a very specific model of intentional causation for granted. It should be equally evident that this is a model I oppose.

ally stated is a vestige of a way of thinking about mental causation which the emergence of the problem has itself revealed to be unfruitful. Token states have not helped us with the problem of mental causation; why then not just go back to the original question: namely how can a *person's* mental properties—e.g. her believing that *p* or desiring that *q*—be causally relevant to what she does or says? And in response to this question, perhaps we should now pose another—namely why shouldn't they be? What is supposed to be standing in the way of a quite straightforward acceptance of the causal relevance to action of a person's mental properties?

There is not space here to treat all the many different lines of thought which have led philosophers to the conclusion that mental properties can have no causal relevance to anything. But I shall say something rather brief in an attempt to explain why I believe that the sort of counterfactual account of causal relevance that I favour, together with a clear distinction between causal relevance, on the one hand, and causal efficacy and extensional causing on the other, ought to provide us with the means of rebutting most attempts to show that mental properties cannot be causally relevant to human actions.

First, there is the general point to be made that a purely counterfactually based account of causal relevance, of the sort that I have endorsed, ought to provide, in principle, the means of offering a very liberal view of the sorts of factors which may be invoked in causal explanations. If in order to decide whether or not some fact was causally relevant to some effect, we are simply to ask ourselves questions of the form 'Would *E* still have happened if *p* hadn't been the case?' or perhaps 'Would *E* have been as likely to happen if *p* hadn't been the case?', there seems, on the face of it, no reason why any distinction of levels should enter our deliberations, no reason why any exclusionary physicalist account of the nature of causality should figure in our thoughts. *E*, for example, could perfectly well be a social effect, like a riot, and *p* a social fact, e.g. the fact that *S* died in police custody. The counterfactual account of relevance simply licenses us to say, if we decide that the riot would not have happened if *S* hadn't died in police custody, that *S*'s dying in police custody was causally relevant to the riot.[7] There is simply no reason, on the face of it, given this view of the causal relevance of facts, to think that social or psychological or historical or economic

---

[7] Provided, of course, that the explanation is a causal explanation according to the 'general categorial' considerations discussed in Ch. 6.

explanations are awkward—that there is any difficulty about their causal status. If there is a problem, then, the case for that idea will need to be carefully made out; it is not simply built into the conception of causation offered here that physics, being the place where the 'causal work' is done, is really the only science capable of offering causal explanations which do not stand in need of vindication by physics.

The traditional way of making out the case for the view that there is a difficulty about the causal status of higher-level explanations, such as psychological explanations, of course, has been by way of the concept of causal overdetermination. It has been argued, for example, that psychological explanations of action are problematic because, given what we know about the neurophysiological antecedents of bodily movement, any attribution of causal relevance to mental as well as to physical factors would involve commitment to two parallel sets of causes of human action, the one physical, the other mental. But where causal relevance (as opposed to the relation I have called *causing*) is concerned, the spectre of overdetermination may be simply illusory. There seems, on the face of it, to be no reason for thinking that the causal relevance of one set of facts (say, a set of physiological facts) to some other fact or to a particular event precludes the relevance of any other sorts of fact (e.g. psychological facts) to that same fact or event—if causal relevance is just a matter of certain sorts of counterfactual being true. If that is all causal relevance amounts to, then facts of all sorts of different kinds and at all sorts of different levels can be causally relevant to others, without there being, as it were, any competition amongst them for space in the causal order. For example, there would seem to be no immediate problem about holding simultaneously both that the fact that I believed that it was raining was causally relevant to the fact that I picked up an umbrella as I left the house, and that the fact that neurons N_1–N_{100} fired was causally relevant to that same fact; since it is true, presumably, both that I wouldn't have picked up the umbrella if I hadn't thought it was raining *and* that I wouldn't have picked up the umbrella if neurons N_1–N_{100} hadn't fired. What reason have we for thinking that this amounts to causal overdetermination?

Someone might want to argue that if I could specify all the physical facts which were causally relevant to my picking up the umbrella as I left the house, I would have given the *complete* causal explanation of why I did so—and that therefore there is simply no room for the recognition of further causally relevant facts at different levels. But even if one accepts, say, that a supervenience relation holds between physics and other discourses, and so that there is a sense in which the physical facts fix all the facts at higher levels,[8] thus permitting that, perhaps in *some* sense of 'complete', a physical causal story about why some effect occurred would be a complete account, it does not seem to follow that facts at those higher levels are simply rendered incapable of functioning autonomously as causal *explanantes*. This, it seems to me, is what Jackson and Pettit's account of the workings of program explanations showed. Just as dispositional facts are not rendered causally irrelevant by the fact (if it is one) that a 'complete' explanation of the effects which they are brought in to explain is available at the categorical level, so no higher-level fact of any kind is made causally redundant by the existence of causal explanations of the same effect at other levels. It is just not true that there is no room for multiple layers of causally relevant facts in the causal explanation of a single effect.

What is crucial here, I think, about the recognition of the distinction between causing and causal relevance is that facts do not compete for causal space in the same way as particulars. Facts are tolerant of other facts in the community of causal *explanantes*; they do not need to fight one another for *Lebensraum* in the way that events seem to have to do. The worry about overdetermination is fuelled by a concern that we cannot permit two simultaneous and independent chains of particular events to cause a single effect, except perhaps in exceptional circumstances. But permitting facts at different levels to be causally relevant to the same effect does not involve any commitment to two (or more) distinct chains of particular causes. Once we reject the idea that all causal explanations invoke causal relations between particulars, then, we ought to be able to shake ourselves free of the picture according to which different causal explanations need to be shown to be invoking the same particulars if they are to be reconciled, one with another. The way would seem to be open for a straightforward recognition of the causal relevance of psychological facts to human action.

Another fear about permitting causal status to psychological explanations is based on the thought that the realm of causality is

---

[8] I am not opposed to this claim; in fact, it seems to me that this is the correct way of stating what is true about the primacy of physics.

the realm of strict law. Causal explanations, the thought goes, are distinguished by their dependence on relations of causation between particulars, and relations of causation between particulars must be understood, in turn, to be instances of general laws. But the account of causal explanation I have offered here has made no central use whatever of the concept of law. Doubtless there are no strict laws relating the possession of certain beliefs and desires to certain sorts of action, but neither are there any strict laws relating the weakness of bridges to their collapsing, or relating the fact that trains fail to hoot when they should to their being involved in accidents, or relating increases of unemployment to increases in the crime rate (though there may be rough generalizations to be made in all these cases). I am tempted, then, simply to deny that causal explanations have anything essential to do with strict laws at all. And once this nettle is grasped, there is no longer any bar to granting causal status to psychological explanations on the grounds that psychology is not a realm which is governed by strict laws.

It seems to me, then, that the force of at least some of the arguments which have made philosophers feel that there is a problem about the causal relevance of mental properties may be partly diminished, once we adopt a distinction between causing and causal relevance, and accept that the conditions governing the latter are really very undemanding—that almost any kind of fact can be causally relevant to an effect, compatibly both with a variety of other facts at numerous different levels also being causally relevant to that effect, and with the absence of any strict laws covering the case. I do not say that the problem of mental causation is hereby solved—that there are no good questions to be answered about how psychological causal explanations relate to their neurophysiological counterparts. But there is no chance of answering a good question unless we first ask one. I believe that philosophy of mind, during the period in which it has been dominated by the models of causation and the conceptions of states against which I have argued here, has been asking questions whose very intelligibility is impugned once those models and conceptions are recognized for the misrepresentations they are; and while it remains in the grip of the associated pictures, there is little chance of our arriving, through the debates thus engendered, at any genuine enlightenment concerning the mind–body problem.

5. CONCLUDING REMARKS

In these final two chapters, I have tried to show how the conclusions of previous chapters—in particular, the distinctions made earlier between particulars and facts, and between causing and causal relevance, together with the critique of the network model of causation which I offered in Chapter 7—might be brought to bear on certain questions and issues in the philosophy of mind. I hope to have made persuasive the contention that the token identity theory is not only false but unintelligible, applied to such things as beliefs and desires; that Stich's argument for eliminative materialism relies on a premiss which can be seen to be straightforwardly false when the role of psychological states in causal explanation is properly understood; and that the recognition of the distinction between causing and causal relevance ought to help us dispose of at least certain sorts of worry about the causal irrelevance of mental properties. But I have said very little about what, in general, ought to replace the conceptions and models of the mind and its place in causality which I have suggested are misconceived. Where should we turn in order to formulate our legitimate philosophical concerns about mentality and its relation to the physical world?

In general, it seems to me that the arguments of this book provide support for the view that the best hope for a theory of mind with ambitions to describe the relation between mental and physical realms is to give up on particularist relations like identity and composition—relations between individual things—and to turn instead to relations which can hold between facts—e.g. causal dependence, supervenience, perhaps constitution, understood as a relation between states of affairs. For the feature of mentality which argues most strongly for its incorporation into a physicalistic picture of the world—its role in the causal explanation of action—is, as we have seen, best understood, at least in the centrally important case of the propositional attitudes, in terms of the sentential variety of causal explanation. What we need to understand is not how one kind of individual, causally efficacious entity (the mental kind) relates to another (the physical kind); but rather how facts about what people believe, desire, intend, etc. relate to facts about the way things are with them, physically speaking. These, I have urged, are two different sorts of question, and it is wrong to suppose that the second sort reduces to the first. One might put the point (though this would be to overstate the case) by saying that the ontology of mind ought to be an ontology of facts, not an ontology of particulars. This overstates the case because of course we will need to speak of particulars too, not least the particulars with which we are ourselves identical. But we ought not, if I am right, to think of the mind as a network of interacting, causally efficacious events and states, whose operations lie behind and explain our intentional actions. If I have made it plausible that this model of the mind is a serious misrepresentation, this book will have achieved its aim.

REFERENCES

ALLEN, R. L., *The Verb System of Present-Day American English* (The Hague: Humanities Press, 1966).

ANSCOMBE, G. E. M., 'Causality and Determination', in Anscombe, *Collected Philosophical Papers*, ii (Oxford: Blackwell, 1981), 133–47.

ARISTOTLE, *Physics*, tr. R. P. Hardie and R. K. Gaye, in *The Complete Works of Aristotle*, 2 vols., i, ed. J. Barnes (Princeton: Princeton University Press, 1984), 315–446.

ARMSTRONG, D. M., *A Materialist Theory of the Mind* (London: Routledge & Kegan Paul, 1968).

——*Belief, Truth and Knowledge* (London: Cambridge University Press, 1973).

——*Nominalism and Realism*, vol. i of *Universals and Scientific Realism*, 2 vols. (Cambridge: Cambridge University Press, 1978).

AUSTIN, J. L., 'Unfair to Facts', in Austin, *Philosophical Papers*, 2nd edn. (Oxford: Oxford University Press, 1970), 154–74.

BAKER, L. R., 'Metaphysics and Mental Causation', in Heil and Mele (eds.), *Mental Causation*, 75–95.

BENNETT, J., *Events and their Names* (Oxford: Oxford University Press, 1988).

BLACKBURN, S., 'Losing your Mind: Physics, Identity and Folk Burglar Prevention', in Greenwood (ed.), *The Future of Folk Psychology*, 196–225.

BLOCK, N. (ed.), *Readings in Philosophy of Psychology*, 2 vols. (London: Methuen, 1980).

——'Can the Mind Change the World?', in G. Boolos (ed.), *Meaning and Method: Essays in Honor of Hilary Putnam* (Cambridge: Cambridge University Press, 1990), 137–70.

BOYD, R., 'Materialism without Reductionism: What Physicalism does not Entail', in Block (ed.), *Readings in Philosophy of Psychology*, i. 67–106.

BROAD, C. D., *Scientific Thought* (London: Routledge & Kegan Paul, 1923).

CAMPBELL, K., *Abstract Particulars* (Oxford: Blackwell, 1990).

CHILD, W., *Causality, Interpretation and the Mind* (Oxford: Oxford University Press, 1994).

CHISHOLM, R., 'Events and Propositions', *Nous*, 4 (1970), 15–24.

266 *References*

——'States of Affairs Again', *Nous*, 5 (1971), 179–89.

CHOMSKY, N., 'Remarks on Nominalization', in D. Davidson and G. Harman (eds.), *The Logic of Grammar* (Encino, Calif.: Dickenson, 1975), 184–221.

CHURCHLAND, P. M., 'Eliminative Materialism and the Propositional Attitudes', *Journal of Philosophy*, 78 (1981), 67–90.

CHURCHLAND, P. S., *Neurophilosophy* (Cambridge, Mass.: MIT Press, 1986).

CORNMAN, J., 'The Identity of Mind and Body', *Journal of Philosophy*, 59 (1962), 486–92.

DAVIDSON, D., 'Causal Relations', *Journal of Philosophy*, 64 (1967), 691–703; repr. in Davidson, *Essays on Actions and Events*, 149–62.

——'The Logical Form of Action Sentences', in N. Rescher (ed.), *The Logic of Decision and Action* (Pittsburgh: University of Pittsburgh Press, 1967), 81–95; repr. in Davidson, *Essays on Actions and Events*, 105–22.

——'The Individuation of Events', in N. Rescher (ed.), *Essays in Honor of Carl G. Hempel* (Dordrecht: Reidel, 1969), 216–34; repr. in Davidson, *Essays on Actions and Events*, 163–80.

——'Events as Particulars', *Nous*, 4 (1970), 25–32; repr. in Davidson, *Essays on Actions and Events*, 181–7.

——'Mental Events', in L. Foster and J. W. Swanson (eds.), *Experience and Theory* (Amherst: University of Massachusetts Press; London: Duckworth, 1970), 79–101; repr. in Davidson, *Essays on Actions and Events*, 207–25.

——'Eternal vs. Ephemeral Events', *Nous*, 5 (1971), 335–49; repr. in Davidson, *Essays on Actions and Events*, 189–203.

——'The Material Mind', in P. Suppes, L. Henkin, A. Joja, and G. C. Moisil (eds.), *Proceedings of the Fourth International Congress for Logic, Methodology and Science* (Amsterdam: North-Holland, 1973), 709–22; repr. in Davidson, *Essays on Actions and Events*, 245–59.

——*Essays on Actions and Events* (Oxford: Oxford University Press, 1980).

DRETSKE, F., *Explaining Behavior: Reasons in a World of Causes* (Cambridge, Mass.: MIT Press, 1988).

——'Mental Events as Structuring Causes of Behavior', in Heil and Mele (eds.), *Mental Causation*, 121–36.

FALES, E. H., *Causation and Universals* (London: Routledge, 1990).

FELDMAN, F., 'Identity, Necessity and Events', in Block (ed.), *Readings in Philosophy of Psychology*, i. 48–55.

FODOR, J. A., *Psychosemantics* (Cambridge, Mass.: MIT Press, 1987).

——'Fodor's Guide to Mental Representation', in Greenwood (ed.), *The Future of Folk Psychology*, 22–50.

FREGE, G., 'Letter to Jourdain', letter VIII/12, in *Wissenschaftlicher Briefwechsel*, ed. G. Gabriel, H. Hermes, F. Kambartel, C. Thiel, and

A. Veraart (Hamburg: Felix Meiner, 1976); tr. as *Philosophical and Mathematical Correspondence* by H. Kaal, abridged by B. McGuinness (Oxford: Blackwell, 1980), 78–80.

——'On Sense and Meaning', in *Translations from the Philosophical Writings of Gottlob Frege*, ed. and tr. P. Geach and M. Black, 3rd edn. (Oxford: Blackwell, 1980), 56–78.

GALTON, A., *The Logic of Aspect* (Oxford: Oxford University Press, 1984).

GOLDMAN, A., *A Theory of Human Action* (Englewood Cliffs, NJ: Prentice-Hall, 1970).

GREENWOOD, J. D. (ed.), *The Future of Folk Psychology* (Cambridge: Cambridge University Press, 1991).

HACKER, P. M. S., 'Events and Objects in Space and Time', *Mind*, 91 (1982), 1–19.

HEIL, J., and MELE, A. (eds.), *Mental Causation* (Oxford: Oxford University Press, 1993).

HEMPEL, C. G., *Aspects of Scientific Explanation* (New York: Macmillan, 1965).

HONDERICH, T., 'Causes and *If p, even if x, still q*', *Philosophy*, 57 (1982), 291–317.

——'The Argument for Anomalous Monism', *Analysis*, 42 (1982), 59–64.

——'The Union Theory and Anti-individualism', in Heil and Mele (eds.), *Mental Causation*, 137–59.

HORGAN, T., 'The Case against Events', *Philosophical Review*, 87 (1978), 28–47.

——and TYE, M., 'Against the Token Identity Theory', in LePore and McLaughlin (eds.), *Actions and Events: Perspectives on the Philosophy of Donald Davidson*, 427–43.

——and WOODWARD, J., 'Folk Psychology is here to Stay', *Philosophical Review*, 94 (1985), 197–226.

HORNSBY, J., 'Which Physical Events are Mental Events?', *Proceedings of the Aristotelian Society*, 81 (1980–1), 73–92.

——'Physicalism, Events and Part–Whole Relations', in LePore and McLaughlin (eds)., *Actions and Events: Perspectives on the Philosophy of Donald Davidson*, 444–58; repr. in Hornsby, *Simple-Mindedness: A Defence of Naive Naturalism in the Philosophy of Mind* (forthcoming, 1997).

——'Agency and Causal Explanation', in Heil and Mele (eds.), *Mental Causation*, 161–88.

——*Simple-Mindedness: A Defence of Naive Naturalism in the Philosophy of Mind* (Cambridge, Mass.: Harvard University Press, forthcoming, 1997).

JACKSON, F., and PETTIT, P., 'Functionalism and Broad Content', *Mind*, 97 (1988), 381–400.

——'In Defence of Folk Psychology', *Philosophical Studies*, 59 (1990), 31–54.

——'Program Explanation: A General Perspective', *Analysis*, 50 (1990), 107–17.

——'Causation in the Philosophy of Mind', *Philosophy and Phenomenological Research*, 50, supp. vol. (1990), 195–214.

——'Structural Explanation in Social Theory', in D. Charles and K. Lennon (eds.), *Reduction, Explanation and Realism* (Oxford: Oxford University Press, 1992), 97–131.

JOHNSTON, M., 'Why Having a Mind Matters', in LePore and McLaughlin (eds.), *Actions and Events: Perspectives on the Philosophy of Donald Davidson*, 408–26.

KENNY, A., *Action, Emotion and Will* (London: Routledge & Kegan Paul, 1963).

KIM, J., 'On the Psycho-physical Identity Theory', *American Philosophical Quarterly*, 3 (1966), 227–35.

——'Events and their Descriptions: Some Considerations', in N. Rescher (ed.), *Essays in Honor of Carl G. Hempel* (Dordrecht: Reidel, 1969), 198–215.

——'Phenomenal Properties, Psychophysical Laws and the Identity Theory', *Monist*, 56 (1972), 177–92.

——'Causation, Nomic Subsumption and the Concept of Event', *Journal of Philosophy*, 70 (1973), 217–36; repr. in Kim, *Supervenience and Mind*, 3–21.

——'Noncausal Connections', *Nous*, 8 (1974), 41–52; repr. in Kim, *Supervenience and Mind*, 22–32.

——'Events as Property Exemplifications', in M. Brand and D. Walton (eds.), *Action Theory* (Dordrecht: Reidel, 1976), 159–77; repr. in Kim, *Supervenience and Mind*, 33–53.

——*Supervenience and Mind* (Cambridge: Cambridge University Press, 1993).

KRIPKE, S. A., 'Naming and Necessity', in G. Harman and D. Davidson (eds.), *Semantics of Natural Language* (Dordrecht: Reidel, 1972), 253–355; rev. and enlarged as *Naming and Necessity* (Oxford: Blackwell, 1980).

LEECH, G. N., *Towards a Semantic Description of English* (Bloomington: Indiana University Press, 1969).

LePORE, E., and McLAUGHLIN, B. P. (eds.), *Actions and Events: Perspectives on the Philosophy of Donald Davidson* (Oxford: Blackwell, 1985).

LEWIS, D. K., 'An Argument for the Identity Theory', *Journal of Philosophy*, 63 (1966), 17–25; repr. rev. in Lewis, *Philosophical Papers*, i. 99–107.

—— 'Psychophysical and Theoretical Identifications', *Australasian Journal of Philosophy*, 50 (1972), 249–58; repr. in Block (ed.), *Readings in Philosophy of Psychology*, i. 207–15.

—— 'Causation', *Journal of Philosophy*, 70 (1973), 556–67; repr. in Lewis, *Philosophical Papers*, ii. 159–213.

—— 'Causal Explanation', in Lewis, *Philosophical Papers*, ii. 214–40.

—— *Philosophical Papers*, i (Oxford: Oxford University Press, 1983).

—— *Philosophical Papers*, ii (Oxford: Oxford University Press, 1986).

LOMBARD, L. B., *Events: A Metaphysical Study* (London: Routledge & Kegan Paul, 1986).

MACDONALD, C., *Mind–Body Identity Theories* (London: Routledge, 1989).

MACKIE, J. L., *The Cement of the Universe* (Oxford: Oxford University Press, 1980).

MARTIN, R. M., *Events, Reference and Logical Form* (Washington: Catholic University of America Press, 1978).

MELLOR, D. H., *The Facts of Causation* (London: Routledge, 1995).

MILL, J. S., *A System of Logic*, 8th edn. (1843; London: Longmans, 1873).

MORTON, A., *Frames of Mind* (Oxford: Oxford University Press, 1980).

MOURELATOS, A. P. D., 'Events, Processes and States', *Linguistics and Philosophy*, 2 (1978), 415–34.

NAGEL, T., 'Physicalism', *Philosophical Review*, 74 (1965), 339–56.

OWENS, D., *Causes and Coincidences* (Cambridge: Cambridge University Press, 1992).

PAPINEAU, D., *Philosophical Naturalism* (Oxford: Blackwell, 1993).

PEACOCKE, C., *Holistic Explanation* (Oxford: Oxford University Press, 1979).

PEIRCE, C. S., 'Apology for Pragmatism', in Peirce, *Collected Papers*, iv: *The Simplest Mathematics*, ed. C. C. Hartshorne and P. Weiss (Cambridge, Mass.: Harvard University Press, 1933).

PUTNAM, H., 'The Nature of Mental States', first pub. as 'Psychological Predicates', in W. H. Capitan and D. D. Merrill, *Art, Mind and Religion* (Pittsburgh: University of Pittsburgh Press, 1967), 37–48; repr. in *Mind, Language and Reality*, 429–40.

—— 'Brains and Behaviour', in R. J. Butler (ed.), *Analytical Philosophy: Second Series* (Oxford: Oxford University Press, 1963); repr. in Putnam, *Mind, Language and Reality*, 325–41.

—— *Mind, Language and Reality*, vol. ii of *Philosophical Papers* (Cambridge: Cambridge University Press, 1975).

QUINE, W. V. O., 'Speaking of Objects', in *Ontological Relativity and Other Essays* (New York: Columbia University Press, 1969), 1–25.

ROBINSON, W. S., 'States and Beliefs', *Mind*, 99 (1990), 33–51.

RORTY, R., 'Mind–Body Identity, Privacy and Categories', *Review of Metaphysics*, 19 (1965), 24–54.

RYLE, G., *The Concept of Mind* (London: Hutchinson, 1949; repr. Harmondsworth: Penguin, 1983).

SCHMITT, F. F., 'Events', *Erkenntnis*, 20 (1983), 281–93.

SHAFFER, J., 'Could Mental States be Brain Processes?', *Journal of Philosophy*, 58 (1961), 813–22.

SIMONS, P., *Parts: A Study in Ontology* (Oxford: Oxford University Press, 1987).

SMART, J. J. C., 'Sensations and Brain Processes', *Philosophical Review*, 68 (1959), 141–56; repr. with slight revisions in C. V. Borst (ed.), *The Mind–Brain Identity Theory* (London: St Martin's Press, 1970), 52–66.

STICH, S. P., *From Folk Psychology to Cognitive Science: The Case against Belief* (Cambridge, Mass.: MIT Press, 1983).

STOUTLAND, F., 'Davidson on Intentional Behaviour', in LePore and McLaughlin (eds.), *Actions and Events: Perspectives on the Philosophy of Donald Davidson*, 44–59.

STRAWSON, P. F., 'Particular and General', *Proceedings of the Aristotelian Society*, 54 (1953–4), 233–60; repr. in Strawson, *Logico-Linguistic Papers* (London: Methuen, 1971), 28–52.

——'Causation and Explanation', in B. Vermazen and M. B. Hintikka (eds.), *Essays on Davidson: Actions and Events* (Oxford: Oxford University Press, 1985), 115–35.

TAYLOR, B., *Modes of Occurrence: Verbs, Adverbs and Events* (Oxford: Blackwell, 1985).

VENDLER, Z., 'Verbs and Times', *Philosophical Review*, 66 (1957), 143–60.

——'Causal Relations', *Journal of Philosophy*, 64 (1967), 704–13.

——*Linguistics in Philosophy* (Ithaca, NY: Cornell University Press, 1967).

WILLIAMS, D. C., 'The Elements of Being', *Review of Metaphysics*, 7 (1953), 3–18 and 171–92.

WILSON, N. L., 'Facts, Events and their Identity Conditions', *Philosophical Studies*, 25 (1974), 303–21.

INDEX

abstract nouns 106
abstract objects 21, 131, 135, 162,
    166, 242 n.
abstract particulars 106 n., 137 n.
    see also token states; tropes
actions 24 n., 33–4 n., 70, 101, 139,
    148, 153, 159, 206, 223
    causal explanation of 221–2, 225,
    227, 232, 242–5, 248, 250,
    252–6, 258–64
adjectives 240
    attributive position within gerundive
    nominals 114
    temporally sensitive 98–9
adverbial modification:
    in relation to aspect 87, 98
    in relation to gerundive
    nominals 114
adverbs, semantics of 76, 92, 153
akrasia 206
Allen, R. L. 85–6, 95
Ancient Criterion of Change (ACC)
    58–63
anomalous monism 5, 20, 44, 46,
    137 n., 233, 234 n.
Anscombe, G. E. M. 140 n., 182 n.,
    200
Aristotle 63 n.
Armstrong, D. M. 1 n., 5 n., 12 n.,
    109 n., 113
aspect 11, 77, 84–8, 91, 98–9, 101
    imperfective 84–5, 87–8, 91, 96,
    101
    inclusive 85–6, 95
    intrusive 85–6, 95
    perfective 84–7, 91, 96, 98
Austin, J. L. 113

Baker, L. R. 210 n.
because 140–1, 146–8, 150–5, 157,
    162–3, 167, 170, 181, 197,
    252

beliefs 6, 15, 106, 111–12, 117–19,
    127, 130–4, 201, 205, 221–3,
    234–7, 238 n., 240, 242–3, 245–6,
    247–54, 256–9, 262–3
    in causal explanation of action
    148–9, 211, 221–3, 225, 227,
    234, 242–3, 251–2, 258
    subject-relative 132, 148
Bennett, J. 6 n., 8 n., 10, 19–21, 40,
    41–7, 50–5, 56, 100, 106 n.
Blackburn, S. 205 n.
Block, N. 211, 257 n.
Boyd, R. 20 n.
bridge laws 256
British Empiricists 12
Broad, C. D. 7 n.
broad-object events, *see* events

Campbell, K. 135–6, 137 n., 138, 199
causal chains 207–9, 261
causal efficacy 14, 105, 135, 150, 151,
    156, 159, 161–2, 169, 185–6,
    189–93, 198–202, 205, 212–13,
    218–19, 222, 228–9, 234, 243–6,
    254, 259, 263–4
causal explanation 13, 15, 105, 134,
    135, 138–54, 156–67, 168–87,
    189–91, 195, 200–1, 206–9, 211,
    216, 222, 225–7, 229–31, 232,
    242–3, 245–6, 247, 251–3,
    259–63
causal laws 136, 178–9, 255, 257,
    262
causal overdetermination 244, 260–1
causal power, *see* causal efficacy
causal relations 23, 135–8, 141, 143,
    147, 151–2, 154, 156, 159–67,
    172, 174, 192, 195, 197, 201–2,
    207, 209–10, 212, 221, 223, 225,
    228–30, 246, 252, 255, 261–2
    'natural' 162–3, 171, 175, 183–5,
    197, 200

causal relevance 13–14, 137 n., 149–50, 161, 169, 174, 186–8, 190–201, 205–6, 212–13, 219–20, 225–6, 228–31, 232, 245, 247, 249, 253, 255–63
causal role 213, 221–2, 224, 226–31, 245, 251–4
causation 11, 13, 14, 64, 65, 134, 135–9, 141–55, 158–61, 163–7, 168–9, 171–2, 177, 185–6, 193–4, 197, 200, 205, 207–8, 212, 214–17, 219, 221, 225, 229, 232, 245, 249, 253, 259–60, 262–3
  general categorial notion of *cause* 170, 175, 180, 182–4, 194, 259 n.
  mental 222–3, 254–6, 258–9, 262
  network model of causation 14, 205–14, 216–18, 221–31, 232, 234, 243–5, 250, 263–4
change 7, 8 n., 9 n., 10, 57–72, 74, 75, 95, 99, 100–1, 198, 210, 215
  relational 59 n.
changeless events, *see* events
Child, W. 140 n., 146 n., 157 n., 168–75, 179–80, 183
Chisholm, R. 7 n., 11, 37
Chomsky, N. 107–8, 110, 112 n.
Churchland, P. M. 15 n.
Churchland, P. S. 15 n.
cognitive science 248, 250
composition 15, 20, 22, 28, 44, 59 n., 65–70, 72–4, 77, 99, 246, 263
conditions 109, 135, 209
  causally relevant 218–21, 225–6, 228–30
congruence 206
constitution 20, 22, 28 n., 44, 59 n., 94, 119, 133–4, 254, 263
constitutive relationships, between facts 176–7, 254, 263
content:
  as individuative of propositional attitudes 131–2, 240
  mental 105, 201, 205–6, 211 n., 232–3, 235, 249, 256
contingent existence, as criterion of particularity 22, 36–7
continuants 66–7, 73–4, 97, 100, 138
Cornman, J. 118 n.
correspondence theory of truth 27, 40
count nouns, see nouns
counterfactuals, 13, 178–9, 181, 185, 190–1, 193–8, 200–1, 228, 245, 259–60

Davidson, D. 4–5, 7 n., 9 n., 11, 25–6, 37, 44, 46, 60 n., 76–7, 137 n., 138, 141–2, 145, 152–5, 163–5, 167, 168, 170, 205–6, 213–16, 220, 223–4, 234 n., 243 n.
definite descriptions 23, 34–5, 38, 41 n., 49, 115, 154, 159
demonstratives 31, 33, 38, 40, 50, 114
dependence relation 72, 183, 185, 197, 201, 245, 253–4, 263
desires 6, 106, 111–12, 118, 131, 133–4, 159, 201, 205, 211, 221–3, 226–7, 234, 245–6, 247–50, 252–3, 256–9, 262–3
developments 83–4
dispositions 186–9, 209, 261
Dretske, F. 5 n., 207 n.
dualism 1–3
  property dualism 29
dynamic strategy 57–8, 65, 68–72, 74, 75

eliminative materialism 14–15, 105, 134, 201, 206, 224, 232, 247–9, 251, 254, 256, 263
epiphenomenalism:
  and anomalous monism 137 n., 256
  of content 14, 232, 247, 256–8
EPTs, *see* properties, exemplifications of
event-describing sentences 23–4, 26, 29–30
events 2–14, 19–33, 34 n., 35, 37, 40, 41–55, 56–74, 75–8, 83–101, 111, 153, 211, 224, 234, 239–41, 244, 251, 257–8
  broad-object 60, 62, 64
  and causal explanation 135–6, 139–40, 142–5, 150, 153–4, 159, 174–8, 190, 196, 225, 254, 260
  and causation 137–8, 144, 150, 154–6, 158–9, 163, 165–6, 170–4, 178, 184–6, 193, 195, 199–201, 206–23, 225–6, 229, 234, 255, 261, 264
  changeless 60, 62, 64, 69–71, 101
  composite 60, 62, 64–5, 68–9
  descriptions 47–8, 51, 54–5, 95, 215
  essences of 216, 218 n.
  and identity 238–9, 241
  individuation of 22–7, 33, 41–2, 46–7, 50

mental 20, 22, 28–30, 46, 48–53, 92–4, 132, 211 n., 222–4, 233–4, 238, 241–3, 255–8, 264
names of 41–2, 54, 95
non-paradigmatic 90–2, 94, 144 n.
physical 47, 49, 52–4, 92–4, 223–4, 233–4, 238, 241, 245, 255
predications 83–4, 87–92, 94, 97, 100, 111, 152–3, 155, 167, 171, 176
as relata of 'natural' relations 171
restrictive conception of (RCE) 61, 64
spatial location 21–2, 65–7, 90
subjectless 60–2
exemplifications of properties, *see* properties
existential generalization:
account of sentential causal claims 152–5, 157–60
over events 25–6
explanation 23–5, 27, 40, 146, 163, 166, 169–70, 175–7, 184–5, 188–9, 216, 221, 229
see also causal explanation
explanatory contexts 23–5, 29, 40–1
externalism 15

facta 164 n.
fact-like entities 20–1, 27, 38, 115
facts 9 n., 10, 13–15, 19, 21, 27, 33–4 n., 35–7, 39–40, 112–15, 205, 263
and causation 135, 138, 147, 151, 161–7, 168–70, 174, 183, 185–7, 192–5, 197, 200–1, 209, 212–13, 218–20, 225, 227–31, 245–6, 253, 258–64
identity conditions for 27, 38–40, 230
Fales, E. H. 136–8, 143
Feldman, F. 28–9, 37
fine-grainedness 27, 37, 161, 230, 245
Fodor, J. A. 205, 222–3, 251
folk psychology 94, 133–4, 189, 205–6, 221, 223–7, 239, 242–3, 248, 250–4
Frege, G. 52 n., 236 n., 240–1
functionalism 9, 11, 12 n., 105, 201, 222–3, 227, 233, 251
fusion:
nonzonal 44–7
zonal 44

Galton, A. 84 n., 85, 87
generalizations 178–82, 242
gerundive nominals, *see* nominals
Goldman, A. 6 n.

happenings 9–10, 23, 25, 56–7, 60, 65, 70–1, 95, 158, 241
Hempel, C. 23
Honderich, T. 136 n., 214 n., 255 n.
Horgan, T. 5 n., 21 n., 224, 243 n., 244
Hornsby, J. 24 n., 33 n., 57 n., 64 n., 65

identity 15, 119, 134, 233, 235–9, 242–4, 246, 254, 256, 263
conditions for events 21, 23, 25–7, 28–31, 50, 52–5, 224; *see also* events
individuation of
identity statements 52–5, 117, 119, 128, 234–8, 240–4, 246
two-route identity statements 53–5, 240–1, 244
identity theory 3, 12 n., 15, 29–30, 44, 47–54, 94, 117–19, 128, 223–4, 227
imperfect aspect, *see* aspect
indexicality 209
individuals 90, 96, 120, 124, 126, 129, 134
instances of properties, *see* properties
intentional realism 233, 251
introspection 53, 93
isomorphism 206, 208, 213, 221, 224–5, 227, 230–1, 243–5

Jackson, F. 14, 169, 186–91, 193, 197–8, 200, 251, 261
Johnston, M. 255 n.

Kenny, A. 5 n., 81–3, 88, 110
Kim, J. 5 n., 6n, 8 n., 9 n., 10, 19–30, 36, 37, 40, 41, 42, 47, 50, 56, 62, 100

laws, *see* causal laws
Leech, G. N. 88
Leibniz's Law 96, 119, 224
Lewis, D. K. 2 n., 12 n., 195 n., 205, 207, 227
Lombard, L. B. 7 n., 10–11, 37, 58–64, 66, 100

Macdonald, C. 6 n., 7 n.
Mackie, J. L. 194, 207 n.

Martin, R. M. 9
masses 90, 96, 99, 120, 124
  mass nouns, *see* nouns
  mass quantification 112, 119, 160
matter 66, 77, 97, 99
Mellor, D. H. 135 n., 141, 156 n., 164 n.
mental events, *see* events, mental
mental states, *see* states, mental
Mill, J. S. 145, 163 n., 206, 207 n.,
  213–16, 220–1
mind-body problem 1–2, 9, 15, 206,
  221, 232, 262
modes of presentation 236, 239, 241
Morton, A. 242 n.
Mourelatos, A. P. D. 5 n., 82–5, 87–9,
  91, 111–12

Nagel, T. 119
names 23, 236–7
  of events, *see* events
  proper 115
network model of causation, *see*
  causation
nominalism 124
nominalization 13, 89, 93, 94, 107,
  111–12, 115, 158–9, 164, 193,
  245, 253
  transcriptions 89, 91, 98, 111–12,
  119, 160, 171
nominals 96, 100, 106–7, 109–14,
  118, 140
  derived 107–9, 111–15, 118
  genitive 126
  gerundive 96, 107–9, 111–14, 118–
  19, 129
  stative 12–13, 111, 113, 115–16,
  158–9
nonzonal fusion, *see* fusion, nonzonal
nouns:
  count 50, 51, 88–90, 111–12, 119,
  122–32, 240
  mass 88–90, 112, 127–30
  stative 111–12, 119, 148–9

objects:
  as causal relata 136–7, 143
  events as changes in 59–67
  non-spatial 67, 162
  physical 66, 99, 100, 136, 209,
  234–7, 240–1, 244
  restrictive conception of (RCO) 61–
  2, 64
obtaining 57, 99
occupation 66, 240–1

occurrences 83, 88–90, 100–1, 241
omissions 209
Owens, D. 179–81

Papineau, D. 134 n., 206
part-causing 213, 216, 219–20, 231
particularism 15, 133, 232, 234, 257,
  263
particularity, *see* particulars
particulars 6–7, 10, 13, 19–24, 26, 27,
  30, 33–8, 39 n., 40, 50, 52–5, 56,
  75, 113–15, 120, 125, 128–9,
  133, 205, 232, 234, 242–6, 249,
  251, 254, 263–4
  and causal explanations 136–7,
  139 n., 169, 174, 195, 253, 258
  and causation 152, 156, 159–60,
  162, 168–71, 183–6, 192, 195–7,
  199, 201, 208, 212–21, 225–6,
  230, 245–6, 253, 258, 261–3
  spatiotemporal 8 n., 22–3, 36–7, 123–
  4, 129, 162, 185, 197, 199, 201,
  240–1
part-whole relation, *see* composition
Peirce, C. S. 120–2, 125
perfective aspect, *see* aspect
performatives 87 n.
persons 33
Pettit, P. 14, 169, 186–91, 193, 197–
  8, 200, 251, 261
physical objects, see objects
physical-causal isomorph (PCI) 224
physicalism, 9, 10, 11, 14–15, 28, 31,
  32, 38, 47, 105, 128, 133–4, 205,
  227, 233, 246, 247, 254–6, 258–
  9, 263
  see also token physicalism
process explanations 14, 169, 186,
  189–92, 197, 200
processes 2–6, 11, 74, 76–7, 80, 83–5,
  87, 89, 91, 94–101, 109 n., 110,
  111, 224, 234, 252
  and causal explanation 135–6
  and causation 137–8, 209
  mental 132
process predications 83–5, 87–91,
  97, 111
program explanations 14, 169, 186,
  189–93, 197, 200, 261
properties 14, 19, 21, 27, 28–31, 33–
  4, 35 n., 36, 39, 41–4, 46–7, 50,
  55, 58, 61–4, 107–9, 111, 112,
  124–6, 134
  categorical 187–90

and causal explanation 135–7, 150,
  173, 178, 187–92, 255–6
and causation 161, 169, 189–90,
  182, 198–200, 209, 211, 218–19,
  255–8
compared with state types 107–9
dynamic 61–2
exemplifications of (EPTs) 6, 8 n.,
  10, 19–22, 26–7, 28–38, 39–40,
  41, 62, 124, 126
instances of 6, 41–51, 54, 107,
  124–6, 130, 136 n., 161–2, 174,
  193, 198–200; *see also* properties,
  exemplifications of; tropes
intrinsic 33, 34 n., 39, 109, 219
mental 28–30, 46–7, 133, 137, 232,
  247, 253–7, 259, 262–3
microphysical 169, 189, 191, 198
negative 43
physical 46–51, 133, 192, 200,
  211 n., 256
relational 32–3, 34 n., 35, 39, 115,
  219
spatial 33, 36–7
static 61–3
temporal 33, 36–7, 90
propositional attitudes 111–12, 118,
  130–2, 234, 242, 250–3, 256, 263
propositions 37–8, 40, 112
punctual occurrences 83–4
Putnam, H. 2 n. 12 n.

quality space 62–4
Quine, W. V. O. 11

reasons, for action 253
reductionism, in philosophy of
  mind 38, 257
reference 25–6, 33–5, 38–9, 41, 47,
  49, 52, 54–5, 95–6
relational properties, *see* properties,
  relational
relations:
  intellectual 165–7, 168, 184–5, 197
  natural 162–3, 165–7, 169–73, 175,
    184–5, 197, 208
  as universals 36
relevance, causal, *see* causal relevance
restrictive conception of an event
  (RCE), *see* event, restrictive
  conception of
restrictive conception of an object
  (RCO), *see* object, restrictive
  conception of

Robinson, W. S. 117
Rorty, R. 119 n.
Ryle, G. 1–2

Schmitt, F. F. 106 n.
secret life requirement 20–1, 28, 30–6,
  38, 40, 50, 55, 115, 161
sentential causal claims 13, 23–4, 141,
  145–65, 167, 168–9, 171–2, 174,
  178, 181, 183, 187, 189, 191–3,
  196, 200–2, 205, 211, 213, 225,
  245, 252, 263
  with negative *explanantes* 152, 156,
    167, 171–2
  with stative *explanantes* 152, 157–
    61, 167, 171–2, 213
sets 8, 21–2, 63
Shaffer, J. 119 n.
Simons, P. 74 n.
singular causal claims 13, 135 n.,
  138–9, 141–5, 147, 149–56,
  158–60, 163–5, 167, 168,
  178–83, 193, 200–2, 205, 245,
  252
  event-citing 142–5, 147, 149, 153–
    4, 158–9, 164, 201
  thing-citing 142–3, 147, 149
singular terms 24, 25, 26, 27, 54, 115,
  139–42, 148–51, 153, 165, 171,
  197, 208, 218
situations 83
Smart, J. J. C. 119
sortal concepts 51, 68, 237–40, 244
space 66, 240–1
spatial properties, *see* properties,
  spatial
spatiotemporal particulars, *see*
  particulars, spatiotemporal
spatiotemporal zones 43, 46
spatiotemporality, as criterion of
  particularity 22, 36–7
standing conditions 145, 210–11,
  215–16, 219–20, 231
states 2–6, 8 n., 10, 11–15, 40, 56–8,
  72–4, 75–8, 80–1, 83–5, 88, 97,
  99, 100, 101, 105–10, 112, 115–
  20, 128–9, 211, 224, 227, 232,
  234, 239–40, 244–6, 251–2, 257–
  8, 262
  as arrangements of objects in
    space 116–17
  of the brain 117–19, 134,
    233–4, 236–7, 239–40, 243,
    251

states (*cont.*)
  and causation 136–7, 144, 150,
    158–9, 171, 174, 176, 209, 211,
    214–15, 217, 219-23, 227, 242,
    245–6, 250, 264
  and identity 236–40, 246
  mental 15, 94, 119, 201, 213, 222–
    3, 233–4, 238, 242–5, 247, 249–
    52, 254–8, 263–4
  physical 119, 213, 238, 242–5,
    254–5
  'state of ...' locution 115–19, 240
  types 108–9, 115, 120, 134, 227
states of affairs 37, 112–15, 136,
    154 n., 173, 177–8, 209, 212,
    229, 245, 263
stative predications 13, 83–4, 88, 108,
    110–14, 119, 176
  and causal explanations 146, 176
Stich, S. P. 15 n., 205, 242 n., 250–2,
    263
Stoutland, F. 255 n.
Strawson, P. F. 106 n., 108, 140 n.,
    165–7, 169–71, 175, 182 n.,
    183–5, 196–7, 200
subjects, of propositional attitudes,
    257–8
substances 35, 42–3, 54, 73, 77, 113,
    129, 133, 135; *see also*
    continuants, things
  constitutive 21–2, 28, 30, 32
supervenience 15, 116, 162, 254, 261,
    263

Taylor, B. 8 n., 57
temporal parts 73–4, 81, 90, 95, 97,
    99–101
temporal properties, *see* properties,
    temporal
temporal shape 11, 72, 75, 97–101
temporal strategy 57, 71–2, 74, 75–8
tenses, continuous 78–81, 85, 88
'theory-theory' 242 n., 252
Thesis of Universal Nonzonal
    Fusion 44–7
things, as causes 136–8, 140, 142–3,
    150–1, 186, 199–200, 209
time schemata 78, 110
times, constitutive 21, 26, 28, 31, 32

token identity theory 14–15, 19, 29–
    30, 44, 46–55, 94, 118, 133, 201,
    205, 223–4, 232–5, 237–9, 241–
    6, 247, 254–5, 257, 263
  see also identity theory, token
    physicalism
token physicalism 28, 30–2, 35–6, 38,
    40, 47, 55, 56, 92–4, 133–4, 224
token states 6, 13, 40, 106, 120, 128–
    31, 133–4, 201, 205–6, 211–13,
    223, 234, 236–8, 241–5, 249,
    252–6, 258–9
  and causal explanation 135, 138,
    148 n., 159–61, 211, 223, 231
  and causation 159, 161, 172, 174,
    193, 223, 231
tokens 40, 121–34, 256
triples, ordered 8 n., 21–2
tropes 41–3, 45–52, 54–5, 137 n.
  mixed 47–9
two-route identity statements *see*
    identity statements
Tye, M. 224, 243 n., 244
type identity theory 29, 256
  see also type physicalism
type physicalism 28, 30, 133
type-token distinction 28 n., 106, 120–
    30, 132–3, 223, 233
type-token pairs 127, 130

universals 20, 35–8, 125, 134, 198

Vendler, Z. 5 n., 78–83, 85, 87–8,
    110, 113–14, 165, 193
verbs 78–84, 88–9, 100, 110, 113–14
  of accomplishment 78–82, 87
  of achievement 78–81, 87
  of activity 78–83, 87
  causal 140
  performance verbs 81, 83
  static, *see* verbs, stative
  stative 78–83, 88, 101, 110–11,
    157

Wilson, N. L. 8 n., 9 n.
Woodward, J. 5 n.

zonal fusion, se*e* fusion, zonal
zones, *see* spatiotemporal zones